Earnings Accruals and Real Activities Management around Initial Public Offerings

AF183553

Peter Ising

Earnings Accruals and Real Activities Management around Initial Public Offerings

Evidence from Specific Industries

Springer Gabler

Peter Ising
Zurich, Switzerland

Dissertation University of Zurich, 2013

ISBN 978-3-658-03793-2 ISBN 978-3-658-03794-9 (eBook)
DOI 10.1007/978-3-658-03794-9

The Deutsche Nationalbibliothek lists this publication in the Deutsche Nationalbibliografie; detailed bibliographic data are available in the Internet at http://dnb.d-nb.de.

Library of Congress Control Number: 2013950219

Springer Gabler
© Springer Fachmedien Wiesbaden 2014
This work is subject to copyright. All rights are reserved by the Publisher, whether the whole or part of the material is concerned, specifically the rights of translation, reprinting, reuse of illustrations, recitation, broadcasting, reproduction on microfilms or in any other physical way, and transmission or information storage and retrieval, electronic adaptation, computer software, or by similar or dissimilar methodology now known or hereafter developed. Exempted from this legal reservation are brief excerpts in connection with reviews or scholarly analysis or material supplied specifically for the purpose of being entered and executed on a computer system, for exclusive use by the purchaser of the work. Duplication of this publication or parts thereof is permitted only under the provisions of the Copyright Law of the Publisher's location, in its current version, and permission for use must always be obtained from Springer. Permissions for use may be obtained through RightsLink at the Copyright Clearance Center. Violations are liable to prosecution under the respective Copyright Law. The use of general descriptive names, registered names, trademarks, service marks, etc. in this publication does not imply, even in the absence of a specific statement, that such names are exempt from the relevant protective laws and regulations and therefore free for general use. While the advice and information in this book are believed to be true and accurate at the date of publication, neither the authors nor the editors nor the publisher can accept any legal responsibility for any errors or omissions that may be made. The publisher makes no warranty, express or implied, with respect to the material contained herein.

Printed on acid-free paper

Springer Gabler is a brand of Springer DE.
Springer DE is part of Springer Science+Business Media.
www.springer-gabler.de

To my family

Foreword

The present book by Peter Ising ties in with research in the area of earnings management. The procedural method consists of analyzing initial public offerings which are expected to have a high probability for strong incentives to use discretionary behavior. The author derives hypotheses for the US capital market and conducts tests with capacious data.

The first group of hypotheses primarily tests if discretionary reporting during initial public offerings exists. To uncover real activities management, the dissertation includes several accounting items as well as the typically employed accruals. The outcome of the thesis demonstrates that real activities management before and after going public in the US exists. Current literature differs about the existence of accruals management. To shed light on these diverging results, the author takes several dimensions into account. On the one hand, he differentiates between points in time around the IPO and on the other hand between industries. Both issues are not covered sufficiently, yet. Findings show that a differentiation between both subjects can have a substantial influence on results. Furthermore, the thesis includes a separation between profitable and unprofitable companies. This distinction is rarely used in prior literature, but results show interesting implications for research and practice, because plenty of companies in certain industries are unprofitable around the IPO.

The second group of hypotheses focusses primarily on differences between specific accounting items in certain industries. Especially the finance literature examined differences in financial ratios for firms around the IPO. The presented revelation that growth industries use expense accounts to a larger extent than established industries around issuing stock to influence investors supports practitioners in analyzing companies. While prior literature mainly expected the reduction of expenses to increase income, the author evidences abnormal increases in growth industries. The results are a valuable source against the background that growth companies are evaluated by their future prospects.

To conclude, the multi-dimensional approach which combines several research components must be highlighted because it is challenging and gives interesting insights. The selected research questions refer not only to open issues in research, but also offer valuable and detailed guidance for practitioners. I recommend this thesis to researchers and professionals, and wish that it wins the broad readership it deserves.

Prof. Dr. Dieter Pfaff

Acknowledgment

This dissertation is the result of my doctoral studies in Zurich, Switzerland. The time during these years was insightful and enriching. I would like to thank everyone who supported me and made my time at the University of Zurich such a unique experience.

First, I express my gratitude to the supervisor of my dissertation and my academic mentor, Prof. Dr. Dieter Pfaff. During my employment at his Chair of Accounting he was available at all times for arising questions and continuously supported the dissertation. Moreover, he advocated extra-curricular activities such as my IFRS-Accountant diploma or the teaching assignment at the Controller Academy. Especially, I thank him for the academic freedom to pursue my favorite topic at the crossroads of accounting and capital markets. I also thank Prof. Dr. Conrad Meyer for being my second supervisor.

There are many people who have made the dissertation and the work as a researcher a pleasant experience. My thanks go to all my doctoral colleagues, administrative assistants, and friends at the several chairs of business administration for academic and leisure time collaboration. In the course of developing my dissertation I benefitted from the interaction with numerous practitioners and scholars at conferences in Harvard, London, Amsterdam, Prague, WHU Vallendar, and Zurich. Due to the financial support of several scholarships from the Graduate School of Business, I was able to attend these valuable events.

Most importantly, my education and this dissertation would not have been possible without the support of my family. My deepest gratitude goes to my parents. My father Dr. Achim Ising and my mother Heidi Ising encouraged me to follow my interests, gave me guidance, and pointed out how to proceed in life. I very much appreciate the support by my brother Dr. Alexander Ising at every stage in my life. Furthermore, I owe gratitude to Meike for continuous moral encouragement and advice. Many thanks to all for supporting my work!

Peter Ising

Table of Contents

List of Abbreviations and Symbols

#	number/amount
Δ	change
A	total assets
Acc	accruals
adj. R^2	adjusted R-squared
ADR	American depository receipts
AM	accruals-based earnings management
ASales	long-lived asset sales
AvChe	average cash
BV	book value
CEO	chief executive officer
CfO	cash flow from operating activities
CFO	chief financial officer
COGS	cost of goods sold
CRSP	Center for Research in Security Prices
D.ΔDefRev	discretionary change in deferred revenues
D.ΔGrRec	discretionary change in gross receivables
D.ΔInv	discretionary change in inventory
D.ΔRec	discretionary change in receivables
D.Acc	discretionary accruals
D.Adv	discretionary advertising expenses
D.CfO	discretionary cash flow from operations
D.COGS	discretionary costs of goods sold
D.DisExp	abnormal discretionary expenses
D.GAS	discretionary gain on asset sales
D.Prod	discretionary production costs
D.R&D	discretionary research and development expenses
D.SGA	discretionary selling, general, and administrative expenses
DS	domestic accounting standard
e.g.	for example (exempli gratia)
Ed.	editor
Eds.	editors
et al.	et alii, et aliae

etc.	et cetera
FASB	Financial Accounting Standards Board
FIFO	first in first out
GAAP	generally accepted accounting principles
GAS	gain on asset sales
GrRec	gross accounts receivable
IAS	International Accounting Standards
IFRS	International Financial Reporting Standards
Int. A	intangible assets
IntFu	internal funds
IPO	initial public offering
ISales	long-lived investment sales
LIFO	last in first out
M&A	merger & acquisition
MV	market value
N	number
NegD.Acc	negative discretionary accruals
no.	number
No.	number(s)
Non-C. A	non-cash assets
NYSE	New York Stock Exchange
OLS	ordinary least squares
p.	page
PosD.Acc	positive discretionary accruals
PPE	property, plant, and equipment
prof.	profitable
profit.	profitable
R&D	research and development expenses
RAM	real activities management
RD	research and development expenses
Rec	net account receivables
REIT	real estate investment trust
RESET	regression specification-error test
ROA	return on assets

S	sales
SalesGR	growth of sales
SEO	seasoned equity offering
SFAS	Statements of Financial Accounting Standards
SG&A	selling, general, and administrative
SIC	Standard Industry Classification
TAcc	total accruals
UCLA	University of California, Los Angeles
VIF	variance inflation factor
vs.	versus
WRDS	Wharton Research Data Services

List of Figures

List of Tables

1. Introduction

1.1 Motivation

"All that glisters is not gold"[1]

The beginning of the new millennium was characterized by company scandals in accounting around the world (e.g., Enron, WorldCom). This triggered a loss of trust in management, the board, and in the profession of auditing. As a result, various laws and guidelines for enhanced corporate governance and financial reporting were approved. In economic systems, financial reporting is of main interest. The company benefits from a transparent and fair presentation of the financial statements in terms of lower capital costs as well as an increased liquidity.[2]

Accounting represents economic transactions in a comprehensible, verifiable, and decision usefulness way. However, financial deals can be presented in various ways in accounting, depending on the person involved in the valuation, the time horizon, and possible future scenarios. Accounting standards grant a certain amount of judgment when applying accounting policies. To a certain extent, estimations and assumptions must be made, influencing the accounts of assets and liabilities as well as the report of income and expenses. This option permits those preparing the accounts to pass their private information on to outsiders (e.g., possible investors, the regulator).[3] Enhanced transparency of reports is beneficial for outsiders and preferable under the information perspective of financial reporting. However, the other side of the coin is that accounting standards could mean the possibility of a deliberate manipulation of disclosed reporting items. Hence, if managers have the intention of obtaining private gains, they purposefully intervene in the financial reporting process. This subjectivity cannot be eliminated by comprehensive monitoring or exact compliance with accounting standards.

The reporting quality does not rely primarily on accounting principles, but on firm specific and institutional characteristics of incentives for the company and its management.[4] These factors lead to a cost-benefit consideration for the preparers who have a complex and specific structure of incentives within any company and especially in specific circumstances such as

---

1 Shakespeare (1600), Act II, Scene vii.
2 Diamond/Verrecchia (1991); Daske/Hail/Leuz/Verdi (2008).
3 Wagenhofer/Ewert (2007), pp. 288-289; Watts/Zimmerman (1986).
4 Leuz et al. (2003).

initial public offerings (IPO). Insiders (e.g., existing principle stockholders, directors)[5] possess private information about investment possibilities, management quality, and the chance to control future agency costs. Hence, there occurs a typical adverse selection problem. For example, companies have no intention of giving a true and fair view of the company's financial position or they want to comply with the capital market expectations, or they want to signal a specific company value. Therefore, they either opportunistically use discretion (e.g., to increase their own benefit) or signal their private information to the public. Thus, when using one set of accounting standards and the same business transactions, the reports disclosed by two companies can evolve differently.[6]

Opportunistic incentives are present, especially when companies come across important events such as IPOs, SEOs, and M&As where information asymmetry between insiders and outsiders exists.[7] Two recent and very popular examples are the IPOs of Facebook in 2012 (with a market value of $104 billion) where sales estimates had to be corrected immediately before trading began and also, the IPO of Groupon in 2011, which raised $700 million and was valued at almost $13 billion, when shortly thereafter sales manipulation was detected and the share price fell.[8] A better understanding of the accounting surrounding IPOs is useful for capital market participants. Therefore, accounting studies of (earnings) accruals management – primarily in the US – tried to identify abnormal behavior.[9] Prior research infers different conclusions about the issue of discretionary reporting around the IPO.[10] While the results of some studies present outcomes in favor of accruals management, others refute these findings. However, in this thesis three major important issues that have not been well considered in IPO literature are covered.

First, different possibilities exist to follow incentives depending on the period around the IPO. Therefore, a clear distinction between pre- and post-IPO financial reports is necessary. On the one hand, initial shareholders want to increase the issue price in the period before the IPO in order to sell their shares at a high value and increase gains for the company. However, the market scrutiny of regulators and analysts, for example, constrains these incentives in the pre-IPO period. On the other hand, shareholders also want to increase the stock price post-IPO in order to sell their shares after the lock-up period and maximize their benefit. Accordingly,

5 Rule 16 of the 1934 Securities and Exchange Act for the list of corporate insiders.
6 Pfaff/Ising (2010), pp. 292-293.
7 Fan (2007), p. 29; see also Pfaff/Ising (2010, 292-293) for the concept.
8 Groupon (2011); Parry (2012).
9 Healy/Palepu (2001), pp. 418-424; Healy/Wahlen (1999), pp. 369-371.
10 Ball/Shivakumar (2008).

these parties have a substantial opportunistic interest in using discretion in accounting in the years surrounding the IPO.[11] This myopic behavior of insiders has already been shown in prior literature.[12]

Second, when setting the share price, earnings are usually seen as the most important and sometimes the only valuable accounting item in prior literature and they are in the focus of both the press and consumers.[13] Correspondingly, these studies suggest that (upward) accruals management represents discretion and that the alternative would be non-existent earnings management in general. However, studies find that other accounting items are value relevant as well.[14] This means they are not only a means to an end for higher earnings. These items can be influenced by real activities management. Consistently, a survey in the US led by Graham et al. (2005) finds that managers who have to cope with greater scrutiny prefer real activities management (RAM) over accruals-based earnings management (AM), because these techniques are less likely to be detected by regulators, analysts, or auditors, for instance.[15] Therefore, the greater the scrutiny, the stronger the motivation for using RAM instead of AM.[16] Pronounced scrutiny is present around IPOs. Nevertheless, prior literature usually does not test for RAM around IPOs, but this is essential since AM and RAM can be used as substitutes and not coercively as complements.[17] Therefore, a closer look at different operating figures should give deeper insight into the diverging discretion of companies going public.

Finally, companies differ depending on various aspects such as profitability, growth, or investment strategy. Therefore, investors value accounting items that are specific to the company. For example, while managers and investors in profitable firms prefer high income, loss companies have to demonstrate their worthiness through sales.[18] Similarly, these specifics are true for diverging industries. In the years around IPOs there are eminent dissimilarities between companies in different business sectors. Usually, studies of earnings management combine various industries in one sample. Consequently, companies in these industries are

---

11 Ahearne et al. (2012, 3-4) find that CFOs and CEOs use discretion.

12 Bhojraj et al. (2009), p. 2363.

13 Armstrong et al. (2009), p. 2; Teoh et al. (1998c), pp. 175-176.

14 Guo et al. (2005), p. 425, for example.

15 The terms real activity management, real activity manipulation, and real earnings management are employed interchangeably.

16 Cohen/Zarowin (2010), p. 15.

17 Cohen/Zarowin (2010); Cohen et al. (2008), p. 781; Zang (2012).

18 *Loss firms* equal "unprofitable" firms. They are characterized by having an income smaller than zero. Similarly, *loss groups* include only loss companies while industries are termed *"unprofitable" industries* if the majority of firms are loss companies.

expected to behave similarly which is a strong assumption. However, they differ in having distinct company characteristics. Hence, the incentives of companies and the corresponding financial reporting goals diverge. Taking all these differences into account can clarify the opacity of incentives and resulting earnings management around IPOs.

1.2 Objective

Several issues can be identified which arise from the fact that incentives are present around IPOs. While prior literature has already addressed many specifics, there are some aspects that deserve further attention. The accounting literature rarely differentiates between diverging incentives around the issue and interests of issuers in various industries concerning accounting numbers. This study serves to close the gap. To address these subjects an empirical study in the US can add value to the ongoing discussion about IPOs and their financial reporting issues.

By examining the particularities of earnings management around the time of IPOs, this thesis provides new evidence about the discretionary behavior before and after the IPO when different incentives are present. Additionally, investors value specific reporting items in varying industries and profitability. The examination of these additional aspects helps to differentiate between the results of prior research where contradicting outcomes exist. Hence, the awareness of capital market participants can be enhanced and information asymmetry reduced. This sheds light on financial reporting and its underlying incentives. The corresponding research question can be formulated as follows:

Do companies use earnings accruals and real activity management in various accounting items differently depending on the time period around the IPO and industry specifics, and do profitable and loss companies behave differently?

This thesis aims at giving new insight into discretionary reporting in the years surrounding IPOs in particular industries and in individual accounting items. The outcome provides academics, investors, analysts, and regulators with a better understanding of accounting around IPOs.[19]

[19] The study does not try to assess earnings quality. However, while earnings quality is a broader concept than earnings management, it partially includes the discretion in earnings and henceforth, it is touched upon in the study because discretionary accruals are a possible measure of earnings quality (Dichev et al., 2012).

2. Initial Public Offerings

2.1 Process of an IPO

The process of going public in the US is governed by the Securities Act of 1933. Usually, if companies decide to go public, an underwriting bank supports the process. After the due diligence, the offering prospectus is prepared. This document includes general information about the firm, future prospects, the competitive environment, and audited financial statements for the most recent three years. With the prospectus the company and its underwriter(s) promote the issue in road shows.[20]

The process of setting a price for an IPO starts at the time the issue is registered and filed with the Securities and Exchange Commission (SEC). In the preliminary or the amended prospectus, the company makes a range of prices available which are built on expectation from the company and constitute possible offering prices.[21]

The time line of the IPO process is portrayed in Figure 1. The process of going public starts some months or years before the issue. The last 365 days before the IPO is defined as year -1 and portrays the pre-IPO results. Then follows the IPO and the shares are made available to the public. Only a part of the shares are available, because initial shareholders sell around 15-20 percent of a company.[22] The remaining 80-85 percent of shares are restricted from sale for a certain time period. This is called the lock-up period.[23] In these months company insiders are not allowed to sell their shares for usually 180 days after public trading started.[24] This period is designed to prevent a stock from experiencing a high volatility, which might occur if too many shareholders sell at the same time. The market could interpret this behavior as revealing private information and the price would fall dramatically.

The time line shows the first 365 days after the IPO as year +1 (post-IPO). Actually, the lock-up period can expire before or after the end of the financial year +1, depending when the company goes public and when the next financial year-end is due. However, the lock-up

[20] Fan (2007), p. 29; Singer (2007), p. 49; Teoh et al. (1998c), pp. 177-178.
[21] Lowry/Schwert (2004), p. 5; Lowry/Schwert (2002), pp. 1173-1174.
[22] Bradley et al. (2001); Ofek/Richardson (2001), p. 22.
[23] DuCharme et al. (2001), p. 370. In primary offerings, the proceeds flow to the company for corporate expansion, for example, whereas in a secondary offering, the proceeds go to the owners for selling their shares. Typically, IPOs combine both methods.
[24] Field/Hanka (2001), p. 471.

period is most often six months and the earnings reporting lag is one to three months after the end of the financial year. Therefore, the lock-up period ends in close proximity to the financial statements of year +1 and its announcement.

Some prior studies used the notation "year 0" instead of "year +1" to refer to the first financial statements after the IPO. However, there are also some studies that use year 0 for all financial statements that are due in the whole calendar year of the IPO. This means some of these dates are before and some are after the IPO.[25] The outcome is a mixture of pre- and post-incentives when using these year 0 results and can bias the findings and their interpretation. To better differentiate between pre- and post-IPO statements, the terms year -1 and year +1 year clearly indicate the time period of the statements and the associated incentives.

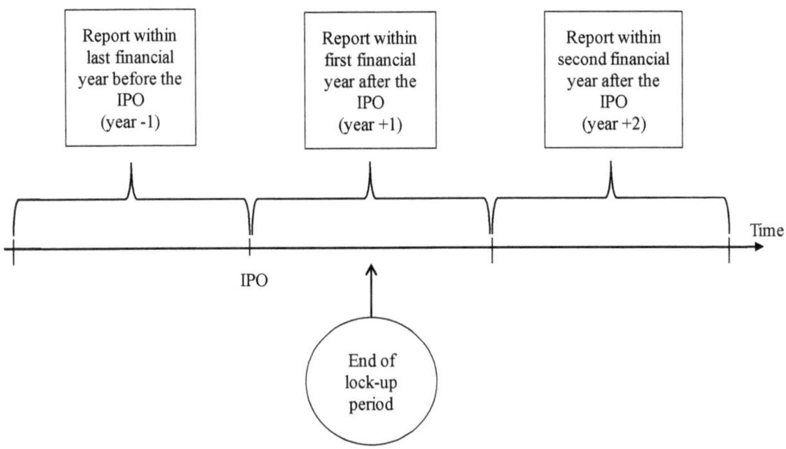

Figure 1: Time Line of IPO Years

[25] DuCharme et al. (2004), p. 34; Teoh et al. (1998b), p. 1936; Teoh et al. (1998c), pp. 178-179.

2.2 Motivations for Going Public

The decision to go public is important for every company and depends on various factors. Prior research mainly examined underpricing and long-run performance of IPOs but paid little attention to the reason for the listing on a public exchange. However, there are several motives which partly contradict each other and therefore, they are difficult to include into one theory.[26] Some are presented here.

The first motive is the minimization of capital costs to optimize the capital structure.[27] This motive is supported by Fama/French (2004, 267) who argue that more unprofitable firms go public due to lower capital costs. Capital costs decline due to spreading the risk of equity owners and lowering borrowing costs because of transparency and reputation, for example. Therefore, issuing equity minimizes the cost of capital and thus maximizes the value of the firm. This helps shareholders to sell their stocks at a high price. Another motive is to increase bargaining power with banks. Being present in the equity market reduces the cost of capital due to more pellucidity about the company.[28]

A third motive could be that companies become a takeover target and shareholders want to establish a market price when they intend to cash out or sell the company at a higher value than without the issue.[29] This can also be true for venture capitalists and underlines the intention of shareholders as well as the management to increase the share price.[30] Again, there are studies that partly disprove this motive which leaves only a part of companies that have this notion in mind.[31] The aforementioned motive also includes that an IPO itself could indicate an overvaluation of the company because shareholders intend to sell at the peak of valuation. Then investors would be conspicuous about the step towards public listing. However, there are studies that find counterintuitive arguments.[32] Therefore, this motive is true for only a part of the companies.

Fourth, a motive for going public certainly is the intention to create publicity or reputation for the firm.[33] The IPO causes the firm to become known to the public which can help to make

26 Brau (2010), pp. 18-19; Pagano et al. (1998), p. 36.
27 Baxter (1967); Modigliani/Miller (1958); Modigliani/Miller (1963); Stiglitz (1969).
28 Pagano et al. (1998).
29 Lerner et al. (2005); Zingales (1995).
30 Black/Gilson (1998).
31 Brau et al. (2010).
32 Ritter (1991).
33 Maksimovic/Pichler (2001); Pagano et al. (1998).

the company more interesting to investors than a firm that operates in the dark. Furthermore, it sometimes has a first mover advantage in the niche of an industry and indicates that it intends to grow intensively in the future. This motive might be relevant especially for small Internet companies or those operating in the Technology industry, but less for companies that are already well-established.

Furthermore, if the shareholders want to cash in, then maximizing the share price is of interest. The associated adverse selection problem inherits the informational asymmetry between the issuer and possible investors. The larger the gap of information between the two parties, the lower the share prices and the higher the underpricing.[34] Since more informational symmetry leads to lower underpricing, an improvement of understanding of the financial report would decrease this anomaly.[35] Therefore, earnings management studies can help to decrease the information asymmetry.

The results of the motives are tested in several studies and indicate that they apply to specific samples of companies.[36] This supports a differentiation between particular sets of firms and underlines the importance of separating companies into subgroups when examining them.

For all companies there exist pros and cons for an IPO which are associated to the motives. On the one hand, companies have a number of benefits when issuing stock.[37] It is the first opportunity for a firm's shareholders to receive money for the value of their ownership stake and diversify their property.[38] Additionally, the corporation receives financing and implements a capable ownership structure.[39] Another benefit from going public is the minimization of the cost of capital and the facilitation of takeover activity.[40] It advances the growth process of a company while later in the life cycle of a company growth usually declines. Further benefits include the increase of publicity, attraction to top executives etc. However, not only the motives and benefits are decisive when companies go public, but prior literature finds that IPO markets are cyclical over time in terms of the amount of companies

34 Leland/Pyle (1977), p. 371-372; Rock (1986), pp. 188-189.
35 Arthurs et al. (2008), pp. 277-279.
36 See for example Pagano et al. (1998) and Brau (2010, 7).
37 The aspects are primarily intended for US IPOs. However, they are similarly true for IPOs in Europe, although the likelihood of going public and the underlying motivations may differ due to structural, cultural and other differences.
38 Pagano et al. (1998), pp. 36-42; Zingales (1995), p. 425.
39 Mello/Parsons (1998), p. 80-82.
40 Brau/Fawcett (2006), p. 406; Schöber (2008), pp. 44-49.

issuing stock and proceeds raised.[41] Accordingly, companies should file the issue in hot markets or after periods of high underpricing.[42]

On the other hand, there are also disadvantages when becoming publicly traded. The direct and indirect costs of going public include the registration and underwriting (which account for around 15 percent of the raised funds), underpricing, employing a more sophisticated financial reporting standard and report in short time intervals, as well as the agency problems generated by a separation between ownership and control to a larger extent.[43] Additionally, the new investors have specific interests and can try to influence the behavior of the company in contrast to the founders' interest.[44]

Overall, there are several motives for going public with the corresponding benefits and downsides, but all include that shareholders sell a part of their stakes in the company and try to receive a high price which fosters earnings management.

2.3 Industry Differences

When going public, companies are valued dependent on several factors including their industry. For example, the future development of the industry has to be taken into account or the peer group (for calculation of the multiples etc.) of existing companies from the same industry.[45] Prior literature finds evidence for differences in industries; therefore, a discrepancy between companies can be expected. Following the Internet bubble, some studies examined financials of IPOs in the Internet and Technology industries and evidenced their difference to other industry sectors. Usually, this procedure means that the (control) sample is a mixture of various industries. However, this assortment of industries mixes influences and varies in itself if specific industries differ in amount of companies. To overcome this problem, studies should focus on one industry at a time instead of mixing industries in the (control) sample.

Some researchers include the Internet and Technology industries which are specific in their financials for several reasons. Internet companies usually have an income lower than zero when going public whereas Technology companies are ambiguous concerning profitability. Furthermore, Internet companies are even younger and grow faster than established

41 Ibbotson/Jaffe (1975); Ibbotson et al. (1988).
42 Lowry/Schwert (2002); Pastor/Veronesi (2005).
43 Jensen/Meckling (1976), pp. 306-309; Ritter (1987), pp. 271-272; Zingales (1995), p. 425.
44 Pagano/Röell (1998), pp. 188-191.
45 Dong/Michel (2012), p. 2.

companies. Other characteristics of these companies are their rapid growth, a predominant equity financing, and the fact that these firms are not valued by their earnings.[46] Similarly, the science (Biotech) industry also shows negative income when going public and it is valued by its R&D expenditures, for example.[47] The specifics of these industries are long-term research and development investments that are meaningful for their future competitiveness. Depending on the results of these projects, companies can create benefits for investors which have to cope with the associated risks. Investments in R&D are expensed as incurred and produce losses over years before the company receives benefits. This attracts venture capital investors in these three industries which take the current risk for future benefits. In contrast to these R&D-intensive industries, Construction, Manufacturing, and Wholesale industries are usually profitable when going public, more commercially established, older, and grow less strongly. However, their growth is stronger than companies in the same industry which are already publicly traded. Moreover, earnings are value relevant for investors while R&D investments are not important in these well-established industries.[48] They are financed by debt as well as equity in contrast to the above industries which are mainly financed by equity.[49] These industries are equipped with many tangible assets. Therefore, they obtain more possibilities of accounting flexibility in reporting earnings which enables them to extend the discretionary amounts over several accounts and obscure the discretion. Firms with many tangible assets can, for example, lower estimates of bad debt, increase inventory valuation, or sell assets for gains instead of merely focusing on sales management to boost reported earnings.[50]

46 Bowen et al. (2002); Damodaran (2012); Davis (2002); Hand (2003).
47 Guo et al. (2005); Lévesque et al. (2012).
48 Bassioni et al. (2004), p. 46; Chan/Chan (2004), p. 210.
49 Graham et al. (2005); Fedyk et al. (2012); Joos/Zhdanov (2004).
50 Singer (2007), p. 21.

3. Discretionary Reporting

3.1 Definition

The management in companies has a variety of opportunities to influence financial reporting.[51] U.S. GAAP standards allow judgment in aspects of recognition and measurement within the bounds of legitimacy. Earnings management is the term usually used when describing discretion in accounting and reporting. Healy/Wahlen (1999, 368) define it as follows: "Earnings management occurs when managers use judgment in financial reporting and in structuring transactions to alter financial reports to either mislead some stakeholders about the underlying economic performance of the company or to influence contractual outcomes that depend on reported accounting numbers." Earnings management takes place within the boundaries of GAAP, so it differs from fraud. Yet, its consequences can be the same.[52] The term is usually connoted with a negative meaning in literature. However, the influence can have various intentions. First, it can be beneficial when using accounting flexibility to signal private information to outsiders. Second, it can occur in a gray area if manipulation is opportunistic or economically efficient. Finally, it is malicious if the company misrepresents or conceals the financial situation of the company.[53] When using the term earnings management several aspects have to be considered. There are different instruments, purposes, and the corresponding timing that influence the meaning of this term. A common characterization of choices is given in Table 1.

This table shows that earnings management can overstate or understate accounting numbers within GAAP while neutrally means no earnings management. When violating GAAP, fraud is present. Conservative reporting means that the liability accounts are overstated while the asset side is understated. This can be done by aggressively recognizing provisions or understating sales, for example. Aggressive accounting includes the understatement of liabilities and the overstatement of assets. Examples are deflation of bad debt provisions or exaggeration of sales. Fraudulent accounting includes the violation of GAAP by illegally manipulating sales accounts, for example.

---

[51] DeAngelo (1988), p. 18.
[52] Dechow/Skinner (2000), p. 239.
[53] For different intentions of earnings management see Fields et al. (2001), Ronen/Sadan (1975), and Schipper (1989).

Table 1: Characterization and Examples of Reporting Types[54]

Reporting type	Accounting choices
	Within GAAP
Conservative	Excessively aggressive recognition of provisions or reserves Overvaluation of acquired in-process R&D in purchase acquisitions Overstatement of restructuring charges and write-offs
Neutral	Earnings that result from a neutral operation of the process
Aggressive	Understatement of the provision for bad debts Drawing down provisions or reserves in an overly aggressive manner
	Violating GAAP
Fraud	Recording sales before they are "realizable" Recording fictitious sales Backdating sales invoices Overstating inventory by recording fictitious inventory

The term earnings management, references to earnings as the only line item of interest although it includes all aspects of discretionary reporting. Originally, earnings management research examines earnings as the most important variable for investors. Meanwhile, the literature stream refers to various accounting items which are managed by companies in accounting and in real activities. For example, Cohen/Zarowin (2010, 9) label RAM as "real earnings management" which emphasizes their focus on the resulting influence on earnings and not on the influenced accounting items (i.e., activities) themselves. However, these line items are managed by real activities and they are used as valuation items by investors. Hence, their importance during IPOs can be higher than for (negative) earnings. To remove earnings from the center of interest and deflect the spotlight on other accounting items that can be of high interest during the IPO, the term "discretionary reporting" is used and it is more capacious and differentiates between the management of earnings, only, and discretion in various accounting items. Hence, this thesis concentrates on the discretion of several line items. It makes more sense to use a broader term if the goal is to examine valuation purposes of various items that are managed both in accounting and by real activities.[55] The aspect of

[54] Adapted from Dechow/Skinner (2000, 239).

[55] It would be confusing to talk about earnings management and meaning other line items that are influenced. The result of the activities displays in earnings, of course, but in this study the intention is to influence specific line items for valuation purposes. To divide between EM and RAM the title says "earnings accruals".

the term “reporting” is founded on the intention to report specific numbers which are influenced by real activities and used in valuation, yet there are many more possibilities to use discretion in reporting.[56] In this thesis, discretionary reporting is equivalent to earnings management in prior literature and includes the management of earnings (accruals), sales, and R&D, for example.[57] Furthermore, it is in line with previous studies when using earnings as a measure of accruals. Looking at individual accounts (such as sales) helps to split up aggregate accruals for valuation purposes and moreover, additional items can be tested for real activity management. In other words, accruals management is only one way to influence earnings while the management of individual accounts typically intends to impact earnings, but it can also be used to influence the valuation of a company if investors value the individual account. Therefore, the title of the thesis differentiates between accruals – that focus on resulting earnings – and real activities that additionally include other accounting items and their purpose in terms of valuation.

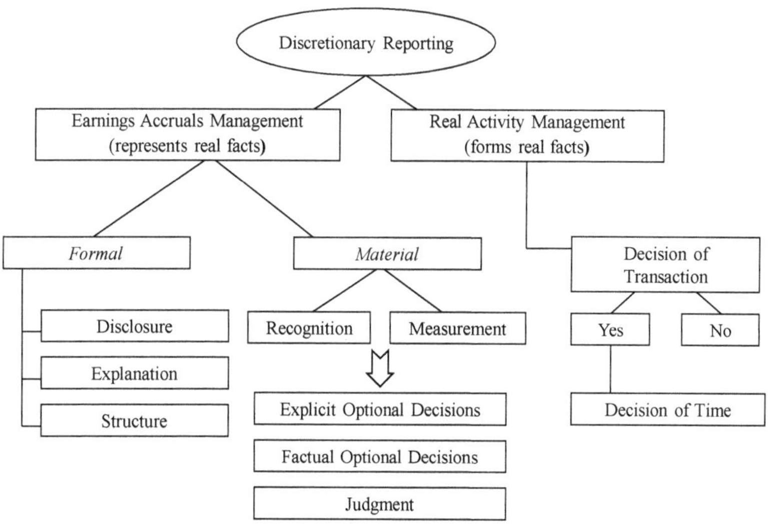

Figure 2: Types of Discretionary Reporting[58]

[56] See Healy/Wahlen (1999, 369) for an example.

[57] Similarly in German, the word “Bilanzpolitik” is used which names only the balance sheet, although other parts of the financial statements are affected, too. This is why “Rechnungslegungspolitik” is a better term when describing these practices. See Pfaff/Ising (2010), pp. 294-295.

[58] Adapted from Baetge et al. (2004, 154) and Hofmann (2008, 87).

Figure 2 exhibits the differentiation between (earnings) accruals management and real activity management. While accruals represent past business activities, real activities arrange business actions as desired by managers. Accruals management differentiates between formal and material procedures. The formal aspect includes tolerance in disclosure, explanation, and structure while the material aspect refers to recognition and measurement. The latter aspects include explicit and factual optional decisions as well as judgment of managers. Real activity management includes actions taken by managers to influence business activities and the corresponding outcomes. Discretion is possible in the aspect of using this leeway or not and when to use it.

While this thesis concentrates on discretionary reporting, it touches the concept of earnings quality because the latter has a broader scope and partly includes the concept of discretionary reporting. Current research has not reached consent about the definition of earnings quality.[59] Quality cannot be directly observed, so the concept of quality in earnings is an abstract one and can be derived from the goals of financial reporting.[60] On the one hand, there are some qualitative measures which cannot be measured empirically (e.g., comparability, understandability). However, there are existing measures which are used as empirical proxies for this quality (e.g., timely loss recognition, earnings smoothing[61]). Basically, the definitions depend on specific earnings properties reliant on the view of researchers, standards setters, investors or analysts, for example.[62] Conditional on the preferred outcomes the definitions and measures of earnings quality diverge.

3.2 Earnings Accruals and Real Activities Management

3.2.1 Earnings Accruals Management

All accounting records that modify the sum of cash flow for financial reporting purposes to generate a summary measure of firm performance in a given period are so-called accruals.[63] Accruals arise as the discrepancy between the timing of cash flow (from operations) and the

[59] See Schipper/Vincent (2003, 98) who define it as economic income whilst Penman/Zhang (2002, 237) designate it as a good indicator of future earnings, as examples.

[60] Wagenhofer/Dücker (2007), p. 266.

[61] This proxy is disputed. Some researchers view smoothed earnings as a measure of high quality earnings (e.g., Francis et al., 2003) whilst others point out the contrary (e.g., Bhattacharya et al., 2003, p. 649).

[62] Goncharov (2005), pp. 5-6.

[63] FASB (2010), OB17-19.

accounting recognition of the transaction.[64] Expected future cash flow is accrued while cash flow from past periods is deferred according to the underlying business transaction and preparers' discretion. Therefore, accruals exhibit a tradeoff between relevance and reliability. In accruals, the information content about future cash flow is relevant, yet they are less reliable than cash flow.[65] Examples of accruals are the difference between earnings and cash flow at year end or in one transaction. The reconciliation of cash flow to earnings inherits several reconciliation positions. Another example is the difference between sales and cash flow. To reconcile cash flow to sales, accounting employs receivables. Depreciation serves to reconcile the cash payment of an asset to the respective accounting periods of usage. The cash flow of an asset has to be allocated to financial periods.

Primarily, accruals support investors in estimating the company's performance over time. Accounting standards instruct preparers when and how to use accruals. Accrual accounting has several hitches. To estimate cash inflows and outflows over time, the preparer has to make decisions which are complex. On the one hand, judgments can be erroneous due to the complex business environment and resulting managerial inaccuracies (unintentional errors). On the other hand, opportunistic incentives can cause preparers to do intentional errors. Both kinds of inaccuracies reduce the quality of accruals as well as earnings. There are three concepts to measure the quality of accruals.[66] First, the magnitude of accruals or the ratio of accruals to cash flow from operations. The second concept focusses on examining the estimation error of accounting accruals. Finally, studies can test for discretionary accruals.[67] These are a common measure in earnings management studies.

The problem in using discretionary accruals is that they are not observable. Therefore, several methods of estimation have been developed. In studies of AM researchers usually measure earnings or sales management by separating the discretionary from the respective non-discretionary part of accruals. Non-discretionary accruals arise from transactions in the current period which are regular for the firm concerning factors such as the performance level, industry conventions, and macro-economic events. On the other hand, discretionary accruals arise from transactions or accounting treatments executed with the purpose of managing results. However, accruals reverse over the lifetime of a company. Current literature estimates discretionary amounts by regressing total accruals on accounting items which explain

64 Healy (1985), p. 86.
65 Sloan (1996).
66 See Goncharov (2005), p. 9 for the concept.
67 For example, the first concept is used in Leuz et al. (2003, 511) and similarly in Penman (2001, 611), the second one in Dechow/Dichev (2002, 36), and the third one in Healy (1985, 89).

accruals. The amount of accruals which is unexplained is referred to as the residual of this model. It equals (non-adjusted) discretionary accruals for the company and is tested for significant anomalies compared to the control group and/or a matched company (adjusted discretionary accruals).

Earnings are the summary measure of individual accounts. When looking at total accruals, derived from earnings, there is no information about the influence of separate accounts. It makes sense to inspect these accounts if they are a good proxy for discretionary accruals, which result from preparer's judgment and have a significant impact on the earnings figure. This single account approach is useful to understand the preparer's procedure, but it only looks at one component of many to build earnings.[68] Examples of single accounts are bad debt provisions, allowance and provision for loan losses, and loss reserves.[69]

3.2.2 Real Activity Management

3.2.2.1 Overview

Companies can use accruals to manage earnings and other accounts, however, these techniques have a high risk of being detected by capital market participants. Therefore, managers can make use of real activities to influence earnings and other accounting data.[70] RAM is defined as actions managers take that differ from normal business practices.[71] RAM takes place in real activities and not only in accounting methods of generally accepted accounting principles (GAAP) which represent those actions.

AM has been thoroughly examined in accounting literature for many years while RAM is recently receiving more attention. However, RAM is not tested comprehensively in an IPO environment or divided by industry. Such an examination can give further understanding of companies' behavior.

RAM offers a more direct way than AM to assess discretionary behavior by managers. However, the ability of correctly estimating real abnormal activities is a crucial point and

68 Francis (2001), p. 314.

69 For the three examples see McNichols/Wilson (1988), Wahlen (1994), and Petroni (1992), respectively.

70 Schipper (1989); Ising (1975).

71 Roychowdhury (2006). Yet, he uses the term real activities "manipulations" instead of "management" and thereby emphasizes the negative and illegal aspects.

difficult to handle because factors such as the economic environment and performance of the firm also play an important role.

Usually, operating and investment decisions affect cash flow whereas accruals management does not. Another difference between AM and RAM is the time when they are employed. While accruals can be adapted at year-end, real activities must be arranged primarily during the year or in the last quarter. However, RAM is more costly than accruals management and hence it reduces firm value due to actions that are not in line with optimal business behavior.[72] In contrast to accruals, real activities management is not obligatory to reverse in the future. An account can be influenced over several time periods and returned instantly to a normal level without going to the opposite direction or spending can be cut lower than the common amount.[73] However, an overinvestment in certain business activities will usually not last over a long time period if the regular business activities suffer from this behavior.

The distinction of discretionary reporting by accounting items in terms of AM and RAM is not always clear. For example, sales can be influenced by accounting decisions as well as by real activities. Companies either bring forward sales from upcoming years or they cut prices to accelerate sales. Similarly, COGS and change in inventory can be influenced by AM and RAM.[74]

Real activities management influences different business activities. Hence, a closer look at diverse operating figures should give a deeper insight into the diverging discretion of companies. Concerning RAM, this study focuses on sales, cash flow from operating activities (CfO), research and development (R&D), selling, general, and administrative expenses (SG&A), advertising expenses, discretionary expenses, change in inventory, cost of goods sold (COGS), production costs, and gain on asset sales (GAS).

3.2.2.2 Sales

Sales are one of the most important figures in accounting to display the performance of companies. They include the information of price and amount of the sold products. Especially growth firms are seen as dependent on revenues rather than expenses, for example.[75] Companies from the Internet and Technology industries are detected employing sales

72 Ewert/Wagenhofer (2005), p. 1112; Graham et al. (2005).
73 For a study specifically concerning reversals of earnings accruals management see Dechow et al. (2012).
74 Roychowdhury (2006).
75 Ertimur et al. (2003); Ghosh et al. (2005); Stubben (2006), p. 2.

management.[76] Likewise, profitable industries such as Construction are interested in high sales to increase their share price.[77] Although sales exhibit high costs when being detected, firms with high gross margins benefit largely from overstating them.[78] Sales management has proven crucial concerning discretion of companies. Therefore, using sales management influences the perception of performance for outsiders. An increase in sales postulates growth in the amount of buyers (regional or diversified group of buyers) and a better market penetration, for example.

Typical examples are bill-and-hold transactions. Buyers receive the invoice although shipment has not occurred, yet. Hence, the seller is still in control of the corresponding rights and duties. Furthermore, more lenient credit terms or price discounts towards customers can increase the amount of sold products. Additionally, companies can use channel stuffing (trade loading) and send products to dealers which will be sold in the next period. Either dealers are obligated to accept these products or companies can send these unasked, for example. However, this can have long-term consequences like the return of goods and excess inventory or fluctuating demand. Temporarily increasing sales volumes are likely to reverse. The surplus of sales leads to higher earnings (when margins are positive), but cash flow will be lower relatively to sales.[79]

Besides revenues, there is the account of gross accounts receivable which includes receivables plus the allowance for doubtful accounts. This account can be managed through real business activities (e.g., more lenient credit terms) or accounting estimates. Furthermore, the account of deferred revenue mirrors the cash receipt of a transaction that has not yet been closed (advanced payments or unearned revenue). Influencing gross accounts receivable has future cash consequences whereas deferred revenue does not.[80] Both accounts have received little attention in prior literature.

[76] Dechow/Schrand (2004), p. 42; Feroz et al. (1991); Levitt (1998), p. 18; Nelson et al. (2002); Pfaff/Ising (2010), p. 296; Turner et al. (2001). Yet, the high frequency of detection can also mean that sales management is more likely to be detected than other line items.
[77] Krolle/Sommerkamp (2010), pp. 49-50; Stubben (2010), p. 696.
[78] Stubben (2006), p. 8.
[79] Cohen/Zarowin (2010), p. 8.
[80] Caylor (2010), p. 83. It is important to note that deferred revenues can be managed by discretion in accounting, only. Nevertheless it is included with real activity sales for clarity reasons.

3.2.2.3 CfO

Cash flow from operations is well discussed in tests of earnings management. It can be influenced by various real activities while accrual accounting has no cash consequences. A typical example is real sales management such as channel stuffing.[81] This procedure usually decreases cash flow in terms of revenues since the products are not yet paid. Income increasing RAM will not always affect abnormal CfO and earnings in the same direction. There are several real actions with ambiguous effects on CfO. Especially, expense accounts can heavily influence this item and will be a main driver of the outcome.

3.2.2.4 R&D

According to the Financial Accounting Standards Board (FASB), costs of R&D projects must be expensed as incurred because of the uncertainty of future benefits resulting from the investments (SFAS No. 2).[82] Prior accounting literature suggests that R&D expenses are an accounting item which is used for discretionary reporting.[83] It is a popular measure to influence the share price but rarely examined in earnings management and especially not around IPOs.[84] R&D is a line item of high internal discretion. While companies can influence cash inflow from operations only to a certain extent, they can internally influence R&D expenses quite severely by management decisions. There might be some ongoing R&D projects which are resource intensive, but costs can be cut by management and do not only rely on external factors. Contrarily, cash inflow has to be generated externally and relies to a much smaller extent on management discretion. The earnings fixation hypothesis suggests investors are interested in earnings and expenses are cut. On the other hand, in industries with high R&D expenses, it is probable that investors focus on this accounting item since it is an indicator for innovative strength and future potential.[85] This means additional spending in R&D could signal future benefits to investors (signaling hypothesis).[86] Either cutting R&D spending to manage income or increasing it to depict future benefits helps to influence

---

81 Roychowdhury (2006).

82 Only for certain kinds of software the FASB permits the capitalization (SFAS No. 86). This differs from International Financial Reporting Standards (IFRS) which allow the recognition of development costs if certain conditions are met (IAS 38.57).

83 Darrough/Rangan (2004), pp. 2-3.

84 Bushee (1998), pp. 306-307; Dechow/Sloan (1991), p. 52; Graham et al. (2005), p. 40; Gunny (2010), p. 857; Hand (2005), pp. 615-616; Hsu (2009), pp. 264-265; Sievers/Klobucnik (2012), pp. 1-3.

85 Griliches (1984).

86 Darrough/Rangan (2004), pp. 2-3. See Trueman (1986) for the signaling hypothesis and Stein (1989) for the earnings fixation hypothesis.

investors. In sum, all companies have expectations to influence R&D expenses around the IPO as elaborated above for accruals.

3.2.2.5 SG&A

Another important accounting item is SG&A expense, although it is mainly ignored as a single line item in the accounting literature about earnings management around IPOs.[87] Prior accounting studies suggested that SG&A expenses are influenced when specific incentives are present.[88] Since SG&A is a catchall category for overhead expenses, it is involved in various business activities and growth firms are less efficient than more mature companies. SG&A can be managed by several real actions with an ambiguous outcome.

U.S. GAAP does not allow recognizing intangible assets such as brands, customer loyalty, or human capital as accounting assets. However, these assets are partly created by expenditures in SG&A and can be seen as investments with future benefit to the firm rather than simply increasing discretionary expenses. Hence, by cutting these expenditures the economic consequence may not materialize in the short-term, but in the long-term. Furthermore, SG&A expenses usually include certain other manageable expenditures such as employee training, maintenance, travel, rent, and salaries. If spending of SG&A is largely made in cash, lowering these expenses reduces cash outflows and also increases earnings. This leads to higher abnormal CfO in the current financial year but could decrease future CfO. Nevertheless, SG&A also includes stock-based compensation, commissions to outside sales representatives, legal and consulting fees, all of which can be high for IPO firms and difficult to influence. Going public may induce high costs on this accounting item.

3.2.2.6 Advertising

If discretionary expenses are examined for RAM by the sum of several accounts (including advertising expenses), the implied conclusion suggests that the aggregate effects of the components can be attributed to their sum, but not to the three parts equally. To extend prior literature, discretionary expenses have to be split up. In their survey Graham et al. (2005) find that advertising expenses are an item of possible influence and is used for managerial

[87] Roychowdhury (2006); Cohen/Zarowin (2010).
[88] Gunny (2010), pp. 857-858; Taulli (2012), p. 88.

discretion to meet earnings targets.[89] However, prior earnings management studies usually do not use this accounting item in their models of real activities management.[90]

Reducing or boosting advertising expense compared to R&D can mean a more immediate impact on sales. While reducing advertising increases cash flow and profit, it may have long-term downsides. On the other hand, increasing spending in this account might generate short-term upsurge in sales and profit. Furthermore, if managers want to meet certain earnings benchmarks, they focus on short-term goals and advertising can play an important role.

3.2.2.7 Discretionary Expenses

Discretionary expenses consist of R&D, SG&A, and advertising expenses. If a company reduces these expenses, they can increase earnings or boost cash flow. This depends on the fact if the company settles its obligations in cash. Yet, the reduction of these accounts can lead to decreased cash flow in the future, as mentioned above.

Discretionary expenses inherit the respective incentives of the three accounting items. In many prior studies it is tested as a single measure for RAM, but usually not around IPOs.[91] The inclusion of this account supports the comparability of the study to prior literature and its behavior around issues. If the three specific items are managed, then discretionary expenses are supposed to be managed equally.

3.2.2.8 Change in Inventory

The change in inventory during the year is another typical measure of real activities management. It is part of the commonly used production costs as sum of COGS and change in inventory.[92] If companies overproduce goods to lower COGS, they generate excess inventory that has to be sold in future periods and generates higher inventory holding costs. If they lower their inventories, they save money by fewer storage costs but have fewer products at hand. In either way, companies can influence these costs depending on their interest. However, if companies overproduce goods and increase inventories, they have to cut down production in the next periods if the demand stays constant and prior inventories were adequate. Contrarily, if companies lower production to decrease inventory holding costs

89 Graham et al. (2005), p. 32.
90 For an exemption see Cohen et al. (2009, 1-2).
91 Gunny (2006).
92 Chen et al. (2010), pp. 14-15; Enomoto et al. (2012), pp. 8-9.

towards the end of the year, they have to increase production in the next year to satisfy customers at a given demand level. Companies can use both approaches when following the specific incentives. However, change in inventory is linked to COGS and production costs. Looking at this specific account gives more information than only taking the aggregate measure of production costs into account.

3.2.2.9 COGS

COGS are the direct costs attributable to the production of the sold goods. This amount includes the cost of the materials as well as direct labor costs used in creating the good. It excludes indirect expenses such as distribution costs and sales force costs. Obviously, COGS depend on the type of business and hence vary from industry to industry.

Typical measures of the firm's profitability are profit margins. The gross profit margin is calculated by gross profit divided by revenue. Gross profit results from revenues minus COGS. A high percentage is superior for this ratio. It is an indicator of performance and profitability within the industry. Furthermore, it is useful for the valuation of companies. Capital market participants are interested in these numbers for specific years as well as in trends over several periods, especially around IPOs.

COGS are part of production costs as used in this study. COGS are important for issuers around the IPO as a measure for the company's gross margin. Investors are interested in this accounting item to figure out at what cost companies produce their goods.

Overproduction decreases COGS, but they can increase when the resulting marginal costs are higher than the fixed costs. A company can produce more units than necessary for a normal business year and thereby spread the fixed overhead costs over a larger number of units. This reduces the fixed costs per unit. The reduction in the fixed costs per unit should not be offset by the increase of marginal cost per unit, so the total cost per unit declines. In this manner, COGS can be reduced by an increase in production that is higher than necessary and report higher operating margins. Conversely, the production costs will increase whilst sales not necessarily. This leads to a higher production costs to sales ratio. If this is the case, cash from operations will decrease and allotment costs increase.

Furthermore, COGS could be influenced by accrual manipulation of inventories. For example, by delaying or speeding up of depreciation.[93] The LIFO vs. FIFO methods can be used to change the profit. The gross profit margin indicates that companies try to lower COGS and increase their margin to demonstrate a healthy company to investors.

3.2.2.10 Production

Production costs are the sum of change in inventories and COGS. Hence, they should be similar to the mixture of the outcomes of the two line items. Reasons for using this additional measure of real activity management are manifold. Including production costs is consistent with many former studies whereas others use only inventory or COGS. However, for comparison reasons it is preferable when presented in split and combined form.

Accrual manipulation to lower COGS through the inventory account (e.g., delaying write-offs of obsolete inventory) should not affect production costs and hence these costs display real activities management. Prior studies on RAM include production costs when examining specific events and present a valuable benchmark for results around IPOs.[94] The findings for inventories and COGS can be ratified by this accounting item. Upward manipulation of sales by price discounts results in abnormally high production costs relative to sales due to lower margins than for regular prices. Sales are increasing and have lower margins but production costs are increasing with the regular variable costs.

Furthermore, overproduction results in lower COGS but higher inventories. Since sales are not changed from overproducing goods, production costs increase. The opposite effect is true for producing fewer goods than needed and companies sell these goods from the available stock which can put companies at risk of delivering problems but decreases production costs.

3.2.2.11 GAS

Gain on asset sales consists of sold assets that can be realized at a value higher than the carrying amount. The decision to sell and the timing can be influenced by managers. It increases cash and income. On the other hand, managers can keep certain assets for periods

[93] To prevent misinterpretation from abnormal COGS only, the results of inventories and production costs give a comprehensive insight. For example, companies can postpone write-downs and decrease COGS by accrual measures.

[94] Gunny (2010); Roychowdhury (2006).

when gain is more useful to the company. Especially, firms with negative earnings are expected to increase gain on asset sales, indicating that these sales should lift low profit. The possibilities for managers for the sale of assets and increasing earnings designate that the accounting item is a possible target of discretion around the IPO. There are only few studies in prior literature which use this account as a RAM tool.[95]

3.3 IPO Specifics

3.3.1 Agents and Motivation

The majority of prior literature on earnings management during IPOs focuses on the US. In this environment the shareholder value aspect is prominent.[96] It postulates the augmentation of the company value, aligning the corporate policy to the interests of the shareholders which also benefits the managers.[97] Earnings are usually seen as the main indicator of performance in companies' reporting and therefore, Rappaport (1986) declares them as a meaningful component for the value of the share price.[98] Usually, managers in the US receive share based-payments (e.g., options) when the company goes public. Consequently, managers have high incentives to use discretion in earnings when issuing equity.

When separating ownership and control, accounting information can relieve agency problems originating from adverse selection and moral hazard. The problem of adverse selection is connected to the decision usefulness approach. On the other hand, the problem of moral hazard is connected to the positive accounting theory. This means accounting and especially earnings take the role of valuation and stewardship. Typically, shareholders require relevant and reliable information which seems to constitute a tradeoff. Solutions are still undergoing current debate. Concerning the agency theory, accounting information should lower information asymmetries between ownership and control as well as between small and large shareholders and debtors.

There are several motives for using earnings management. These are embedded in communication or contracting with shareholders and stakeholders. Managers can communicate their information to stakeholders and form expectations. On the other hand,

95 Gunny (2010); Bartov (1993).
96 Rappaport (1986), p. 1.
97 Rappaport (1986), p. 7-12; Claussen (2006), p. 314.
98 Rappaport (1986), p. 13.

contracts can include accounting figures to measure remuneration (bonus plans). Both aspects include expectations and decisions which can be influenced by earnings management. Agents show discretionary behavior if they have incentives to alter financial statements. This might be caused by a maximization of their utility function.

Prior studies suggest that capital market incentives are the most significant ones.[99] The players involved in this setting are the management, financial statement users, and gatekeepers. The management is responsible for reporting. Usually, it includes the chief executive officer, the chief financial officer (and the chief accounting officer or controller).[100] In general, the boards of directors have to approve significant decisions, however, management decides on operations and finance. By the insider knowledge, they are better informed than outsiders and able to perform earnings management. Due to this information managers can try to improve their compensation which is linked to financial results and/or the share price by bonuses, or options, for instance.[101] These aspects are especially present around IPOs when new shares are distributed to the management level for aligning the interests of shareholders and management to reduce the principal-agent problem. Additionally, managers can be evaluated on the basis of the firm's stock price.[102]

Besides shareholders and managers, there are gatekeepers. They are required to make financial statements more reliable. This includes auditors, analysts, and the press, for example. These groups reduce information asymmetry between firms and potential investors at the IPO by verifying and interpreting the financials.[103] Nevertheless, as prior accounting scandals demonstrated they cannot avoid manipulation, but at least reduce it. Auditors play an important role when examining the financial statements. Their reputation is at stake if misstatements are detected. Similarly, regulators want to preserve good accounting behavior and examine IPOs very closely to assure a functioning capital market. Since incentives of discretionary behavior are very high when selling shares, companies are under increased scrutiny by these capital market participants before the IPO. Within these groups there are still diverging incentives. For example, the shareholders either want to sell at a high price at the IPO or want to sell later. Accordingly, incentives are present at different points in time.

---

99 Cohen/Zarowin (2010), p. 12; Fields et al. (2001); Healy/Wahlen (1999).
100 The Sarbanes-Oxley Act of 2002, section 302.
101 Hall/Murphy (2002); Healy (1985).
102 Armstrong et al. (2009), p. 1.
103 Monitors prevent market failure, see Akerlof (1970).

The management supplies financial statements to users. These include (potential) shareholders, creditors, employees etc. Since the stock market plays an important role in the US, companies are expected to communicate information.[104] An instrument for transmission of news is earnings, for example. Few studies find that loss companies are valued by other means.[105] When companies issue shares, investors verify the quality of the company by the prospectus and the included financial reports, for instance. Investors use accounting information to value companies on the capital market and to find appropriate share prices. The price is important for the company to receive more cash during the IPO and for managers who are compensated with options or if their bonus is connected to the share price. The connection of earnings and market price is found in prior research.[106] This creates incentives for managers to influence the performance of the company. In inefficient markets investors cannot see through that behavior. Especially around IPOs, the information asymmetry is high due to a low information level of the issuing firm. Users rely primarily on the offering prospectus they receive at the IPO.

3.3.2 Discretionary Reporting

3.3.2.1 Time

When going public the companies are under heightened scrutiny but aim for an elevated share price. After the IPO managers can profit from share-based payments. They build on the fact that accrual-based earnings management in one period must reverse in another. According to the literature there are two streams of hypotheses. The first one follows the idea that the issuer receives the proceeds of an IPO and therefore, they are self-evidently interested in a higher share pricing.[107] Managers want to influence the pricing decision of investors by improving their financial picture in the IPO prospectus. Therefore, they use discretion in the last financial statement before the shares are issued. Investors and analysts rely heavily on these accounting numbers in making their calculations of the company value.

The second stream follows the idea that firms rather report conservatively before the IPO since firms are under heightened scrutiny of investors, auditors, the SEC, analysts, and others

---

104 Dechow/Schrand (2004).
105 Bartov et al. (2002); Rajgopal et al. (2002).
106 Ball/Bartov (1996); Easton/Harris (1991); La Porta et al. (1997); Lowry/Schwert (2004), pp. 4-5; differently Cheng/Firth (2000).
107 Healy/Wahlen (1999); Teoh et al. (1998b).

(see chapter 3.3.2.2).[108] But after the IPO, managers can benefit from a higher share price when the lock-up covenants for the management, the investment bank, and other insiders (e.g., venture capitalists) terminate. This gives managers incentives to use discretion in accounting post-IPO. To answer the phenomenon of when managed numbers and opposing incentives in the time horizon around IPOs are most likely and when the reversals can be expected, specific years have to be examined.

A mixture of these streams is the idea that particularly income and sales are under special surveillance of the SEC before the issue occurs. Firms could choose to use discretion on other accounting items before the IPO because RAM is less probable to be discovered, but additionally they might use AM thereafter. Not only income is of particular interest for investors and investment banks when valuing firms, but also other accounting numbers depending on the respective industry. A further substantial contribution to the literature would be a broader view of the value relevant numbers and related industry groups.

Usually, companies use accounting flexibility over several periods. With the elasticity of GAAP they can prepare future discretion or have to reverse past discretion. This means that negative accruals management today can support upward management in the next periods. On the other hand, after upward accruals management companies have to reverse accruals in the following period(s). This transitory aspect is especially true for AM over the lifetime of a company. Prior literature already evidenced that the economic process which influences the firm's RAM has a multi-period component, too.[109] An overinvestment in certain business activities usually happens in a short time frame. In the subsequent years spending is cut to a normal level or even inverted to a lower level than the industry average.[110] During an IPO this can mean that companies start using discretion in accounting items already some time before the IPO to benefit from the positive reversal in the IPO year.

Therefore, it is obvious to check for discretion in the years before and after the IPO, when discretionary reporting is expected. A choice can take on the opposite (algebraic) sign in the following years; yet, the reversals are not coercively significant. Another possibility is to influence accruals after the IPO and observe the reversal of discretion in the following years. If no significant accruals management is evidenced in the two years around the IPO, the reversals could be visible in the more distant surrounding years. Therefore, taking only one or

108 Ball/Shivakumar (2008), for example.
109 Cohen et al. (2013), pp. 15-16.
110 Dechow et al. (2012) examine the reversals of earnings accruals management.

two years into account is not enough for a comprehensive examination, especially if incentives exist over more than one year. Current studies find this issue to be mainly neglected in prior research, but advocate its application.[111] Accordingly, while the pre- and post-IPO years are examined, other years around the IPO are also of interest.

3.3.2.2 Inflation vs. Deflation

Prior literature mainly claims that managers influence earnings around the IPO with the purpose of boosting the share price.[112] However, existing discretionary reporting literature neglects a differentiation between AM and RAM to evidence their occurrence around IPOs. It is important to distinguish between incentives before and after an IPO by explicitly separating the years in the process of going public. This displays the dissimilarities according to the respective motivations in the literature streams. In these years, issuers are confronted with varying incentives.

The procedure of accruals management carries costs for the management. Especially around IPOs, the costs of accrual-based earnings management are opposed to the incentives of earnings management. These costs include the scrutiny by capital market participants, the impending penalty of uncovering the behavior, and the effort to reach a certain financial target, for example. Consequently, some authors disprove that earnings are artificially inflated at the IPO.[113] The systematic and upward influence is challenged, since this would alarm regulators, investors, analysts, underwriters, auditors, the press, shareholders and others who would intervene or take legal actions against it.[114] Ball/Shivakumar (2008) and Venkataraman et al. (2008) even assume conservative accounting at the IPO, because there exists a higher risk of legally and regulatory consequences if manipulation of accounting is detected. This relies on the fact that at the IPO the scrutiny of financial reporting is high due to increased interest of market participants. A retrospective revelation would be possible since accruals are only rescheduled from future periods and cannot be used anymore in the upcoming years. According to these studies, detection would lead to consequential costs due to an increase of capital costs as well as a damage of the firms' and managers' reputations.[115] Ball/Shivakumar (2008) find in their study that issuers in UK exhibit a higher asymmetric timeliness than non-

[111] Baber et al. (2011), p. 1190; Dechow et al. (2012), p. 276.
[112] Dechow/Skinner (2000); DuCharme et al. (2001); Healy/Wahlen (1999); Lo (2008).
[113] Armstrong et al. (2009), p. 2.
[114] Beneish (1998).
[115] Ball/Shivakumar (2008), p. 325; Venkataraman et al. (2008); Venkataraman et al. (2004).

issuers.[116] This supports their theory of conservative accounting. Venkataraman et al. (2008) conclude that auditors are exposed to a higher process risk and hence act more conservatively.

It is important to note that conservative accounting usually leads to negative accruals management while current research mainly focuses on positive (or absolute) earnings management. However, the negative side alone is also of importance and is linked to other line items as well as other years in the same accounting item. In fact, negative discretion in years before the IPO can be helpful to disclose higher amounts in the post-issue years or indicate increasing earnings to investors. If accruals management is examined over several years, the alteration of signs plays a key role in the behavior of companies.

[116] Asymmetric timeliness is a conservative approach which recognizes economic losses earlier than gains.

4. Literature Overview

4.1 State of Research

There is a large amount of prior literature that examines accruals management. Furthermore, initial public offerings deliver an interesting setting with pronounced incentives. Therefore, accruals management around IPOs has been in the focus of accounting and finance literature.[117] While the magnitude of discretionary accruals in the offering year used to be of main interest, the connection to future operating performance and the stock price attracted increasing notice.[118] Large positive discretionary accruals seem to be negatively correlated with returns in the following year. Due to the complex situation of an IPO, the subsequent studies tried to explain the influence of third party intermediaries in discretionary accruals. On the one hand, companies can be backed by venture capitalists or private equity companies; on the other hand, the governance within companies can play an important role (e.g., CEO turnover, presence of an audit committee).[119]

Studies present accruals management around IPOs as self-evident due to the prevailing incentives of managers as well as shareholders who systematically try to achieve a higher issue price by influencing investors with high earnings.[120] This is beneficial for the company as well as the shareholders in the short-term, whereas in the future the stock price will drop in line with accrual reversals. However, some findings in the accounting and in the finance literature contradict this notion and indicate that accruals are not inflated.[121] Furthermore, the relation between discretionary accruals and subsequent stock returns might not result from inflated earnings, but from the correlation of cash flow and stock returns or due to signaling reasons.[122]

The divergent results in earnings management literature can follow from the mixture of several aspects such as years and industries. For example, mixing pre- and post-IPO financial reports can lead to erroneous outcomes. For example, Teoh et al. (1998c) state that pre-IPO

117 Some of the first studies examining earnings management around IPOs were Aharony et al. (1993) and Friedlan (1994).
118 Teoh et al. (1998b); Teoh et al. (1998c).
119 Katz (2006); Morsfield/Tan (2006); Venkataraman et al. (2008); Wongsunwai (2013).
120 Dechow/Schrand (2006); Dechow/Skinner (2000); DuCharme et al. (2001); Healy/Wahlen (1999); Lo (2008); Teoh et al. (1998b); Teoh et al. (1998c).
121 Armstrong et al. (2009); Ball/Shivakumar (2008); Dechow/Skinner (2000).
122 Fan (2007); Ritter/Welch (2002).

results for accruals are similar to the post-IPO findings.[123] Others find abnormally low discretionary accruals, but usually these studies use calendar years as reference to determine pre- and post-IPO while the IPO year itself is defined as year zero.[124] This thesis uses the IPO date to separate pre- and post-IPO periods and includes no "year zero". For the year after the IPO the majority of studies discover abnormally high discretionary accruals.[125] Therefore, a mixture of years should be avoided and a separation of financial reports which are due before or after the IPO is essential.

For a better understanding of earnings management around IPOs prior literature makes several suggestions. For example, Bernard/Skinner (1996), Healy/Wahlen (1999), and McNichols (2000) recommend specific settings where models can be applied with a certain focus. Beaver/Engel (1996) propose focusing on individual industries while McNichols/Wilson (1998) focus on certain constituents of models. Bernard/Skinner (1996) and Cecchini et al. (2012) suggest concentrating on certain accounting items. Additionally, Aaker/Gjesdal (2010) and McNichols (2000) advocate a combination of specific industries and accruals models.

4.2 Earnings Accruals Management

4.2.1 Teoh et al. (1998b)

The study of Teoh et al. (1998b) was one of the first to find positive discretionary accruals predicting long-run stock prices. This evidence is important to subsequent earnings management studies because it gives the fundamental aspect that investors seem to value accruals. The sample includes 1'649 IPOs between 1980 and 1992. They evidence diverging performance between aggressive and conservative earnings accruals management. Further earnings management research repeatedly refers to this study and its caveats.

Although the study does not include explicit pre-IPO years, it concludes that incentives and results would be similar to post-IPO findings. Actually, the study includes all financial reports which end in the calendar year of the IPO. This results in a mixture of pre- and post-IPO financial statements and the corresponding incentives. Furthermore, this thesis diverges in differentiating between industries, specific IPO years, and other accounting items than

[123] Teoh et al. (1998c), p. 204, endnote 4. See also Teoh et al. (1998b), p. 1936.
[124] Armstrong et al. (2009); Venkataraman et al. (2008).
[125] Armstrong et al. (2009); Fan (2007); Teoh et al. (1998b); Teoh et al. (1998c); Venkataraman et al. (2008).

earnings. Including these aspects could provide explanations for subsequent performance that do not rely on earnings accruals.

4.2.2 Ball/Shivakumar (2008)

Ball/Shivakumar (2008) examine accruals management before the IPO in the United Kingdom. They use 393 (overall IPO sample) and 172 (accruals tests) companies between 1992 and 1999 from the London Stock Exchange. They chose this country because there is financial data available before the IPO when firms are private and as soon as going public they can restate this information for the prospectus. Ball/Shivakumar (2008) want to examine if scrutiny before the IPO is high enough to avoid manipulation. The authors analyze up to two years before the IPO with the Jones model. They find that companies report more conservatively before going public instead of the commonly postulated earnings inflation scenario.

An associated aspect of their study concentrates on the Teoh et al. (1998b) paper because these authors claim that earnings are inflated before the IPO. Ball/Shivakumar (2008) question the hypothesis and the results of Teoh et al. (1998b) and evidence different outcomes, based on scrutiny around IPOs.

Including pre-IPO years adds substantial insight in IPO research, because earnings accruals have to reverse in the future. Nevertheless, including further years around the IPO would illustrate differences between these years and the corresponding incentives. Moreover, earnings accruals are only one measure of discretionary behavior. The thesis differs in adding real activity measures that could explain specific behavior in real aspects. Furthermore, dividing the sample by industries, adding real activity measures and finally employing these aspects on the US capital market with many more companies substantially improves research.

4.3 Real Activities Management

4.3.1 Roychowdhury (2006)

One of the first papers to examine the management of operational activities is Roychowdhury (2006). He includes 4'252 US companies in the years between 1987 and 2001. The author argues that there is little other research in this area, except, evidence of decreasing R&D.[126] Roychowdhury uses real activities models which are essentially based on Dechow et al. (1998). The study focuses on real activities that have "the primary objective of meeting certain earnings thresholds".[127]

The purpose of the study is to identify real activities management around the zero earnings threshold. Results show that firms try to avoid losses by sales management, employ overproduction to lower COGS, and reduce discretionary expenses to improve their profit.

First of all, the development of empirical methods to detect real activities establishes new possibilities that can be applied in various earnings management settings. Three new real activity measures are introduced. The first one is a model for the normal level of operating cash flow. The abnormal amount should indicate sales management by price discounts. The second model includes production costs, and the third one tests for abnormal discretionary expenses. While these three accounting items are used as the only indicators, there are many more items which have not been included in this setting. Accruals cannot illustrate the discretionary behavior to the same extent. Hence, the study ignores earnings accrual models.

Roychowdhury focuses on earnings while other accounting items are only a means to an end. In other words, real activities have the purpose to influence earnings, usually in the upward direction. Nevertheless, an interesting aspect to concentrate on is the fact that investors do not merely focus on earnings around IPOs, but include additional financial items for valuation purposes. More precisely, real activities influence certain line items – other than earnings – which can be the main purpose of managers intent and the influence in earnings is only a subordinated result. The fact that investors value other accounting items and the aspect of expense accounts being signals of future benefit for loss firms is important for an IPO surrounding.

Another interesting aspect is that Roychowdhury (2006) controls for industry differences as well as growth of firms and identifies both of them as an influencing variable. However, using a cross-sectional overall sample as a mixed industry approach does not examine differences in specific industries nor does it include changes of items after the specific event. Importantly, focusing on earnings as the outcome of the three measures would neglect effects of other accounting items alone on capital market participants around IPOs. Real activities being a

---

126 This thesis evidences contrary outcomes for the IPO setting where different incentives exist.

127 Roychowdhury (2006), p. 336.

means to an end for earnings manipulation makes sense in this approach, but is insufficient in an IPO setting.

4.3.2 Gunny (2010)

The study of Gunny (2010) examines earnings accruals and real activities management with the respective influence on future performance concerning earnings benchmarks. The study adds additional measures of real activities (SG&A and gain on asset sales) and introduces expected direction of discretionary behavior in certain accounting items (e.g., R&D, SG&A). The author covers more than 4'028 companies in the years from 1988 to 2002. Gunny (2010) finds that companies that just meet earnings benchmarks reduce R&D and SG&A to increase income, lower prices to inflate sales, and overproduce to decrease COGS. These firms show a better future performance than firms that miss benchmarks.

As in Roychowdhury (2006), the focus of discretionary behavior rests on the resulting earnings. In an IPO environment, this neglects that real activity measures could have a value by themselves for capital market participants. Especially, specific industries or loss firms could use other means for influencing outsiders. The findings of intentionally decreasing R&D and SG&A is in line with the common sense concerning inflated earnings for profitable firms, conversely, they do not test if this might not apply to loss firms or specific industries. Applying the measure around IPOs should enhance understanding of discretionary behavior.

4.4 Multi-Dimensional Approaches

4.4.1 Cohen/Zarowin (2010)

Cohen/Zarowin (2010) examine accrual-based and real activity management at seasoned equity offerings (SEO). The sample consists of 1'151 companies traded on the US exchange markets between 1987 and 2006. The authors employ the three measures of Roychowdhury (2006) plus discretionary accruals. They find that firms engage in accruals as well as real activities management. The usage of these measures depends on the associated costs. The authors contribute the discovery of a combination of accruals and real activity management at SEOs with varying accents, also in time. Specifically, Cohen/Zarowin (2010) test if real activities have a greater influence on performance than accruals management. The suggestion of using accruals and real activities management in a capital market event study is substantial.

Similar to Roychowdhury (2006), the effects of all manipulation measures on earnings are in the focus. Nonetheless, measures like R&D can also be seen as a valuable account with signaling effects instead of categorizing it as a mere expense account. Then, it would no longer be a means to an end but valuable in itself. This is similarly true for SG&A which is not examined. Dividing companies into groups of profitability or growth provides additional insight to verify industry characteristics (around IPOs). Assessing SEOs and associated incentives gives valuable comprehension since capital market events give good insights for research and practitioners. This is equally true for an IPO setting.

4.4.2 Fedyk et al. (2012)

Although the study of Fedyk et al. (2012) is a working paper to date, it is included due to its certain analogy to this thesis and its specific approach. The authors analyze 3'434 US companies in the years from 1989 to 2006. They examine discretion in three accounting items which are all used by investors to value companies. These items are earnings, sales, and R&D. Fedyk et al. (2012) mention that there may be many more accounting items, but these are ignored because they focus on items which are found to be value relevant. The authors include three specific industries and an aggregated industry sample. Investigating earnings management in the year after the IPO adds interesting insights. Fedyk et al. (2012) employ a method that lets them decide if discretion in these items is used simultaneously because managers have various possibilities to influence capital market participants and not only earnings. This is especially true for emergent companies. The authors find discretion in certain accounting items, especially for sales and R&D, but not for earnings in specific industries. The idea to differentiate between industries should be adapted for years around IPOs. The selective approach of RAM around IPOs exists for certain companies.[128]

Fedyk et al. (2012) concentrate on the post-IPO year. Hence, there is no additional information of dissimilarities between specific years around IPOs in the combination with real activity management, although these time periods were found to differ. It is an interesting literature gap which would add substantial knowledge about characteristics around IPOs.

Taking three accounting items into account which are value relevant is an interesting contribution. Yet, there exist other value relevant accounting items as well which are neglected, but have been identified in the finance literature. These additional line items and

[128] A prior version of this paper is Singer (2007).

models have to be included for further contributions of issues concerning real activity management (see chapter 5.2.2).

Another interesting aspect in this thesis that differs to Fedyk et al. (2012) is to assess profitable industries with corresponding subgroups. Adding single industries with mainly profitable companies enhances understanding of IPO firm behavior and the dissimilarities to unprofitable industries. This assists to examine the characteristics of industries and potential differences. Overall, it remains an empirical question whether discretionary behavior in several line items is present around IPOs and differs over time as well as by industries.

5. Hypotheses and Models

5.1 Hypotheses Development

5.1.1 Research Aspects

As seen in the above chapters, there are several interesting aspects to examine in financial discretion around IPOs. Some are built on theoretical and empirical background while others were already identified in non-IPO settings by prior research. First, incentives for discretion in accounting items differ depending on time period around the IPO. In these years companies overstate, understate, or do not use any discretion in line items. It is important to differentiate between the time periods before and after IPOs. Second, companies use different accounting items to influence investors. Earnings are only one measure to examine discretion besides other figures. Third, the difference between industries has to be taken into account. They vary in their incentives for discretion in line items depending on investors' focus in company valuation. Hence, some prior studies suggest concentrating on industry and item specific models.[129] Finally, the dissimilarity between all, profitable, and loss companies in the same industry and in a similar industry group has to be considered. These categories of companies can also differ in their incentives of discretion in specific accounting items. Furthermore, the various studies that examine earnings management use varying models for the same accounting item which can lead to different outcomes. To make sure the study is comparable to a major part of prior literature; several models for one line item should be used.

The following two groups of hypotheses include the above aspects of discretion in financial reporting. The first set of hypotheses focuses on the diverging incentives of AM and RAM dependent on time period around the issue. The second set concentrates on specific industry differences and the respective influence in discretion of particular accounting items.

According to prior literature, discretionary behavior around IPOs exists. Yet, tests for the specific categorizations which are analyzed here are missing. However, results for these aspects are very helpful for future research and practice. Therefore, the following basic hypothesis (alternative form) is tested for all accounting items as a first step: Companies use discretionary behavior around an IPO. This hypothesis is tested for each year (years -2 to +3),

[129] Aaker/Gjesdal (2010), p. 44; Lang/Lundholm (1996), pp. 608-609.

group, and industry. The basic hypothesis helps to visualize the differences in each specific year around the IPO. Consequently, they are predominantly presented in the results section.

5.1.2 Hypotheses for Periods around IPO

5.1.2.1 Distinction between Years

The issuing companies and shareholders want to realize a high price for the shares to receive more financial benefits from the IPO. A financial report vitally influences the pricing decisions and valuation by investors.[130] Depending on the incentives it is obvious that shareholders have a substantial opportunistic interest to influence accounting numbers which are crucial to investors.[131] However, some more aspects have to be taken into account than in prior literature when examining discretion around IPOs.[132] One characteristic is that incentives around the issue differ over time; therefore, several adjacent years have to be included. Furthermore, the reversal effect of accruals and measures other than earnings, i.e. real activity accounts, are of importance in these time periods.[133]

Usually, earnings accruals studies examine discretion at IPOs including the pre- or post-IPO year or year zero, only. However, there is additional information encompassed in the other years around the issue. For example, the second year before the IPO can inform about the company performance before going public.[134] Moreover, investors that anticipate discretionary reporting in the year before the IPO look at several prior periods to compare changes over the years.[135] Managers can take advantage of that by influencing investors' perception (by negative or positive discretion).

Additionally, most prior studies for earnings management around IPOs do not take the reversal effect of accruals into account which prior literature finds to be important.[136] Implicitly these studies assume that any effect in year -1 or +1 does not result from year -2 but

---

130 Benveniste (1989), pp. 344-345; Lowry/Schwert (2004), pp. 4-5; Roosenboom (2012), pp. 1653-1654; Teoh et al. (1998c), pp. 175-176; Zhang (2012), p. 332. IPO prospectuses include prior year financial statements of the last three years, usually (SEC, 2013).

131 Ahearne et al. (2012, 3-4) find that incentives for CFOs and CEOs to use discretion are present. The legal aspect of discretionary reporting is not part of this study. The discretion takes place in a grey area which is not assessable for outsiders.

132 Some of the first studies examining earnings management around IPOs were Aharony et al. (1993) and Friedlan (1994).

133 The reversal effect for non-IPO firms is also addressed by Dechow et al. (2012).

134 Year -3 is not included due to unavailable data in COMPUSTAT.

135 Year -2 is included in the offering prospectus but not available before when the respective financial year ends.

136 Dechow et al. (2012).

is initiated in the specific year when their examination starts. They take for granted that no discretion is present in year -2, because a possible influential behavior in that period could optimize pre- or post-IPO results by reversals. For example, companies could use negative discretion in accruals to benefit from the reversals in future years. There is rare evidence in prior literature that the systematic of reversals is used before the IPO to profit in future years. Furthermore, there is no evidence that RAM is non-existent around the IPO. If it would exist, it would have a further impact on accruals.

However, if companies would inflate accruals in year -2, the downward reversal would probably be present in years -1 and +1. Yet, these years are of major importance for the shareholders in receiving a higher price. Hence, managers' possible intention to positively influence year -2 is neutralized because the downward reversal would deteriorate the more important years -1 and +1.[137] Usually, a negative influence in year -2 would leave companies with fewer options in discretion for years -1 and +1 because accruals reverse in the short-term and RAM would have to be consistently employed from year -2 to several following years. Additionally, year -2 is under increased scrutiny by investors when analyzing the issue. Another reason that no positive discretion is present arises from the fact that investors follow the development of the financials over years and prefer increasing benefits. Since capital market participants could detect discretionary behavior, this period is not expected to be biased. In sum, in contrast to prior studies, more than one pre-IPO year is of interest and has to be included in the study. Yet, this time period has attracted only little attention in prior literature and is not well-examined for US data.[138]

Furthermore, prior studies were criticized that earnings management might be detected due to the situation of IPO companies (e.g., abnormal performance, growth, costs of going public). If no discretion is present in year -2, it would support that models are not coercively biased by the circumstances for issuers around IPOs, at least not for the overall situation of going public (except specific costs).

Only few studies of discretionary reporting around IPOs systematically use the last report before the IPO while the others use the first one thereafter (or even a mixture of both).[139] There exist arguments in support of both approaches. If companies try to influence their

---

137 Accounting rules are applied retrospectively for the IPO prospectus and can be biased by issuers.

138 A rare exemption is the study of Ball/Shivakumar (2008) who examine data up to three years before the IPO for companies in the United Kingdom. Since data availability for US in COMPUSTAT is sparse, additional data had to be hand collected.

139 Fedyk et al. (2012), p. 20; Liu (2009); Morsfield/Tan (2006); Teoh et al. (1998b), p. 1936.

offering price and the corresponding proceeds, they have to use the last annual or quarterly report before the IPO.[140] However, if shares are issued shortly before the end of the reporting period, investors have a higher interest in the quarterly reporting right before the IPO than in the annual report of the prior year which was published some months ago. Furthermore, the incentives of company insiders and major shareholders are still present in year +1.[141]

Concerning accruals, companies could also employ negative discretion in pre-IPO reporting to influence post-IPO results since accruals have to reverse in the future and can help to improve results in year +1 etc. Consequently, pre-IPO reports are of interest when studying the influence of discretionary behavior on IPO pricing and the discretion could spill to post-IPO pricing as well. Current studies find this issue to be mainly neglected in prior research.[142] In sum that means, both years around the IPO are of interest for further research and their possible differences should be examined.

Due to the fact that in this study the period +1 comprises the first 365 days after the issue and period +2 covers 730 days, discretion in the first annual report after the issue is included in time period +1 and accordingly in +2 for the second report.[143] However, annual reports are published some time after the end of the financial year. Managers and other insiders want to influence the share price after the lock-up period because of share-based payments.[144] If the first annual report after the IPO is published within timely proximity to the issue, the second report still includes discretionary behavior due to influenced quarterly financials.[145] In other words, the first as well as the second report after the IPO can be biased and can contain discretionary reporting. Furthermore, investors such as venture capitalists keep the majority of investments in companies on average for two years after the issue.[146] This means not all initial investors sell their shares at the end of the lock-up period. In sum, year +2 is also expected to exhibit some significant discretionary behavior.

Yet, in the third year after the IPO no discretionary behavior is anticipated due to lowered and dispersed incentives of insiders and major shareholders. These could still be willing to sell their shares, but not with the same initial intensity and not everyone at the same point in time as for the IPO and the end of the lock-up period. Before these two dates, the shares are not

140 Ball/Shivakumar (2008), p. 327. Note that scrutiny is present, but mainly for positive earnings and sales.
141 The end of the holding period can happen to be before or after the end of the first post financial year.
142 Baber et al. (2011), p. 1190; Dechow et al. (2012), p. 276.
143 Cohen/Zarowin (2010) proceed similarly when analyzing up to three years before and after SEOs.
144 Wongsunwai (2013), pp. 296-298. He analyzes especially venture capitalists.
145 See also Field/Hanka (2001) and Wongsunwai (2013) for the importance of the lock-up period after IPOs.
146 Gompers/Lerner (2002), p. 266.

transferable for insiders and come to the market at once while in the third year after the IPO regular trading is ongoing with no specific point in time to sell and with no corresponding incentives as before.[147] The third year after the IPO is the last to be examined, because from year +4 incentives from other circumstances heavily overlap the link to the IPO.[148]

Overall, there are credible incentives that companies use either positive or negative AM and RAM around the IPO. The notion from the argumentation above for all accounting items is that companies use discretion in financial statements in years -1 to +2 around an IPO. However, in years -2 and +3 less discretion is expected.[149] The succeeding hypothesis summarizes the before mentioned aspects for years, industries, and the groups of companies (overall, profitable, and loss groups):

Main hypothesis concerning periods: In years -1 to +2 companies use discretion in certain accounting items proportionately more frequently than in years -2 and +3 around an IPO.[150]

For all accounting items, the difference in time periods is expected. Accordingly, the hypotheses for the specific accounts are listed below in Figure 3 (without hypotheses Sales 2 and CfO 2).[151]

---

147 Yet, significant results are present due to other reasons (e.g., beating earnings targets).

148 Data for years -4 and -3 to run the corresponding calculations are not available in COMPUSTAT. The same time horizon of years -2 to +3 is used by Armstrong et al. (2009) to test for earnings accruals.

149 The formulation indicates that IPO years should be significant compared to the so-called non-IPO years (years -2 and +3). If year -2 is missing due to a lack of data, one could argue that the null hypothesis is rejected only, if the combined years of -1 to +2 are significant and year +3 finds insignificant results since year -2 is usually rarely significant compared to other years. Yet, if year -2 is missing, no final decision can be made. This comparative methodology is employed to focus on differentiation between years around the IPO and not only on IPO versus non-IPO companies.

150 All hypotheses are stated in alternative form. Here, the null hypothesis is: In years -1 to +2 companies *do not* use discretion in certain accounting items proportionately more frequently than in years -2 and +3 around an IPO. In the results, the significance level indicates to what extent the null hypothesis can be rejected and the alternative hypothesis is accepted.

151 A list of all hypotheses is included in the appendix.

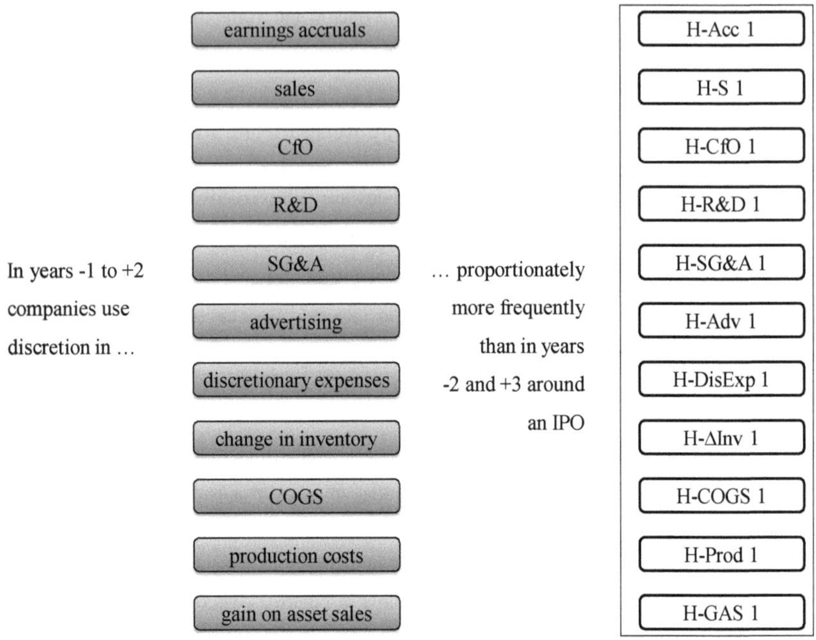

Figure 3: Overview of Hypotheses Set 1

The basic hypothesis states that discretionary behavior around the IPO exists. It is important to note that the hypotheses have to be tested and presented for all industries separately. In Figure 3, the hypotheses do not explicitly mention the industries due to clarity reasons in their formulation and due to the fact that these specific hypotheses are not expected to substantially differ between industries. Likewise, this is the case for the differentiation between groups of sample firms (all, profitable, and loss companies) which are presented in the results.

5.1.2.2 Specifics of Sales and CfO

5.1.2.2.1 Hypothesis Sales 2

As mentioned before, earnings are not the only important accounting item around IPOs, but other figures also play a decisive role for valuation. The valuation literature promotes that sales is a significant item for all companies.[152] Hence, sales management can have a major influence on investors.[153]

When earnings are negative they are not used for valuation techniques. Then investors have to apply other accounting items to perform their calculations. Contrarily, sales play an important role irrespective of profitability. Therefore, they are essential for profitable as well as loss companies in all industries; especially for growth firms, which rank sales higher than other accounts.[154] Additionally, there exist more relaxed possibilities to influence sales instead of earnings over a long time period.[155] Consequently, their discretionary amount is expected not to be negative in the years of high incentives around the IPO. The alternative would be to lower sales before the issue and boost them afterwards or use sales accruals in the short-term that reverse in the long-term. However, this is not expected since insiders prefer short-term value around IPOs. Thus, the hypothesis for years -1 to +2 can be formulated more exact as follows:[156]

Hypothesis Sales 2 (H-S 2): Companies do not show significantly negative discretion in sales in years -1 to +2 around an IPO.

5.1.2.2.2 Hypothesis Cash Flow 2

Cash flow from operations (CfO) is used by practitioners in numerous valuation techniques such as the discounted cash flow model etc.[157] However, CfO can be influenced upward only to a certain degree dependent on factors such as the market. Cutting expenses is an option to increase cash flow, but it can lead to future losses if these expenses are required for the persistent and regular business activities.[158] Lowering expenses can be one trait to influence cash flow, but other discretionary accounting behavior can have a negative effect. For example, intensify R&D spending to display future growth or price reductions which increase sales, both result in a relatively lower CfO. Hence, according to prior literature, the results on cash flow are ambiguous when companies use discretion and no direction can be postulated. However, the notions from prior literature are only partly appropriate for this study. Due to

[152] Bartov et al. (2002), p. 327; Damodaran (2012), pp. 543-550; Davis (2002), p. 446 and p. 464.
[153] Here, sales management and the corresponding hypotheses refer to all models of change in accounts receivable, in deferred revenue, and in gross receivable.
[154] Ertimur et al. (2003); Ghosh et al. (2005); Graham et al. (2005), p. 20; Meyer (2009), pp. 57-58; Stubben (2006), p. 2.
[155] See projects of FASB to improve revenue recognition, for example: FASB (2013).
[156] The null hypothesis is stated as follows: Companies use negative sales management from years -1 to +2 around an IPO.
[157] Block (1999), p. 87; Roosenboom (2012), p. 1653.
[158] A typical example is cutting expenses for salaries which can lead to decreased productivity in the future.

the existing incentives around IPOs, sales management is expected. RAM of sales (such as channel stuffing and more lenient credit terms) have a negative impact on cash flow from operations in terms of sales.[159] Due to abnormally high sales as control variable, CfO will rather be abnormally low. Similarly, overproduction to loer COGS leads t abnormally low CfO. Another reason for expecting low CfO is fueled by the managers' belief that outsiders prefer earnings over cash flows as the key metric.[160] Especially growth firms are not valued by cash flow before the issue.[161] This supports the notion that companies rather exhibit negative discretionary CfO in years -1 to +2 than influencing them positively. Therefore, the hypothesis for CfO can be formulated more exactly: Abnormal cash flow from operations will not be positive, but it is expected to be negative or – if no discretion exists – normal in years -1 to +2. Consequently, the specific hypothesis is:

Hypothesis CfO 2 (H-CfO 2): Companies do not show significantly positive discretion in CfO in years -1 to +2 around an IPO.

5.1.3 Hypotheses for Specific Industries

5.1.3.1 High-Growth vs. Well-Established Industries

While the first set of hypotheses focused on the differentiation in years and on the direction of discretion, the second set refers to group specific differences. This means dissimilarities in industries in terms of growth and profitability as well as profitable and loss groups within one industry. The time periods around IPOs still play an important role, but they are not compared to other time intervals as in set one.

Prior finance and accounting literature find different financial patterns for certain industries, especially for the Technology and Internet industries, but usually they did not test for earnings management.[162] Since the characteristics and financials in these industries vary compared to well-established industries, a differentiation between high-growth and well-established industries during IPOs should give new insights for earnings management research.[163] Industries within each cluster are similar. For example, companies in the Construction and

159 Cohen/Zarowin (2010), p. 8; Liu (2009), p. 40.
160 Graham et al. (2005), p. 5.
161 Myers (1984), pp. 134-136.
162 Joos/Plesko (2005) and Lévesque et al. (2012), for example.
163 The criterion for inclusion in the high-growth industry is the change in sales (at least 35%) around the IPO. Amounts are presented in the descriptive statistics.

Wholesale industries are well-established[164], growing slowly and profitable while Biotech, Internet, and Technology companies are rather young and growing fast. Companies in different industries vary in their incentives to use discretion in several accounting items and not only earnings. However, most studies in the past used earnings as the main value driver for companies in all industry sectors.[165] The limitations in these studies are the centering on earnings and the negligence of industry variation. The anomaly for growth industries inherits that investors primarily focus on other line items.

Prior accounting literature mainly suggests that cutting certain expenses (e.g., R&D expenses) is a popular measure to positively influence current-period earnings and cash flow.[166] This is in line with the earnings fixation hypothesis and would increase the share price.[167] However, especially the finance literature – centered on the resource based theory – finds that R&D and SG&A are important for high tech companies at IPOs.[168] Since these companies are more dependent on future benefits from current R&D projects than slowly growing (well-established) and less R&D-intensive industries. The amount of this item shows the intention of these companies to invest in the future and give suggestions about possible prospective benefits and revenue growth. This behavior would be consistent with the signaling hypothesis.

Consistently, there are hints that R&D is value relevant to investors in specific industries.[169] This might cause companies to increase R&D expenses at the cost of income.[170] Hence – in contrast to common belief in accounting literature – there exists an incentive to inflate R&D around IPOs (years -1 to +2). Therefore, the discretionary amount of R&D expense is expected to be abnormally high and not low for certain industries. Contrarily, well-established companies are highly dependent on positive earnings. Therefore, they rather influence income than the fairly low account of R&D expenses in these industries. Samples in prior accounting studies mainly included companies from these well-established industries which results in an outcome in favor of the majority of companies. The R&D amounts do not coercively have to be negative and significant, since companies in well-established industries are still strongly growing around the IPO, but not as much as in the growth industries. Discretion is expected

164 Well-established companies are usually still growing more around the IPO than companies that already went public some time ago in the same industry.

165 Bédard et al. (2008), pp. 522-523; Brau/Fawcett (2006), pp. 400-401; Teoh et al. (1998c), pp. 175-176.

166 Bushee (1998), pp. 306-307; Darrough/Rangan (2004), pp. 3-4; Dechow/Sloan (1991), p. 52; Graham et al. (2005), p. 40; Gunny (2010), p. 857.

167 Shi/Zhang (2012), p. 2.

168 Lévesque et al. (2012), pp. 47-48.

169 Joos/Plesko (2005), pp. 849-850; Lev/Sougiannis (1996), pp. 108-109; Sougiannis (1994), pp. 63-66.

170 Hand (2005), pp. 615-616; Hsu (2009), pp. 264-265; Sievers/Klobucnik (2012), pp. 1-3.

for the growth industries with Biotech, Internet, and Technology companies rather than for the Construction and Wholesale industries.[171] The corresponding hypothesis is:

Hypothesis R&D 2: In years -1 to +2 companies use positive discretion in R&D proportionately more frequently in high-growth industries (Biotech, Internet, and Technology) than companies in well-established industries (Construction and Wholesale).

Another important accounting item is SG&A expense which can be managed by several real actions. However, it is mainly neglected as a single line item in prior RAM studies and only included in the aggregate measure of discretionary expenses.[172] Prior accounting literature mainly suggested that all companies reduce SG&A expenses to improve earnings and cash flow to influence investors.[173] However, especially in the banking and finance research the valuation literature finds that SG&A expenses are important and investors consider this amount as value relevant in specific industries.[174] Particularly, in high-growth Technology companies SG&A is considered as an investment in growth and implies future revenues. Similar to the arguments for R&D, these facts hint at positive discretionary behavior in SG&A in specific industries.

For well-established industries the argument of SG&A expenses being investments is less valid, because these kinds of companies do not have equally high intangible assets. Low SG&A point to artificially decreased expenses which might be feasible for well-established companies or growth companies after the issue.[175] They can demonstrate an improving organization (better sales efficiency etc.).[176] Yet, SG&A are also influenced by increased costs caused by the IPO. In sum, for growth industries (Biotech, Internet, and Technology) SG&A is mainly expected to be abnormally high around the IPO whilst for industries with established companies (Construction and Wholesale) results can be ambiguous. Therefore, the hypothesis is stated as follows:

171 While the Technology industry is young and growing around the IPO, the ratio of negative income is around 50% in these years.

172 Roychowdhury (2006); Cohen/Zarowin (2010).

173 Gunny (2010), pp. 857-859.

174 Amir/Lev (1996), pp. 18-19; Lévesque et al. (2012), pp. 47-48.

175 Taulli (2012), p. 88. As a practical example, the Technology company Groupon Inc. had SG&A expenses at around 50% of revenue around the IPO and the primary driver was sales staff.

176 These interpretations depend on the specific line items which make up SG&A. They vary between future investments (brands) and inefficiency (sales force) which can be part of future research.

Hypothesis SG&A 2: In years -1 to +2 companies use positive discretion in SG&A proportionately more frequently in high-growth industries (Biotech, Internet, and Technology) than companies in well-established industries (Construction and Wholesale).

The third component of discretionary expenses – besides R&D and SG&A – is advertising. In their survey Graham et al. (2005) find that advertising expenses are an item of possible influence and is used for managerial discretion to meet earnings targets.[177] However, prior earnings management studies usually do not include this accounting item in their models of real activities management and hence no RAM research around IPOs exists.[178] In splitting up discretionary expenses this study extends prior earnings management literature. Advertising expenses could have other effects on capital market participants than other cost accounts of RAM. Cutting advertising can have a more immediate impact on sales than cutting or increasing R&D or SG&A. On the one hand, companies are expected to cut spending in advertising to lower cash outflows and increase earnings as prior literature suggests for cost accounts in general. On the other hand, firms can increase this item for reputational reasons and for creating public attention to a young company. Both will probably lead to short-term changes in sales.

Advertising expenses are typically higher for young and growing companies in unprofitable industries because they are less well known to the public than more mature companies. Additionally, growth firms are mainly valued by other accounts than earnings and therefore, do not increase them by artificially reducing other expenses. Contrarily, well-established companies are primarily valued by earnings and do not intend to deflate income by increasing advertising. However, they do not deflate advertising either, because they need advertising when going public. In sum, advertising is expected to be abnormally high for companies in the Biotech, Internet, and Technology industries but not for the Construction and Wholesale industries. The corresponding hypothesis is:

Hypothesis Adv 2: In years -1 to +2 companies use positive discretion in advertising proportionately more frequently in high-growth industries (Biotech, Internet, and Technology) than companies in well-established industries (Construction and Wholesale).

Discretionary expenses are the aggregate measure of the three aforementioned accounting items. To include this measure anyway, has several reasons. First, showing results for this

177 Graham et al. (2005), p. 32.
178 For an exemption of using discretion in advertising – but in a non-IPO setting – see Cohen et al. (2009, 1-2).

aggregated measure maintains comparability to prior studies which used this item in other circumstances. Second, there is additional information in using this account if, for example, companies use opposing discretion in the three single items which results in an insignificant amount of the aggregated measure. Discretionary expenses are examined in prior literature in relation to beating earnings benchmarks or other thresholds.[179] However, it is not examined for IPOs although this gives a good insight of companies' behavior with expenses that are well influenceable. Since discretionary expenses are the aggregate measure of R&D, SG&A, and advertising, they are expected to exhibit the same directions as in the industries above. Hence, discretionary expenses are expected to be abnormally high for companies in the Biotech, Internet, and Technology industries, but not in the Construction and Wholesale industries. The corresponding hypothesis is:

Hypothesis DisExp 2: In years -1 to +2 companies use positive influence in discretionary expenses proportionately more frequently in high-growth industries (Biotech, Internet, and Technology) than companies in well-established (Construction and Wholesale) industries.

Other RAM measures such as sales, change in inventory, COGS, and production costs, are not presented here because no corresponding hypotheses of growth versus well-established companies are included. Actually, the opposing influence of both high R&D and high SG&A on COGS generates ambiguous results and would make it difficult to disentangle the interpretation.[180]

5.1.3.2 Profitable vs. Unprofitable Industries

Other than high-growth versus well-established industries, there can be a differentiation between profitable and unprofitable industries and companies during IPOs. The criterion to constitute a profitable or unprofitable industry during IPOs depends on the fact if the majority of companies in one industry are profitable or unprofitable in the years around the IPO.[181] Profitable companies have a net income equal to zero or higher while loss companies have a net income lower than zero. While the criterion of growth is usually steady over the years around the IPO, the criterion of profitability may differ in these periods. According to prior literature, a separation in regard to profitable versus unprofitable industries is useful for

[179] Gunny (2010); Roychowdhury (2006).
[180] Lévesque et al. (2012), p. 48.
[181] The fact that an industry is named unprofitable only concerns the time interval around the IPO. In future years these industries can turn profitable for the majority of companies.

investors as well as for research to understand the intuition of accounting numbers around IPOs.[182] Some industries such as the Construction, Manufacturing, and Wholesale industries include primarily profitable companies around the IPO, whilst the companies in the Biotech and Internet industries mainly end these financial years with a loss.[183]

Within one industry, companies are divided by the (algebraic) sign of net income into the profitable and loss subgroups (as well as the aggregated overall group). Positive net income is expected to endure while negative net income is expected to exist temporarily and is considered less information relevant to investors.[184] Accounting literature usually uses the overall sample when testing for earnings management; however, prior studies find that differences in discretionary reporting between profitable and loss companies exist. The finance literature – especially valuation studies – already examined dissimilarities and differentiates between these two groups of companies.[185] Furthermore, Graham et al. (2005) find many differences between these two subgroups in their survey of financial executives.[186] This might result from diverse methods of valuation by investors depending on the corresponding subgroup; and executives want to comply with the methods in the best possible way. Firms are expected to influence the corresponding accounting item which is most likely valued by investors.[187] This is why differences between the two groups around IPOs are expected in specific accounting items and in terms of sign, as well. Not all results are predicted to be different, but some diverge in cases when motivations of the companies vary due to group affiliation (industry or profitability) and the (algebraic) sign of income.

In the profitable industries, earnings are a relevant value driver when investors set the offer price and evaluate companies.[188] However, some prior studies even find conservative accruals which could result from an increased fear of managers during an IPO to use positive earnings accruals management.[189] In fact, negative accruals in years before the IPO can be helpful to disclose higher amounts in the post-issue years or indicate increasing earnings to investors. If earnings accruals management is examined over several years, the alteration of signs plays a key role in the behavior of companies.

182 Aggarwal et al. (2009), p. 253; Fama/French (2004), p. 230; Singer (2007), pp. 21-22.
183 Although the Internet industry has more than 50 percent of profitable companies in year +1, they have fewer than 50 percent in all other years. The Technology companies exhibit varying net income around the IPO and cannot be assigned to a particular group.
184 Graham et al. (2005), p. 20.
185 Joos/Plesko (2005); Liu et al. (2002), pp. 137-138.
186 Graham et al. (2005), pp. 25-26, for example.
187 Fedyk et al. (2012), p. 24.
188 Graham et al. (2005).
189 Ball/Shivakumar (2008); Venkataraman et al. (2008).

In general, due to increased scrutiny on earnings in year -1 conservative behavior of issuers exists. Therefore, the outcomes for accruals will rather be significantly negative or neutral. Since investors highly value earnings in profitable industries, companies are not expected to artificially decrease them. Consequently, earnings in year -1 are unmanaged and earnings in +1 are not the reversal of prior years. In the post-IPO year, abnormally positive accruals are expected, because scrutiny decreases and companies try to influence investors and increase the share price. These accruals will reverse within the next few years. As aforementioned, company insiders still sell their shares after the lock-up period. This prompts companies to reverse accruals later or slower. Additionally, a severe reversal could alarm investors. Therefore, year +2 does not coercively have to be significantly negative, but can still be abnormally positive. Additionally, venture capitalists that sell shares after the lock-up engage less in profitable industries.[190] For these reasons, no specific expectation is used for year +2. The corresponding hypothesis is stated as follows:

Hypothesis accruals in profitable industries (H-Acc 2): Companies in profitable industries (Construction and Wholesale) show no earnings accruals management in year -1, but positive discretion in year +1.

In profitable industries, earnings are a relevant value driver for investors and upward earnings accruals management is expected by prior literature. The alternative was non-existent earnings management. However, there is the possibility of deflating earnings accruals in favor of other accounting items and future reversals.[191] While current research mainly focuses on positive (or absolute) earnings management, the systematic of deflation and reversals is rarely tested in prior studies. In contrast to profitable industries, capital market participants primarily use valuation techniques that do not include earnings but give more weight to other accounting items in unprofitable and growth industries.[192] Hence, loss firms in unprofitable sectors do not manage earnings upward in years -1 and +1. Additionally, if loss firms invest in other business activities (e.g., R&D and SG&A) for valuation purposes while earnings are unimportant, accruals decrease even more (always in terms of sales). Therefore, the anticipation for year -1 is different and for year +1 is vice versa compared to companies of the profitable group formulated above. Venture capital firms are usually engaged in these industries. They keep the majority of their investments in companies on average for two years

[190] Wongsunwai (2013), p. 4.
[191] (Profitable) companies could deflate current accruals and use the reversals for increasing future accruals.
[192] Bartov et al. (2002); Callen et al. (2008); Ertimur et al. (2003); Guo et al. (2005); Hayn (1995); Joos/Plesko (2005); Rajgopal et al. (2002); Roonen/Yari (2008), p. 147; Singer (2007).

after the issue.[193] When selling their stake, venture capitalists want to benefit from the investments. Investors appreciate increasing earnings. Accordingly, positive accruals are expected in year +2 from the reversal of downward accruals manipulation and from the intention of venture capital firms to profit from the sale of shares. The corresponding hypothesis is stated as follows:

Hypothesis accruals of loss firms in unprofitable industries (H-Acc 3): Loss companies in unprofitable industries (Biotech and Internet) exhibit negative earnings accruals in years -1 and +1, but positive accruals in year +2.

5.2 Econometric Models

5.2.1 General

To test the hypotheses, adequate econometric models have to be employed. Companies have several possibilities to use discretion in financial reporting. On the one hand, they can influence reporting (accruals) and on the other hand, they can use real activities. Usually, prior studies implicitly consider earnings accruals as the preeminent and only value driver for companies when testing for discretion in reporting.[194] Differences between industries are mainly ignored.[195] This misconception was addressed in some studies.[196] Since companies differ in growth opportunities, profitability, and investments, managers influence accounting items which are regarded as decisive value drivers. Therefore, several line items have to be tested for discretionary behavior to shed light on the earnings management puzzle. The econometric models have to take different aspects into account. These include differences between industries, time periods around the IPO, and accounting items, of course. The analysis should display the varying discretionary behavior around IPOs dependent on industries, profitability, and accounting numbers.

Several models for earnings accruals and RAM have to be used to test the hypotheses. Prior studies usually use total accruals or sometimes non-cash working capital as the measure of accruals management.[197] Total accruals are calculated as the difference between income before extraordinary items and cash flow from continuous operations. Cash flow accruals can

[193] Gompers/Lerner (2002), p. 266.
[194] Armstrong et al. (2009), pp. 1-2; Baik et al. (2010), p. 1; Pfaff/Ising (2010).
[195] Except in Fedyk et al. (2012), for example.
[196] Bartov et al. (2002); Demers/Joos (2007); Guo et al. (2005).
[197] Teoh et al. (1998b), p. 1936; DeFond/Jiambalvo (1994).

only be derived from 1987 onwards as statements of cash flow became available and include previous year's figures.[198] Whereas working capital accruals can be calculated from the balance sheet and have no time restrictions. Working capital accruals are calculated as change in non-cash current assets less the change in current operating liabilities. Short-term accruals in working capital are more variable than long-term accruals. Therefore, they are mainly responsible for the variance in total accruals.[199] However, working capital accruals are biased when estimated from changes in balance sheet data.[200] This can result from major financing events such as acquisitions, divestitures, or other deals that affect the accounts in consecutive financial reports.[201] These transactions change the working capital accounts in the balance sheet, but they are not reported as accruals in the cash flow statement. Therefore, models with total accruals calculated from cash flow became more popular. Accruals usually reverse within the short- or long-term and are used as an indicator of discretion around IPOs.

Besides accrual models, prior studies use real activity models to test for abnormal behavior in certain accounting items. The idea behind these models is that the respective line item can be explained by other accounts of the company. Predominantly, the level of sales is taken as an explanatory variable because it best describes the ongoing business situation. The abnormal part is considered as intentional behavior.

Prior studies usually use only one model for each accounting item which conveys that they are interpreting their results only according to the specific model or they use the model with the appropriate results. An exception is Dechow et al. (2012) who use five different accruals models.[202] This behavior increases comparability. By including several models to test for discretionary behavior, the results become more substantial if certain models are not clearly superior for research settings.

---

198 The release of SFAS 95 made cash flow statements obligatory.

199 Thomas/Zhang (2002).

200 Hribar/Collins (2002).

201 Ball/Shivakumar (2008, 340) regard this as a caveat in the study of Teoh et al. (1998b) since 16.7% of their IPO firms are affected by an acquisition or divestiture in the IPO year.

202 Dechow et al. (2012), pp. 288-289.

5.2.2 Accruals and Real Activity Models

5.2.2.1 Earnings Accruals Models

Prior literature usually uses only one model per study and line item. In this study various models are considered to test for accruals and real activity management and compare them to each other. To provide a clear picture of the results, only one model for each line item is employed in the main section while the alternative models are presented in the robustness section as sensitivity tests. The five accruals models are from Healy, Jones, Dechow et al. (modified Jones model), Dechow/Dichev and McNichols. These models are considered for several reasons. First, numerous studies find differences between the validity of these models. Some evidence the performance-matched modified Jones model to be more valid while others find the Jones model (but only for balance sheet accruals) to be superior.[203] Further studies prefer other models, but taking these two models into account is essential. Second, usually the research literature and especially studies in American accounting journals link their research to prior studies by using the same setting, including models, and then add their scientific contribution.[204] This procedure helps the reader to compare the contribution to prior findings and the occurrence of several models can be a reason for diverging results in prior studies. Since this study builds on prior literature in American journals, the usage of several models which are commonly used in various studies links this research to other studies. Additionally, recent empirical accounting studies also include various models to analyze earnings and thereby show the difference between the models.[205] While the main section includes the modified Jones model, the robustness section presents the remaining four models for accruals.

The modified Jones model[206] differs from the Jones model in calculating the change in revenues, as it subtracts the change in net accounts receivable (ΔSales-ΔRec). This eliminates the problem of low test power in case of misstated net accounts receivable. The employed model is:

[203] See Dechow et al. (1995, 223) who find evidence for the modified Jones model to be preferable while Kothari et al. (2005a, 178) particularly find the Jones model matched on ROA in certain research settings to produce the most valid results, but for balance sheet accruals. Furthermore, Ball/Shivakumar (2006, 240) evidence that the Jones model is considerably misspecified when researching reduced noise in earnings and in timely loss recognition. All studies use working capital accruals.

[204] DeFond/Jiambalvo (1994), pp. 148-149; Roychowdhury (2006), p. 348.

[205] See Dechow et al. (2012) and Stubben (2010), for example.

[206] Dechow et al. (1995).

$$\frac{TAcc_{i,t}}{A_{i,t-1}} = \alpha_t + \beta_{1,t}\frac{1}{A_{i,t-1}} + \beta_{2,t}\left(\frac{\Delta Sales_{i,t}}{A_{i,t-1}} - \frac{\Delta Rec_{i,t}}{A_{i,t-1}}\right) + \beta_{3,t}\frac{PPE_{i,t}}{A_{i,t-1}} + \varepsilon_{i,t}. \qquad \text{(Acc1)}$$

where

TAcc = total accruals from cash flow;

A = total assets;

ΔSales = sales $_t$ – sales $_{t-1}$;

ΔRec = net accounts receivable $_t$ – net accounts receivable $_{t-1}$;

PPE = gross property, plant, and equipment.[207]

5.2.2.2 Sales Models

Sales management is relatively often detected around IPOs. The measurement for discretion in sales is indirect by calculating abnormal change in receivables. The model of sales management estimates the discretion by regressing the change in receivables (ΔRec) on the change in sales (ΔSales) as well as available financial resources (Funds).[208] The variable funds is calculated as earnings before extraordinary items plus depreciation and amortization expenses minus capital expenditures to control for differences in credit behavior across firms. It is supposed to capture that firms with more available resources can have more lenient credit terms towards customers than firms which are short on resources. However, firms with the same resources can still be detected when using channel stuffing, for example. If the credit policy and the sales mix between cash and credit remain constant, the ratio of accounts receivable to sales (indicated by the coefficient β_1) should also remain constant over time.[209] More lenient credit requirements lead to an increase in receivables relative to sales. Therefore, the model is:

$$\frac{\Delta Rec_{i,t}}{A_{i,t-1}} = \alpha_t + \beta_{1,t}\frac{1}{A_{i,t-1}} + \beta_{2,t}\frac{\Delta Sales_{i,t}}{A_{i,t-1}} + \beta_{3,t}\frac{Funds_{i,t}}{A_{i,t-1}} + \varepsilon_{i,t} \qquad \text{(ΔRec1)}$$

where

Funds = available resources.

207 The subscripts are "i" for the company and "t" for the time period.

208 Roychowdhury (2006); Singer (2007).

209 To include prospective changes in the credit policy or in the sales mix that result from competitive aspects, the model is run in specific industries and years.

When cash has already been received, but revenue is deferred to the next period, then managers have the possibility of manipulating accounting estimates. A model for short-term deferred revenue and accounting discretion is based on Caylor (2010).[210] The assumptions underlying this model include that short-term deferred revenue is associated with future period's sales because deferred revenue includes amounts deferred to the next period. Furthermore, it is linked to cash flow from operations in the current period because the cash related with deferred revenue was gained in the current period. This indicates that variations in short-term deferred revenue are positively related to simultaneous changes in CfO and future fluctuations in sales. The corresponding model is:

$$\frac{\Delta DefRev_{i,t}}{A_{i,t-1}} = \alpha_t + \beta_{1,t}\frac{1}{A_{i,t-1}} + \beta_{2,t}\frac{\Delta Sales_{i,t+1}}{A_{i,t-1}} + \beta_{3,t}\frac{\Delta CfO_{i,t}}{A_{i,t-1}} + \varepsilon_{i,t} \quad (\Delta\text{DefRev})$$

where

ΔDefRev = deferred revenue $_t$ – deferred revenue $_{t-1}$.

RAM models test for real activities management of each dependent variable. Real business activities such as easing credit policies mainly influence gross accounts receivable. This is costly to firms as it relates to accelerating sales when cash has not yet been collected. Furthermore, the management makes subjective estimates of the earned amount of revenue. This is common in industries with long-term construction projects. A model for changes in gross accounts receivable is based on Caylor (2010).[211] The first assumption is that gross accounts receivable are associated with current period's sales because accounts receivable constitute sales accrued in the current period. Second, gross accounts receivable are associated with next period's CfO because the receivable amounts will result in CfO in the next period or later. This infers that changes in gross accounts receivable should be positively related to simultaneous changes in sales and future changes in CfO. The two control variables include any non-discretionary component that is not captured by the other. The model is:

$$\frac{\Delta GrRec_{i,t}}{A_{i,t-1}} = \alpha_t + \beta_{1,t}\frac{1}{A_{i,t-1}} + \beta_{2,t}\frac{\Delta Sales_{i,t}}{A_{i,t-1}} + \beta_{3,t}\frac{\Delta CfO_{i,t+1}}{A_{i,t-1}} + \varepsilon_{i,t} \quad (\Delta\text{GrRec})$$

where

ΔGrRec = gross accounts receivable $_t$ - gross accounts receivable $_{t-1}$.

210 Calyor (2010), p. 86. Deferred revenue is a liability account.
211 Calyor (2010), pp. 85-86.

5.2.2.3 Specific Real Activity Models

The importance of cash flow in practice turns them into an interesting account for investors.[212] Prior literature finds some hints of a systematic distribution of cash flow around a specific threshold.[213] Cash flow from operations is influenced by various business activities and is connected to many accounts. Since sales are important and meaningful for other accounts, cash flow is regressed on sales and change in sales in the current period.[214] For estimating the normal amount, the following multivariate regression model is used:

$$\frac{CfO_{i,t}}{A_{i,t-1}} = \alpha_t + \beta_{1,t}\frac{1}{A_{i,t-1}} + \beta_{2,t}\frac{Sales_{i,t}}{A_{i,t-1}} + \beta_{3,t}\frac{\Delta Sales_{i,t}}{A_{i,t-1}} + \varepsilon_{i,t} \qquad \text{(CfO)}$$

where

CfO = cash flow from operating activities.

Prior literature uses a few different models for R&D. To maintain comparability, they are included in this study, but three of them in the robustness section. The first R&D model concentrates on the level of R&D in the respective year compared to the prior years.[215] The model regresses the R&D expenses (RD) on the lagged R&D expenses, on the average cash holdings (AvChe) as well as on sales growth (SalesGR).[216] Prior year's R&D works as a proxy for the firm's R&D opportunities and persistent activities. The coefficient is expected to be positive. The average cash (AvChe) during the year is a proxy for internal resources available for investments in R&D. Sales growth is expected to be connected to R&D by indicating the further growth of the company and its resources. The following model captures discretionary behavior in accruals and real R&D spending as well as reclassifications. Since the data around the IPO is only partly available, the model is calculated with sales growth within one year.[217] The following model is used:

---

212 Block (1999), p. 87.

213 Burgstahler/Dichev (1997).

214 Cohen/Zarowin (2010), p. 8; Dechow et al. (1998); Roychowdhury (2006).

215 Berger (1993); Singer (2007); whereas Gunny (2010, 863) uses another model which includes market value and therefore, it cannot be used before IPOs.

216 Fedyk et al. (2012), p. 40. They mention no diverging results of the model with sales growth instead of Tobin's Q. There is no possibility to use Tobin's Q in pre-IPO years. Using past sales instead of future sales means that R&D is used according to present information instead of information that is not available to managers when deciding about these expenses.

217 Results are expected to be very similar in years when the model with sales growth from two periods includes sufficient observations for reasonable calculations; therefore, it is included in the robustness section.

$$\frac{RD_{i,t}}{A_{i,t-1}} = \alpha_t + \beta_{1,t}\frac{1}{A_{i,t-1}} + \beta_{2,t}\frac{RD_{i,t-1}}{A_{i,t-1}} + \beta_{3,g,t}\frac{AvChe_{i,t}}{A_{i,t-1}} + \beta_{4,t}SalesGR_{i,t} + \varepsilon_{i,t} \quad \text{(RD1)}$$

where

RD = R&D expenditures;

AvChe = average cash;

SalesGR = sales growth.[218]

Similarly to R&D, there are a few models for estimating abnormal SG&A. These are taken into account as follows. The model of Dechow et al. (1998) expresses expense as a linear function of contemporaneous sales. Applied for the account of SG&A, this model attributes that SG&A are dependent on the sales of a company. Following their model – including an intercept – normal SG&A is estimated as:[219]

$$\frac{SGA_{i,t}}{A_{i,t-1}} = \alpha_t + \beta_{1,t}\frac{1}{A_{i,t-1}} + \beta_{2,t}\frac{Sales_{i,t}}{A_{i,t-1}} + \varepsilon_{i,t} \quad \text{(SG\&A1)}$$

where

SGA = selling, general, and administrative expense.

Discretionary expenses are commonly calculated as the sum of R&D, SG&A, and advertising expenses in prior studies.[220] While R&D and SG&A are rarely examined, advertising expenses are usually not at all in the scope of prior studies when examining RAM.[221] However, advertising expenses can constitute a crucial amount of discretionary expenditures during the year and they are especially important around issues. This makes them an interesting account for RAM research. The model for advertising is based on Roychowdhury (2006) and uses lagged sales as the control variable because advertising depends partially on last year's sales. In the case of advertising expenses this leads to a (low) number of observations before the IPO. The model to calculate normal advertising expenses is:[222]

$$\frac{Adv_{i,t}}{A_{i,t-1}} = \alpha_t + \beta_{1,t}\frac{1}{A_{i,t-1}} + \beta_{2,t}\frac{Sales_{i,t-1}}{A_{i,t-1}} + \varepsilon_{i,t}. \quad \text{(Adv1)}$$

---

218 Note that "change in sales" is deflated by total assets while "sales growth" is deflated by sales.

219 Since most other models for SG&A include a market based variable they cannot be employed here. However, additional models are calculated in the robustness section.

220 Cohen/Zarowin (2010), p. 3; Roychowdhury (2006), p. 339.

221 For an exemption see Cohen et al. (2009), pp. 1-2.

222 Advertising Expenses are not part of SG&A in COMPUSTAT. Sometimes the majority of advertising expenses are higher than SG&A, like for IPOs in the Biotech industry; and sometimes vice versa.

where

Adv = advertising expense.

Finally, discretionary expenditure – as an aggregate measure – is composed of advertising, R&D, and SG&A expenses. Discretion in these single accounts can be used to improve profit margins in the current year. However, long-term results could be influenced negatively. The first model for this item is the same as used in Roychowdhury (2006). It includes prior year sales as the control variable instead of current year sales to avoid influence of discretionary sales in the respective year. This could result in fewer observations before the IPO. Normal discretionary expenses are calculated as follows:

$$\frac{DisExp_{i,t}}{A_{i,t-1}} = \alpha_t + \beta_{1,t}\frac{1}{A_{i,t-1}} + \beta_{2,t}\frac{Sales_{i,t-1}}{A_{i,t-1}} + \varepsilon_{i,t} \qquad \text{(DisExp1)}$$

where

DisExp = discretionary expense.

For analysis of change in inventory, prior literature uses several measures. A study of Aaker/Gjesdal (2010) explicitly focuses on the inventory account. They use several models from different backgrounds. They apply the working capital Jones (1991) model to inventory with change in sales as the control variable. Adapted, it is used as follows:

$$\frac{\Delta Inv_{i,t}}{A_{i,t-1}} = \alpha_t + \beta_{1,t}\frac{1}{A_{i,t-1}} + \beta_{2,t}\frac{\Delta Sales_{i,t}}{A_{i,t-1}} + \varepsilon_{i,t} \qquad (\Delta\text{Inv1})$$

where

ΔInv = change in inventory.

To estimate normal cost of goods sold, a model based on Dechow et al. (1998) is implemented which is also used by Roychowdhury (2006) and extended by an intercept. It employs sales as explanatory variable for any change in this account.[223]

$$\frac{COGS_{i,t}}{A_{i,t-1}} = \alpha_t + \beta_{1,t}\frac{1}{A_{i,t-1}} + \beta_{2,t}\frac{Sales_{i,t}}{A_{i,t-1}} + \varepsilon_{i,t} \qquad \text{(COGS)}$$

223 This model shows similar results as a sophisticated model in the study of Gunny (2010) and therefore, it is used here, because of restricted data availability. While aforementioned measures also used the model with lagged sales, here it is not applied because COGS are linked to current sales. The alternative model is presented in the robustness section.

where

COGS = cost of goods sold.

The aggregate measure of production costs is the sum of change in inventories and COGS. Abnormally high production costs are symptomatic for sales management due to (abnormal) price discounts or symptomatic for management of COGS due to overproduction. Therefore, firms can report higher production margins as well as higher reported earnings. The model used to estimate normal production costs includes sales and change in sales as explanatory variables:

$$\frac{Prod_{i,t}}{A_{i,t-1}} = \alpha_t + \beta_{1,t}\frac{1}{A_{i,t-1}} + \beta_{2,t}\frac{Sales_{i,t}}{A_{i,t-1}} + \beta_{3,t}\frac{\Delta Sales_{i,t}}{A_{i,t-1}} + \varepsilon_{i,t} \qquad \text{(Prod1)}$$

where

Prod = production costs.

The last RAM model is used for estimating the normal level of gain on asset sales. Companies can manage earnings in the short-term when selling (long-term) assets. Data availability for this model is restricted to years after 1986, when an obligation for disclosure was implemented. The model – based on prior studies – regresses gain on asset sales on the explanatory variables of sales, sales growth, asset sales, investment sales, and internal funds. All have been shown to influence the level of these gains.[224] The model for estimating normal gain on asset sales is:

$$\frac{GAS_{i,t}}{A_{i,t-1}} = \alpha_t + \beta_{1,t}\frac{1}{A_{i,t-1}} + \beta_{2,t}\frac{Sales_{i,t}}{A_{i,t-1}} + \beta_{3,t}SalesGR_{i,t} + \beta_{4,t}\frac{ASales_{i,t}}{A_{i,t-1}} + \beta_{5,t}\frac{ISales_{i,t}}{A_{i,t-1}} + \beta_{6,t}\frac{IntFu_{i,t}}{A_{i,t-1}} + \varepsilon_{i,t} \qquad \text{(GAS)}$$

where

GAS = gain on asset sales;

ASales = long-lived asset sales;

ISales = long-lived investment sales;

IntFu = internal funds.

[224] Bartov (1993); Gunny (2010), pp. 864-865; Herrmann et al. (2003). Tobin's Q is replaced by sales growth while market value is replaced by sales, as in the prior models.

It is important to note that earnings can be managed by accounting procedures, not affecting the RAM measures whilst using RAM typically affects earnings.

5.2.3 Research Design

To avoid heteroskedasticity, all variables and the intercept are deflated by lagged total assets, except indicator variables and sales growth. The usage of deflated variables is a common procedure in prior studies.[225] Similarly, it is general convention in the literature to include an intercept as well as an intercept scaled by (lagged) total assets in AM and RAM models to avoid misspecification.[226] Otherwise a spurious correlation between the scaled dependent variable and the scaled independent variable could be present, resulting from variation in the scaling variable (lagged total assets). Hence, the procedure controls for scale differences among firms.[227] The inclusion of an unscaled intercept helps to ensure that the mean abnormal regressand for every industry-year is zero.[228] Prior literature finds improved results and mitigated model misspecification when including the unscaled intercept.[229] Other studies find the omission of the unscaled intercept to be immaterial in contrast to eliminating the scaled intercept.[230] The models use mainly prior year assets and sales. Both are largely available in two and three years before the IPO while other data are not. This explains why there can be a higher number of companies one year before than two years before the IPO.[231]

To calculate the significance of abnormal amounts, several steps have to be followed which are exemplified with the modified Jones model. Nevertheless, all other models can be substituted here due to the equal calculation of other abnormal accounting items. First, total accruals are calculated by earnings before extraordinary items minus cash flow from operations for the whole sample. Second, the cross-sectional modified Jones model is calculated for each year and industry (subgroup) without specific IPO companies (sample companies) to estimate the coefficients of the regression. There are at least eight observations required for each industry-year grouping to ensure reliable coefficient estimates.[232] The

225 Jones (1991), p. 212. Lagged total assets are usually preferred over average total assets as in Ball/Shivakumar (2006) in contrast to Armstrong et al. (2009).

226 Caylor (2010), p. 86; Gunny (2010), p. 863; Kothari et al. (2005a), p. 195; Roychowdhury (2006), p. 344; Singer (2007); Zang (2012), p. 682. No unscaled intercept is employed in Cohen/Zarowin (2010, 6).

227 Barth/Kallapur (1996).

228 The intercepts allows the average regressand for an individual industry-year to be non-zero even when the primary regressors in the model are zero.

229 Compare Kothari et al. (2005a, 195) for the Jones and modified Jones models.

230 Roychowdhury (2006), p. 344.

231 One might think that there can be only as much pre-IPO companies as there are companies two years before the IPO because of data restrictions.

232 Caylor (2010), p. 86.

industry-year coefficients are used on the independent variables of the IPOs to estimate normal (accrual) amounts. The resulting expected accruals are subtracted from the actual accruals to receive the discretionary (abnormal) accruals. The results are not adjusted for performance, yet. Therefore, the next step is the inclusion of comparable companies.

Especially around IPOs, company performance plays an important role. Issuers are comparably young, growing, undergo structural changes, and the IPO usually takes place in hot capital market periods. To control for missing explanatory variables, such as performance and the differentiation between discretionary and non-discretionary accruals, prior literature promotes matching the sample firms with comparable companies. The usual procedure is to follow Kothari et al. (2005a) and match each IPO firm with a non-IPO firm on the basis of industry membership, year, and return on assets (ROA).[233] Matching on industry is based on the same two to four digits SIC code, depending on the number of companies available in each industry subsector.[234] The results of including matched companies are better specified than non-matching approaches and therefore, matching is applied here. A further effect of matching is that the outcome provides more conservative estimates than without matching. Usually, this leads to more non-rejections of the null hypothesis.[235] Some studies include ROA as an additional regressor instead of matching on ROA, but this procedure induces linearity on the relation of performance and accruals which is found to be untrue.[236]

The same procedure for calculating discretionary accruals is used for the matched sample firms of each IPO firm. Finally, this abnormal amount of each matched firm is subtracted from the discretionary accruals of the IPO firm to adjust this amount for performance. The mean difference of each industry-year result is tested (t-test, alternatively the Wilcoxon rank-sum is used for non-normally distributed variables) for significant difference from zero. The results are denoted highly significant for the 1% level or significant for the 5% and 10% levels, respectively. The results for the particular industries are presented for the overall sample as well as for both subgroups of companies (profitable and loss companies).

Any abnormal result indicates that discretion exists. Negative (and significant) results point out that mean abnormal accruals of IPO firms are (significantly) lower than those of matched comparable companies, both controlled for the specific explanatory variables. In other words,

---

233 The company with the closest ROA is used as matched company and the ROA is restricted to a lower than 30 percent difference.

234 For example, the Biotech companies are matched on three or even all four digits of the SIC code.

235 Cohen et al. (2013), p. 28. These authors use an adapted performance matching procedure.

236 Butler et al. (2004); Kothari et al. (2005a), pp. 192-193.

the mean of IPO firms in the specific industry, year, and accounting item is (significantly) lower than the mean of non-IPOs. The same is true for positive amounts or the other accounting items in the study.[237] To test the main hypotheses, additional tests for the combination of the respective two year groups (sum of all company residuals in the two groups are compared: t-test or Wilcoxon rank-sum, depending if the regressand is normally distributed) as well as additional contrast fit models for the five years (-2 to +3) are employed. To decide if a specific hypothesis is rejected or not the tests have to be applied by subgroup, year, and industry. Alternatively, a mixed model approach (fixed effects) and interaction terms can be used. The similar procedure is used for hypotheses set two where industry groups are compared by their discretionary amounts.

The focus of this thesis is on earnings management within GAAP, however, the empirical study might include companies with illegal activities to reach their goals. The study is based on prior literature and picks-up certain accounting items with the respective models which are now examined for different factors (e.g., years, industries). Hereby, the different accounting items make the plot throughout the study. In this way, prior literature can be compared to the presented results. The practitioners view would probably be to present the results by industry.

Concerning the differentiation of the groups within industries, the expectation is that in an industry such as the Biotech, for example, which includes mainly loss companies during the IPO, the result for the overall sample is similar to the result of the loss group. Nevertheless, all respective results from the overall, profitable, and loss samples are documented separately for numerous reasons. First, prior literature usually presents the overall sample, only.[238] For comparison purposes, the overall sample is presented here, too. However, some studies find differences between profitable and loss companies and by presenting the overall sample only, there would be missing information.[239] Furthermore, in this study the categorization emphasizes the difference between the overall sample and the subgroups of profitable and loss firms. Additionally, an interesting issue will come into effect, when profitable and loss firms display opposing results and the mixture is present in the overall sample. In prior studies this would mean that the interpretation is made for the overall sample, although at least one group indicates opposing results. Henceforth, some information about earnings management is lost. For example, if the profitable group shows significantly positive results (in any year and

[237] The studies of Gunny (2010) and Zang (2012) deliver the construct validity of the proxies in RAM models.
[238] Caylor (2010), p. 90; Cohen/Zarowin (2010), p. 10; Dechow et al. (2012), p. 299; Gunny (2010), p. 898; Roychowdhury (2006), p. 349; Zang (2012), p. 688.
[239] Graham et al. (2005), pp. 18-20.

group) and the loss group significantly negative ones, the overall sample could exhibit insignificant results. Hence, the interpretation would be that no discretion is present although this would not be true for the subgroups.

6. Empirical Study

6.1 Sample and Data

The US-capital market is the largest in the world.[240] US-American IPOs offer an excellent data sample. On the one hand there exists an extensive amount of IPOs with a large database and the accounting items are usually available over a long time period. Furthermore, US companies typically offer incentives during IPOs by share-based payments which are of further interest in the empirical study for the years after the issue. Therefore, the data of public companies with their primary exchange in the US are included. The data collection starts in 1987 because this is the first year that has detailed enough numbers to calculate the regressions.[241] Accordingly, cash flow from operations is available from post 1986.[242] The last year taken into account is 2012, providing an IPO-database of 26 years. The financial accounting data are drawn from the industrial annual files of CRSP-COMPUSTAT in November 2012.[243] Extant prior IPO literature consistently excludes American Depository Receipts (ADRs), unit offerings, closed-end funds, and Real Estate Investment Trusts (REITs) offerings. In COMPUSTAT the accounting numbers for the third years (and earlier) before the IPO are basically not documented because of limited data availability for not publicly traded companies in the US.[244] As seen before, the models include lagged values. In the case of year three prior to the issue this means amounts from the fourth year before the IPO would be necessary. There is no available data for this time period. Therefore, year two before the IPO illustrates the beginning of the results description.

---

240 NYSE Euronext (2012).

241 Accruals from working capital data can be collected from 1962 onwards, because COMPUSTAT data prior to 1962 are generally acknowledged to suffer from survivorship bias, see Kothari et al. (1995). Data with missing values are typically eliminated.

242 SFAS no. 95 obligates firms to publish a statement of cash flows for fiscal years ending after July 15, 1988. For some early adopters the report is available from 1987 onwards.

243 Source: CRSP®, Center for Research in Security Prices. Graduate School of Business, University of Chicago. Used with permission. All rights reserved. www.crsp.uchicago.edu. The author acknowledges the data from COMPUSTAT, which were obtained through Wharton Research Data Services (WRDS) and sponsored by University Research Priority Program Finance. The usage of these databases is very common, for example, Cecchini et al. (2012), Ising (2009).
The data format in COMPUSTAT is used with flagged STD. STD indicates that the data are the originally reported and not restated figures. If available, PRE_AMENDS are used. These are data prior making amendments to financial statements following a possible SEC investigation. The number of PRE_AMENDS data is rare. The sample is limited to domestic firms (COMPUSTAT mnemonics: popsrc = D and fic = USA) with the domestic accounting standard (DS) and primary issue tag in the US (COMPUSTAT mnemonic: priusa = 1).

244 Pre-IPO data is enclosed in the offering prospectus and is commonly available for three years prior to the IPO whereas it can also be hand collected from 10-K forms. See also Armstrong et al. (2009, 20) and Katz (2006, 6).

Consistent with prior studies, positive and available values of the following variables are required: cash and equivalents; current assets; current liabilities; property, plant, and equipment; receivables; sales; short-term debt and total assets. Correspondingly, non-missing values of earnings before extraordinary items are mandatory to derive cash flow. As in previous research the standard procedure of winsorizing is applied here.[245] This technique winsorizes all continuous variables at the top and bottom 1% of their respective distributions. This limits the influence of outliers. The final sample includes around 2'823 IPOs and overall 6'601 firms with 60'618 firm-year observations in the years from 1987 to 2012.

All models are tested in particular industries.[246] The selection of industries follows prior literature and tries to include prominent and yet diverging industries to test a broad variety of sectors.[247] The clusters are expected to inherit distinct characteristics. However, there have to be enough companies in the specific industries to estimate the models because companies are classified into groups according to their industry membership. The first group is comprised of chemical, especially pharmaceutical and biological establishments in the Biotech industry. Since most of the chosen companies engage in pharmaceutical preparations or the production of vaccines and similar, it is called the Biotech (Biotechnology) industry.[248] Firms in the Biotechnology industry are those with a four-digit SIC code of 283 or 8731. The decision follows Joos/Zhdanov (2008) who "choose an emerging R&D environment, the Biotechnology industry, because this industry is characterized by long investment cycles with highly uncertain payoffs"[249] where valuation depends heavily on R&D success. The second group contains the Internet firms. Internet firms are indicated by a SIC code of 737. These companies have been shown to differ from non-Internet companies and therefore, they bias findings for an all industry sample.[250] The next group includes (high-growth) Technology companies from computer, electronics, and communication industries. Firms in the technologies exhibit a three-digit SIC code of 355, 357, 381, 382, 384, 386, 481, 873, or two digits of 36. These firms differ from non-Technology companies and their R&D spending is important for capital market participants.[251] The fourth group consists of Construction and Heavy Machinery Manufacturing industries (Construction) with SIC codes 15 to 1799, 3312

[245] Gunny (2010), p. 877. For a discussion of trimming data instead of winsorizing see Kothari et al. (2005b).
[246] For clarity reasons of the thesis, five industries are sufficient. As in prior literature the regulated industries (SIC 4910-4939) and financial institutions (SIC 6000-6999) are omitted as comparable industries due to their special business model.
[247] This procedure fosters comparability to prior literature. A main notion of this thesis is to show differences in industries. Therefore, a mixed overall industry sample is not presented.
[248] Joos/Zhdanov (2008), p. 446. Similarly, Zucker et al. (1998), pp. 290-291.
[249] Joos/Zhdanov (2008), p. 431.
[250] Bartov et al. (2002), p. 322.
[251] Francis et al. (2012), pp. 261-262; Hsu (2009), p. 265.

to 3325, 3510 to 3549, and 37. This group is quite different to the three aforementioned industries. For example, it has fewer intangible assets and rather long-term sales cycles. The last group encompasses Wholesale companies with SIC codes of 50 to 5199.[252] This group has short sales cycles and rather low R&D expenses. The groups are expected to cover distinct characteristics of industries. An overview of SIC is presented in Table 2.

Table 2: Industries and Codes

Industry	*Sub-Industry*	*Industry Codes (SIC)*
Biotech	biological and physical research; drugs	283, 8731
Internet	computer programming; data processing and corresponding services	737
Technology	computer and electronic equipment; analyzing instruments; communications; research services	355, 357, 36, 381, 382, 384, 386, 481, 873 (except 8731)
Construction and ferrous production	building and heavy construction; steel works and iron foundries; production of machinery, engines, transportation, and corresponding equipment	1500 to 1799, 3312 to 3325, 351-3549, 37
Wholesale trade	wholesale trade durable & non-durable goods	5000 to 5199

6.2 Descriptive Statistics

Table 3 illustrates the overall sample of the included companies. The Biotech industry includes 915 companies with 8'732 firm years. The Internet industry comprises almost twice as much companies but only 50% more firm-years. This results from the fact that Internet companies are younger and do not include a long history of data. The largest group is the Technology industry with 2'833 companies and 28'086 firm years. The two smallest industries are the Construction and the Wholesale groups with 617 and 585 companies, respectively. Nevertheless, they include 6'289 and 5'279 firm-years. This results in an overall amount of 6'601 firms with 60'618 firm-year observations which makes it a huge sample.

252 The calculations were repeated for the first year before the IPO without companies from SIC code 5122 and the results are almost exactly the same.

Table 3: Number of Firms and Firm-Years by Industry

	Biotech	Internet	Technology	Construction	Wholesale	*Total*
No. of firms	915	1'651	2'833	617	585	**6'601**
No. of firm-years	8'732	12'232	28'086	6'289	5'279	**60'618**

Table 4 and Figure 4 report descriptive statistics for IPO years. They illustrate the distribution of all IPOs by year (1987 to 2011) and industry.[253] The distribution shows a hot IPO market in the years of 1991 to 2000. It peaks in 1996 for most industries and the overall sample while the peak of the Construction sample occurs in 1993. The lowest IPO activity exists in 2002, 2003, and 2008. This distribution is similar for the overall sample and the individual groups except the Construction industry which has a low in 2009. From there onwards the IPO market seems to recover. Additionally, the findings indicate that in the examined time interval the Technology and Internet industries had more companies go public than the other industries. Furthermore, the Construction and Wholesale industries depict the lowest number. This underlines the importance of differentiating between industries. Mixing all companies in an overall sample results in a biased outcome, for example in favor of the sample with the most companies. The Technology group would comprise over one third of the overall sample as well as over five times the Construction or Wholesale samples.

[253] The overall number of 3'168 IPOs includes all IPOs in these years with available data, but the number can be reduced for calculations if, for example, not enough comparable companies in the same SIC and year are available.

Table 4: IPOs by Industry and Year

	Biotech		Internet		Technology		Construction		Wholesale		*Total*	
Year	#	%	#	%	#	%	#	%	#	%		%
1987	3	*1%*	3	*0%*	17	*1%*	2	*1%*	4	*2%*	**29**	*1%*
1988	8	*2%*	10	*1%*	34	*3%*	4	*2%*	4	*2%*	**60**	*2%*
1989	6	*2%*	7	*1%*	21	*2%*	4	*2%*	3	*1%*	**41**	*1%*
1990	4	*1%*	12	*1%*	31	*3%*	7	*4%*	4	*2%*	**58**	*2%*
1991	27	*7%*	19	*2%*	55	*5%*	6	*3%*	15	*7%*	**122**	*4%*
1992	28	*7%*	42	*5%*	88	*8%*	9	*5%*	10	*5%*	**177**	*6%*
1993	27	*7%*	44	*5%*	105	*9%*	24	*13%*	23	*11%*	**223**	*8%*
1994	24	*6%*	35	*4%*	81	*7%*	24	*13%*	22	*11%*	**186**	*7%*
1995	18	*5%*	89	*10%*	118	*10%*	15	*8%*	18	*9%*	**258**	*9%*
1996	50	*13%*	124	*14%*	134	*12%*	20	*11%*	28	*14%*	**356**	*13%*
1997	27	*7%*	86	*10%*	92	*8%*	22	*12%*	19	*9%*	**246**	*9%*
1998	19	*5%*	71	*8%*	36	*3%*	14	*8%*	14	*7%*	**154**	*5%*
1999	12	*3%*	138	*15%*	73	*6%*	3	*2%*	7	*3%*	**233**	*8%*
2000	30	*8%*	88	*10%*	102	*9%*	8	*4%*	3	*1%*	**231**	*8%*
2001	4	*1%*	6	*1%*	10	*1%*	1	*1%*	3	*1%*	**24**	*1%*
2002	1	*0%*	4	*0%*	3	*0%*	2	*1%*	1	*0%*	**11**	*0%*
2003	4	*1%*	3	*0%*	3	*0%*	0	*0%*	1	*0%*	**11**	*0%*
2004	23	*6%*	18	*2%*	29	*3%*	1	*1%*	5	*2%*	**76**	*3%*
2005	11	*3%*	10	*1%*	21	*2%*	4	*2%*	3	*1%*	**49**	*2%*
2006	24	*6%*	15	*2%*	25	*2%*	9	*5%*	5	*2%*	**78**	*3%*
2007	15	*4%*	23	*3%*	38	*3%*	3	*2%*	3	*1%*	**82**	*3%*
2008	2	*1%*	2	*0%*	5	*0%*	1	*1%*	0	*0%*	**10**	*0%*
2009	3	*1%*	9	*1%*	7	*1%*	0	*0%*	1	*0%*	**20**	*1%*
2010	9	*2%*	14	*2%*	16	*1%*	2	*1%*	2	*1%*	**43**	*2%*
2011	9	*2%*	19	*2%*	13	*1%*	0	*0%*	4	*2%*	**45**	*2%*
Total	**388**		**891**		**1'157**		**185**		**202**		**2'823**	*100%*

Note: # = amount of companies. % = percentage of companies in the respective industry year.

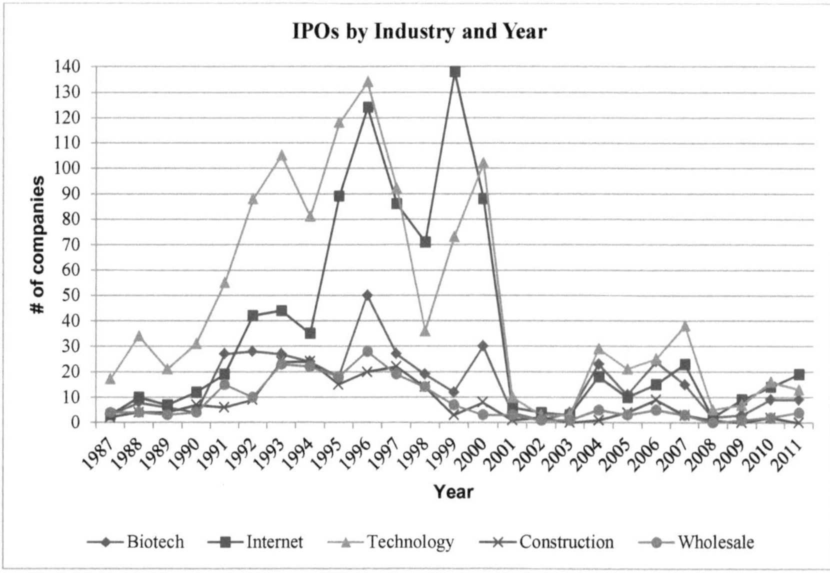

Figure 4: IPOs by Industry and Year

Table 5 illustrates the amount of sample firms by year and the corresponding percentage of profitability while Figure 5 gives a picture of the history of profitability around the IPO. The sample companies in the Biotech industry are obviously the group with the most loss companies over the years. Only around 15% of the companies are profitable when issuing stocks while it seems even decreasing after the issue. This group consists of 1'510 firm years with available data. In the Internet group there are around 40% of profitable firms except for the first report after going public when even 52% of the sample is profitable. This group consists of 3'089 firm years. Technology companies show a quota of around 40 to 50% of profitable companies, except in the post-IPO year the ratio increases to 56%. It is the largest group with 4'068 firm years the sample. The Construction industry consists of mainly profitable companies in all sample years. The ratio varies from 66 to 80%. With only 641 firm years it is the smallest group. In the Wholesale industry, there are around 60 to 80% of profitable firms in the examined time period, with the highest value in the first period after going public. This group consists of 736 firm years.

Table 5: Sample Firms per Year and Percentage of Profitability

Year	-2		-1		+1		+2		+3	
	#	*% prof.*	#	*% prof.*	#	*% prof.*	#	*% prof.*	#	*% prof.*
Biotech	27	*15%*	202	*14%*	388	*15%*	466	*14%*	427	*12%*
Internet	24	*38%*	388	*38%*	891	*52%*	952	*41%*	834	*39%*
Technology	38	*50%*	442	*41%*	1'157	*56%*	1'256	*48%*	1'175	*45%*
Construction	7	*71%*	56	*66%*	185	*78%*	201	*80%*	192	*71%*
Wholesale	7	*57%*	75	*77%*	202	*80%*	234	*73%*	218	*67%*
Total	**103**		**1'163**		**2'823**		**3'109**		**2'846**	

Notes: # = amount of companies. % prof. = percentage of profitable IPO sample companies in the respective industry-year.

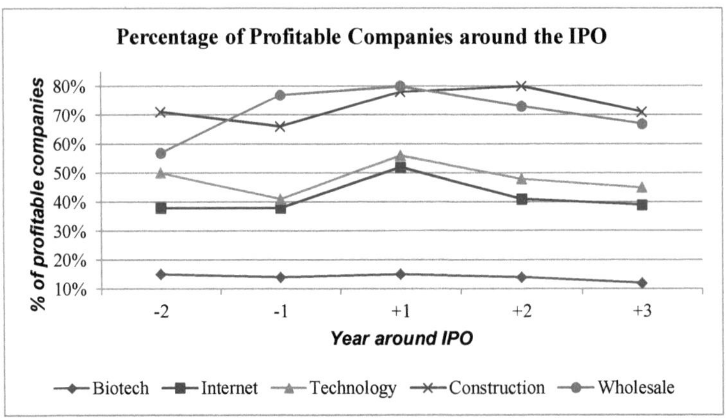

Figure 5: Percentage of Profitable Companies around the IPO

The following Table 6 includes the descriptive statistics for the specific industries in the post-IPO year. It reveals specific characteristics for the five industries. The reported parameters exhibit substantial differences between these industries. This fosters the belief that due to industry and year differences the motivation of applying discretion in accounting varies around the offering. The Biotech companies show the lowest total assets, followed by the Internet industry. From the remaining industries the Construction companies have the highest total assets. The results for sales clearly show that the three growth industries (Biotech, Internet, and Technology) exhibit substantially less sales than the Wholesale and Construction industries. This is similar for sales in percent of total assets. However, as expected from prior literature, the Biotech, Internet, and Technology industries exhibit a higher sales growth rate than the more well-established industries. Yet, their sales growth rate is still quite high compared to companies in the same industry but publicly traded some time ago. As mentioned in the hypotheses, the Biotech, Internet, and Technology industries clearly deviate from the Construction and Wholesale industries.

Non-cash assets are lower for the growth industries than for the other groups which might be a matter of size. The leverage ratio shows that the Biotech, Internet, and Technology industries are lower than the two other industries. This means that the three growth industries do not need much credit after the issue. Obviously, the cash inflow at the IPO is utilized for paying off debts. The amount of total assets in terms of market value indicates that Biotech, Internet, and Technology companies have substantially lower ratios than the Construction and Wholesale industries. Hence, although few assets are in the balance sheet, the market values their future prospects and expectations.

Intangible assets show an ambiguous picture in absolute amounts but a clearer one in relative values. The Construction companies exhibit the highest absolute amount. However, high-growth industries show the highest ratio for intangible assets in terms of sales. The results for R&D expenses are even more striking and support the notions for the hypotheses. R&D in terms of sales is much higher for the growth companies than for the well-established ones, although the Technology companies exhibit a relatively low value. Coherent with the hypotheses, the Biotech, Internet, and Technology industries substantially deviate from the Construction and Wholesale industries.

Table 6: Descriptive Statistics of IPO Companies by Industry

	Biotech	Internet	Technology	Construction	Wholesale
A	88	156	261	314	269
Sales	37	109	182	323	549
% A	*42%*	*70%*	*70%*	*103%*	*204%*
SalesGR	*54%*	*59%*	*43%*	*24%*	*29%*
Non-C. A	46	98	208	291	249
% A	*52%*	*63%*	*80%*	*93%*	*93%*
Leverage	*25%*	*28%*	*31%*	*50%*	*51%*
MV	243	687	549	312	237
A/MV	*36%*	*23%*	*47%*	*101%*	*113%*
Int. A	17	25	64	68	51
% S	*45%*	*23%*	*35%*	*21%*	*9%*
R&D	14	13	14	19	0.3
% S	39%	12%	8%	6%	0%
TAcc	-5.2	-9.6	-14.6	-14.6	-2.9
D.Acc	-.0538	-.0019	.0060	.0198	.0352
PosD.Acc	.0923	.1405	.0921	.0759	.0991
NegD.Acc	-.1398	-.1566	-.1112	-.0781	-.0730
D.ΔRec	.0029	.0159	.0109	.0130	.0127
D.ΔGrRec	.0231	.0915	.0491	.0853	.0449
D.ΔDefRev	.0268	.0708	.0057	.0005	.0004
D.CfO	-.2046	-.0565	-.0577	-.0145	-.0275
D.R&D	.0502	.0192	.0084	-.0036	.0003
D.SGA	.2564	.2453	.1304	-.0046	.0218
D.Adv	.0098	.0097	.0042	.0029	.0018
D.DisExp	.3941	.3405	.1854	-.0051	.0235
D.ΔInv	-.0006	-.0001	.0141	.0094	.0018
D.COGS	.1733	-.1517	-.0158	-.0068	-.0798
D.Prod	.1821	-.1135	.0280	.0232	-.0175
D.GAS	-.0006	.0000	-.0001	.0000	-.0001

Notes: Total amounts are average amounts in millions in the post-IPO year. Discretionary amounts are divided by total assets. Variables are defined as follows: A = total assets. % A = (item above) in percent of total assets. SalesGR = growth of sales. Non-C. A = non-cash assets = total assets minus cash and short-term investments. Leverage = ratio of total liabilities to total assets. MV = market value. A/MV = total assets divided by market value. Int. A = intangible assets. % S = (item above) in percent of total sales. R&D = research and development expenses. TAcc = total accruals. D.Acc = discretionary accruals. PosD.Acc and NegD.Acc = positive and negative discretionary accruals. D.ΔRec = discretionary change in receivables. D.ΔGrRec = discretionary change in gross receivables. D.ΔDefRev = discretionary change in deferred revenue. D.CfO = discretionary cash flow from operations. D.R&D = discretionary research and development expenses. D.SGA = discretionary selling, general, and administrative expenses. D.Adv = discretionary advertising expenses. D.DisExp = abnormal discretionary expenses. D.ΔInv = discretionary change in inventory. D.COGS = discretionary cost of goods sold. D.Prod = discretionary production costs. D.GAS = discretionary gain on asset sales.

The descriptive statistics for discretionary (abnormal) amounts of various accounting items underline the considerable difference between the growth and the well-established industries. Whilst total accruals have a negative mean in all industries, discretionary accruals are positive in three amounts for the more profitable industries. The Internet industry exhibits the highest amounts of all industries in both, the positive and negative discretionary accruals amounts. An interesting aspect turns out when looking at the three discretionary sales measures (changes in receivables, gross receivables, and deferred revenue). The amounts for changes in deferred revenue and gross receivables are usually higher than for receivables, indicating that studies should include these methods when examining sales management. However, most prior studies did not employ these models. Abnormal cash flow from operations is negative in all industries. This is in line with high R&D amounts. Abnormal amounts for R&D are substantially higher for the growth industries than in the remaining two groups. This is equally true for abnormal SG&A amounts, but these amounts are even higher. Again, this suggests including SG&A as well as R&D. Since discretionary advertising amounts are abnormal and also higher for high-growth than for well-established industries, the resulting discretionary expense amount considerably differs between these industries. The abnormal amounts for change in inventory are negative for Biotech and Internet companies but positive for the other three groups. Discretionary COGS are only positive and high for the Biotech industry. The combined measure of abnormal production costs exhibits ambiguous results, yet, the amount for the Biotech industry is strikingly positive. The last measure of gain on asset sales is low and ambiguous for all industries.

The methodology of Pearson measures the degree of association between numerical variables.[254] Table 7 depicts results for the Person correlation of the discretionary amounts in the Biotech industry. Several results are striking. First, discretionary behavior in accruals is present in combination with discretionary sales as well as change in inventory. All accounts can be influenced by discretionary accounting behavior and not necessarily real activities. As expected from their methodological backgrounds (see chapters 3.2.2.2 and 5.2.2.2), change in receivables and change in gross receivables are positively correlated.

Contrarily, the accounts of R&D, SG&A, and discretionary expenses are all negatively correlated to accruals. These items are all expensed as incurred and rely on real activity behavior. This means Biotech companies use accrual as well as real activity management around the IPO. Furthermore, there is striking evidence that discretionary cash flow is negatively correlated to the expense accounts such as SG&A. This is intuitive since expenses reduce cash flow. Connected to this outcome is the fact that Biotech companies use R&D and SG&A inflation as complements. While advertising expenses are positively correlated to SG&A they are not correlated to R&D. This is usually the case due to a closer relation of advertising and SG&A expenses. The aggregate measure of discretionary expenses confirms the employed methods as it is negatively correlated to cash flow and positively correlated to its three components. The very high amount for SG&A is caused by the definition of discretionary expenses which requires SG&A as available variable in the aggregate measure. It has to be included anyhow due to comparison reasons (the same argument is valid for COGS and production costs).

Production costs are the aggregate measure of COGS and change in inventory. The abnormal amount of change in inventory is negatively correlated to COGS which confirms the intuition of real activity management as outlined in chapters 3.2.2 and 5.2.2. Similarly, production costs are positively correlated to COGS but not to change in inventory. As expected, COGS and production costs have many results in common as the very high amount of their correlation confirms. This is caused by the fact that Biotech companies have few inventories as it is the nature of this industry. Finally, there is almost no correlation of gain on asset sales to any other measure.

---

[254] The tables for Pearson include merely the post-IPO year (year +1) due to space constraints. This year seems most suitable since it includes enough observations and important incentives around the IPO. Including the subsamples would induce opacity in presentation and is left to future research. A Spearman correlation matrix is typically used on ordinal outcomes.

Table 7: Pearson Correlation for Discretionary Variables in the Biotech Industry

	D.Acc	*D.ΔRec*	*D.ΔGrRec*	*D.ΔDefRev*	*D.CfO*	*D.R&D*	*D.SGA*	*D.Adv*	*D.DisExp*	*D.ΔInv*	*D.COGS*	*D.Prod*	*D.GAS*
D.Acc	1.000												
D.ΔRec	**.140*****	1.000											
D.ΔGrRec	.084	**.495*****	1.000										
D.ΔDefRev	-.172	.176	-.124	1.000									
D.CfO	-.050	**-.208*****	-.092	**.200***	1.000								
D.R&D	**-.208*****	-.051	.023	.022	.008	1.000							
D.SGA	**-.244*****	.008	.080	**.402****	**-.522*****	**.206****	1.000						
D.Adv	-.075	.158	.230	**.470****	**-.254****	-.142	**.432*****	1.000					
D.DisExp	**-.203*****	-.001	.091	**.327****	**-.524*****	**.194****	**.961*****	**.460*****	1.000				
D.ΔInv	**.221*****	**.216*****	.045	-.089	-.078	**-.151*****	-.041	-.032	-.014	1.000			
D.COGS	-.083	.058	.048	.065	**-.190*****	**.210*****	**-.233*****	-.103	**-.123***	**-.104****	1.000		
D.Prod	-.075	.084	.068	.051	**-.225*****	**.173*****	**-.163****	-.150	-.084	.007	**.979*****	1.000	
D.GAS	.000	.050	.056	.062	-.026	.018	-.028	**.264***	-.020	-.072	-.078	-.095	1.000

Notes: *, **, *** represent statistical significance at 10 percent, 5 percent, and 1 percent levels (two-sided), respectively (emphasized by bold type). The results denote the correlation of discretionary amounts in the Biotech industry in the post-IPO year. Variables are defined as follows: D.Acc = discretionary accruals. D.ΔRec = discretionary change in receivables. D.ΔGrRec = discretionary change in gross receivables. D.ΔDefRev = discretionary change in deferred revenue. D.CfO = discretionary cash flow from operations. D.R&D = discretionary research and development expenses. D.SGA = discretionary selling, general, and administrative expenses. D.Adv = discretionary advertising expenses. D.DisExp = abnormal discretionary expenses. D.ΔInv = discretionary change in inventory. D.COGS = discretionary cost of goods sold. D.Prod = discretionary production costs. D.GAS = discretionary gain on asset sales.

Table 8 documents results for the Person correlation of the discretionary amounts in the Internet industry. Outcomes are similar to the Biotech industry in several aspects, but differ in others. Again, discretionary earnings accruals are positively correlated with receivables and inventory, but not with other accounts. Especially the expense accounts show opposed signs to accruals. Sales management is negatively correlated to abnormal cash flow which is in line with abnormal sales behavior deflating cash flows (see chapter 5.2.2). This outcome is true for all three sales measures.

As expected, cash flows are also negatively correlated to the expense accounts. This is corresponding to the Biotech industry. Additionally, cash flows are negatively correlated to the remaining amounts of change in inventory, COGS, production, and gain on asset sales. The connection of expense accounts and change in inventory is ambiguous. The negative correlation to SG&A can be explained by an enlarged effort to sell products that are in stock. The positive correlation of inventory and COGS (as well as production) to sales can be explained by sales management influencing these accounts. Similarly, inventory plays a minor role in this industry.

Table 9 illustrates outcomes for the Person correlation of the discretionary amounts in the Technology industry. Again, the results are similar as in the industries before. All sales variables are correlated mutually, again. Some differences are present for sales. Receivables are positively correlated to SG&A and advertising expenses which is quite intuitive. Especially, outcomes for gain on asset sales differ. This variable is correlated to accruals which points at a coherent attempt to increase earnings.

Table 8: Pearson Correlation for Discretionary Variables in the Internet Industry

	D.Acc	*D.ΔRec*	*D.ΔGrRec*	*D.ΔDefRev*	*D.CfO*	*D.R&D*	*D.SGA*	*D.Adv*	*D.DisExp*	*D.ΔInv*	*D.COGS*	*D.Prod*	*D.GAS*
D.Acc	1.000												
D.ΔRec	**.209*****	1.000											
D.ΔGrRec	**.140*****	**.461*****	1.000										
D.ΔDefRev	**-.398*****	**.276*****	**.210****	1.000									
D.CfO	**-.056***	**-.212*****	**-.234*****	**-.194***	1.000								
D.R&D	**-.104*****	**.081****	.064	.060	**-.078****	1.000							
D.SGA	**-.246*****	.036	.024	**.281*****	**-.188*****	**.290*****	1.000						
D.Adv	**-.113****	-.037	**.114***	.163	**-.130****	**.135****	**.319****	1.000					
D.DisExp	**-.182*****	.055	**.089****	**.348*****	**-.122*****	**.348*****	**.920*****	**.372*****	1.000				
D.ΔInv	**.144*****	**.097*****	**.081***	-.017	**-.154*****	**.062***	**-.090*****	-.035	**-.137*****	1.000			
D.COGS	.019	**.070****	.039	**-.304*****	**-.329*****	-.008	**-.347*****	**-.092***	**-.465*****	**.183*****	1.000		
D.Prod	.022	**.067****	.049	**-.351*****	**-.354*****	-.000	**-.310*****	-.073	**-.422*****	**.227*****	**.989*****	1.000	
D.GAS	-.007	-.014	-.000	**.267****	**-.105*****	-.022	.012	.007	.010	.021	**.098****	**.111*****	1.000

Notes: *, **, *** represent statistical significance at 10 percent, 5 percent, and 1 percent levels (two-sided), respectively (emphasized by bold type). The results denote the correlation of discretionary amounts in the Internet industry in the post-IPO year. Variables are defined as follows: D.Acc = discretionary accruals. D.ΔRec = discretionary change in receivables. D.ΔGrRec = discretionary change in gross receivables. D.ΔDefRev = discretionary change in deferred revenue. D.CfO = discretionary cash flow from operations. D.R&D = discretionary research and development expenses. D.SGA = discretionary selling, general, and administrative expenses. D.Adv = discretionary advertising expenses. D.DisExp = abnormal discretionary expenses. D.ΔInv = discretionary change in inventory. D.COGS = discretionary cost of goods sold. D.Prod = discretionary production costs. D.GAS = discretionary gain on asset sales.

Table 9: Pearson Correlation for Discretionary Variables in the Technology Industry

	D.Acc	*D.ΔRec*	*D.ΔGrRec*	*D.ΔDefRev*	*D.CfO*	*D.R&D*	*D.SGA*	*D.Adv*	*D.DisExp*	*D.ΔInv*	*D.COGS*	*D.Prod*	*D.GAS*
D.Acc	1.000												
D.ΔRec	**.284*****	1.000											
D.ΔGrRec	**.081****	**.259*****	1.000										
D.ΔDefRev	**-.214****	**.207****	**.221****	1.000									
D.CfO	**-.164*****	**-.244*****	**-.082****	-.015	1.000								
D.R&D	.008	.043	.006	-.019	**-.062***	1.000							
D.SGA	**-.157*****	**.085*****	**.079****	.082	**-.200*****	**.184*****	1.000						
D.Adv	**.088***	**.092***	**.176*****	-.009	**-.130****	-.006	**.092***	1.000					
D.DisExp	**-.115*****	**.082*****	**.120*****	.059	**-.159*****	**.229*****	**.936*****	**.141*****	1.000				
D.ΔInv	**.273*****	**.137*****	**.129*****	**.243*****	**-.210*****	**.063***	.040	**.089***	.021	1.000			
D.COGS	-.039	**.073****	**.071****	.111	**-.259*****	-.020	**-.242*****	.060	**-.276*****	**.092*****	1.000		
D.Prod	.018	**.094*****	**.096*****	.120	**-.304*****	.007	**-.147*****	.062	**-.177*****	**.267*****	**.924*****	1.000	
D.GAS	**.078****	.041	.003	.001	-.056	.009	-.029	-.054	-.023	-.042	.011	-.001	1.000

Notes: *, **, *** represent statistical significance at 10 percent, 5 percent, and 1 percent levels (two-sided), respectively (emphasized by bold type). The results denote the correlation of discretionary amounts in the Technology industry in the post-IPO year. Variables are defined as follows: D.Acc = discretionary accruals. D.ΔRec = discretionary change in receivables. D.ΔGrRec = discretionary change in gross receivables. D.ΔDefRev = discretionary change in deferred revenue. D.CfO = discretionary cash flow from operations. D.R&D = discretionary research and development expenses. D.SGA = discretionary selling, general, and administrative expenses. D.Adv = discretionary advertising expenses. D.DisExp = abnormal discretionary expenses. D.ΔInv = discretionary change in inventory. D.COGS = discretionary cost of goods sold. D.Prod = discretionary production costs. D.GAS = discretionary gain on asset sales.

Table 10 points out results for the Person correlation of the discretionary amounts in the Construction industry. An outstanding finding is that there are fewer significant correlations in this industry than in the high-growth industries. Especially the expense accounts are mainly insignificant, although their negative correlation with cash flow is still present. While earnings accruals and receivables are still positively correlated, the level is higher. This might be caused by fewer possibilities of well-established industries in using discretionary behavior or sales might be more important.

Findings for COGS in growth industries seem to differ substantially from the Construction industry. Whilst in the first mentioned industries COGS used to depict some positive results the findings for Construction point at consistently negative correlations. This might be attributed to other kinds of business activities. Another remarkable finding is that the correlation of COGS and production costs has decreased. This is coherent with the above outcome that industries differ in specific variables. In fact, the Construction industry includes more inventories than the growth industries. As in the Technology industry, gains on asset sales are correlated with earnings accruals and indicate that companies use both methods simultaneously.

Table 11 illustrates outcomes for the Person correlation of the discretionary amounts in the Wholesale industry. Results are mainly in line with findings for the Construction industry. Similarly, there are fewer significant results than in the growth industries. However, findings for sales partially differ. Especially deferred revenues seem to be employed contrarily.

In summary, the results for correlations of abnormal variables show differences between growth and well-established industries. This is coherent with the predictions made in the hypotheses. However, there are similarities in certain accounting items, especially for accruals and the correlation with receivables and gross receivables as well as the correlation of expense accounts with cash flows. Additionally, there are differences between single industries. This is not surprising due to different business activities.

Table 10: Pearson Correlation for Discretionary Variables in the Construction Industry

	D.Acc	*D.ΔRec*	*D.ΔGrRec*	*D.ΔDefRev*	*D.CfO*	*D.R&D*	*D.SGA*	*D.Adv*	*D.DisExp*	*D.ΔInv*	*D.COGS*	*D.Prod*	*D.GAS*
D.Acc	1.000												
D.ΔRec	**.374*****	1.000											
D.ΔGrRec	.029	**.218****	1.000										
D.ΔDefRev	**-.420***	-.062	-.119	1.000									
D.CfO	**-.475*****	**-.194*****	.093	-.118	1.000								
D.R&D	.114	-.054	-.002	.573	.039	1.000							
D.SGA	-.031	.020	-.022	.135	**-.272*****	.039	1.000						
D.Adv	.138	.047	.114	.410	-.125	.162	.222	1.000					
D.DisExp	-.021	.037	.070	.085	**-.292***	-.006	**.923***	.317	1.000				
D.ΔInv	**.408*****	**.207*****	.120	.244	**-.294*****	-.069	.104	.303	.123	1.000			
D.COGS	**-.187****	-.037	-.023	-.17	**-.130****	**-.310*****	**-.178****	.121	**-.152****	**-.132***	1.000		
D.Prod	-.033	-.013	.001	.075	**-.268*****	**-.316*****	**-.142***	.311	-.098	**.240*****	**.775*****	1.000	
D.GAS	**.235***	.131	-.003	.327	-.002	.024	**-.212***	.003	-.176	.089	-.030	-.018	1.000

Notes: *, **, *** represent statistical significance at 10 percent, 5 percent, and 1 percent levels (two-sided), respectively (emphasized by bold type). The results denote the correlation of discretionary amounts in the Construction industry in the post-IPO year. Variables are defined as follows: D.Acc = discretionary accruals. D.ΔRec = discretionary change in receivables. D.ΔGrRec = discretionary change in gross receivables. D.ΔDefRev = discretionary change in deferred revenue. D.CfO = discretionary cash flow from operations. D.R&D = discretionary research and development expenses. D.SGA = discretionary selling, general, and administrative expenses. D.Adv = discretionary advertising expenses. D.DisExp = abnormal discretionary expenses. D.ΔInv = discretionary change in inventory. D.COGS = discretionary cost of goods sold. D.Prod = discretionary production costs. D.GAS = discretionary gain on asset sales.

Table 11: Pearson Correlation for Discretionary Variables in the Wholesale Industry

	D.Acc	*D.ΔRec*	*D.ΔGrRec*	*D.ΔDefRev*	*D.CfO*	*D.R&D*	*D.SGA*	*D.Adv*	*D.DisExp*	*D.ΔInv*	*D.COGS*	*D.Prod*	*D.GAS*
D.Acc	1.000												
D.ΔRec	**.257*****	1.000											
D.ΔGrRec	-.023	**.254*****	1.000										
D.ΔDefRev	**.560*****	-.156	**.531****	1.000									
D.CfO	**-.595*****	**-.240*****	**-.156***	**-.416***	1.000								
D.R&D	-.091	**.176***	.127	-.215	-.102	1.000							
D.SGA	-.067	.087	**.186****	.232	.075	-.003	1.000						
D.Adv	-.135	-.086	-.124	**-.763****	.134	.160	.254	1.000					
D.DisExp	-.034	.087	**.159***	.168	.057	.002	**.976*****	**.368****	1.000				
D.ΔInv	**.497*****	.076	-.097	.304	**-.367*****	-.097	.024	.110	.019	1.000			
D.COGS	.069	-.002	.110	.260	**-.223*****	.064	**-.574*****	**-.327***	**-.574*****	-.062	1.000		
D.Prod	**.248*****	.048	.111	**.379***	**-.378*****	.042	**-.488*****	-.223	**-.469*****	**.169****	**.874*****	1.000	
D.GAS	.006	-.098	.030	.480	-.080	.036	-.106	.209	-.057	-.056	.117	.079	1.000

Notes: *, **, *** represent statistical significance at 10 percent, 5 percent, and 1 percent levels (two-sided), respectively (emphasized by bold type). The results denote the correlation of discretionary amounts in the Wholesale industry in the post-IPO year. Variables are defined as follows: D.Acc = discretionary accruals. D.ΔRec = discretionary change in receivables. D.ΔGrRec = discretionary change in gross receivables. D.ΔDefRev = discretionary change in deferred revenue. D.CfO = discretionary cash flow from operations. D.R&D = discretionary research and development expenses. D.SGA = discretionary selling, general, and administrative expenses. D.Adv = discretionary advertising expenses. D.DisExp = abnormal discretionary expenses. D.ΔInv = discretionary change in inventory. D.COGS = discretionary cost of goods sold. D.Prod = discretionary production costs. D.GAS = discretionary gain on asset sales.

6.3 Empirical Results

6.3.1 Results for Periods around IPO

6.3.1.1 Hypothesis Earnings Accruals 1

6.3.1.1.1 Biotech

In the following chapters, results for the hypotheses are arranged by the particular hypothesis of accounting items, then by industry (Biotech, Internet, Technology, Construction, and Wholesale) and within them by year group (-1 to +2 versus -2 and +3), for all three groups of companies (overall sample, profitable, and loss groups). First, the results for the basic hypothesis for each year group in the specific industry are presented accompanied by the according tables which help to best visualize the differences in each year. Second, the concluding section focusses on the results for the period specifics and the findings concerning the year group comparisons are presented.

Several accrual models are applied in this study. The performance-matched modified Jones model was shown to be the most valid one of the five documented models in prior literature.[255] It is considered as prevalent when arguing with significant and insignificant results while the others are utilized as robustness models in the corresponding section (chapter 6.4.2).[256] The results represent tests for hypothesis H-Acc 1: In years -1 to +2 companies use discretion proportionately more frequently in earnings accruals than in years -2 and +3 around an IPO.

Table 12 presents results for the analysis of discretionary reporting around IPOs for the modified Jones model.[257] The outcomes in the year before the IPO show highly significant negative accruals management for the overall and loss samples.[258] Interestingly, the modified Jones model does not show any significant pattern for profitable companies, but insignificant

---

[255] Kothari et al. (2005a). The other employed models in the robustness section are the models of Jones, Dechow/Dichev, McNichols, and Healy.

[256] This is similar for other accounting items which are also calculated with various models. These models are included as sensitivity checks in the robustness section.

[257] Results are presented with adj. R^2 (adjusted R-squared) because not the whole population can be included due to a lack of data in COMPUSTAT.

[258] It is important to note for the accounting items that the interpretation concerns the discretionary part of each item since the models test the significance of the abnormal discretionary parts and not the whole amount of the items themselves. However, the discretionary part is included in the sum of e.g. accruals of each company (regular accruals plus discretionary accruals equal the reported accruals) and this affects the overall amount.

and negative results. This dissimilarity of groups was not yet identified in prior literature. A negative amount in the accrual model means that discretionary accruals for IPO firms before the issue are abnormally low (for the same year and same three or even the complete four digits SIC code). In the year after the IPO, the overall and loss samples still have significantly low discretionary earnings accruals. Yet, the profitable companies do not show any significance and depict positive values. The results are consistent with Singer (2007).[259] The differentiation between the subgroups gives additional information for investors when evaluating firms since the results emphasize the diverging conclusions for the subgroups. In the second year after the IPO, the results are insignificant.

In the second year before the IPO, results show that firms do not manage earnings significantly. The amount of the results two years before the IPO is almost exactly the contrary to one year before the IPO (0.04 to -0.05 of mean discretionary accruals). This might support the notion that companies use the second year before the IPO as a preparation year for IPO discretionary behavior. In the third year after the IPO, all results are insignificant but positive. Further calculations show that in the Biotech industry, the findings are consistent with the alternative hypothesis H-Acc 1 for the overall and loss groups while the very small profitable group indicates no significance.[260] As expected, there is a significant difference for discretionary accruals between years -1 to +2 and years -2 and +3 for the two major groups.

[259] Singer (2007), p. 58. Fedyk et al. (2012) do not evaluate the two subgroups within one industry, but only the overall sample which is insignificant. The outcomes of the overall groups are not exactly comparable because of the slightly different research design and the authors use 30 percent fewer observations.

[260] Note the formulation of results from statistical outcomes in the thesis: On the one hand, results can reject the null hypothesis of no discretionary behavior and hence the findings are "consistent" with the (alternative) hypothesis that discretion exists. The alternative is that results do not reject the (null) hypothesis of no discretion which means that there is no evidence of discretionary behavior.

Table 12: Earnings Accruals by Year, Group, and Industry

Year	-2			-1			+1			+2			+3		
	all	*profit.*	*loss*	*all*	*profit.*	*loss*	*all*	*profit.*	*loss*	*all*	*profit.*	*loss*	*all*	*profit.*	*loss*
Biotech															
D.Acc	.041	--	.037	**-.050*****	-.008	**-.058*****	**-.057*****	.002	**-.066*****	.011	.013	.010	.008	.008	.008
N	27	4	23	195	29	166	380	56	324	454	63	391	425	52	373
Adj. R^2	.055														
Internet															
D.Acc	-.019	-.048	-.002	**-.029*****	-.017	**-.037*****	-.006	.002	-.015	**.020*****	.011	**.027*****	-.005	-.007	-.004
N	24	9	15	382	147	235	886	458	428	947	391	556	832	326	506
Adj. R^2	.053														
Technology															
D.Acc	-.004	.014	-.024	-.005	**-.017****	.003	**.010****	**.017*****	.000	**.020*****	**.018*****	**.022*****	.004	**.010****	-.000
N	37	19	18	439	183	256	1'144	646	498	1'252	601	651	1'172	527	645
Adj. R^2	.072														
Construction															
D.Acc	-.004	-.014	--	-.013	-.007	-.025	**.026*****	**.024*****	.032	-.001	.003	**-.024***	-.004	-.008	.005
N	7	5	2	56	37	19	181	141	40	201	161	40	191	135	56
Adj. R^2	.040														
Wholesale															
D.Acc	-.029	--	--	-.022	-.016	-.046	**.032*****	**.028*****	**.044****	**.024*****	**.019****	**.037****	.007	.009	.004
N	7	4	3	73	58	15	202	162	40	231	168	63	218	147	71
Adj. R^2	.124														

Notes: *, **, *** represent statistical significance at 10 percent, 5 percent, and 1 percent levels (two-sided), respectively (emphasized by bold type). The results are split by group: overall (all), profitable (profit.), and loss. Results show the means of discretionary accruals (D.Acc), the IPO sample size (N), and the mean adjusted R-squared (Adj. R^2) for the whole sample in one year (there are similar results in all years). Discretionary accruals are calculated using the modified Jones model. Two consecutive hyphens (--) denote less than five available observations.

6.3.1.1.2 Internet

In the year before the IPO, the Internet industry seems to use negative accruals management or is forced to report conservatively because of increased scrutiny of market participants. Especially, loss companies and the overall sample display highly significant and negative results while the profitable group exhibits insignificant amounts. In the first year after the IPO, earnings are unmanaged. In the second year after the IPO, Internet companies exhibit significant and positive earnings accruals for the overall and loss samples. This indicates that especially the loss companies are expected to exhibit positive discretionary accruals to investors. Profitable firms still do not inflate earnings. Interestingly, the model finds significance (5% level) for the overall sample which is usually presented in prior studies. Yet, the results for the subgroups differ.

For the Internet group, the earnings accruals model does not find any significance in the second year before the IPO. Almost all results display negative amounts for the 24 observations. In the third year after the IPO, the model equally detects no discretionary behavior in any group. In the Internet industry, the findings are consistent with the alternative hypothesis H-Acc 1 for the overall and loss groups while the small profitable group indicates no significance. As expected, there is a significant difference for (discretionary) accruals between years -1 to +2 and years -2 and +3 for the two larger groups.

6.3.1.1.3 Technology

In the Technology industry, the accruals model displays no systematic results in the year before the IPO. The modified Jones model finds significant negative results for the profitable subgroup. Hence, profitable firms manage earnings downward in the year before the IPO and are rather conservative as argued by Ball/Shivakumar (2008). This could also mean they postpone accruals for the upcoming years because of the short time reversal of accruals. In the year after going public, management of earnings is present in profitable companies. The model finds significance (1% or 5% levels) for the overall and profitable groups. In the second year after the issue, Technology firms exhibit a systematic pattern in managing earnings upward. All groups display highly significant (1% level) and positive amounts of accruals management for all three subgroups. Since scrutiny decreases after the IPO to a common level, companies influence the line items which are crucial to investors.

In the second year before the IPO, there is no significance. In the third year after the IPO, the findings for earnings accruals indicate that only profitable companies apply discretion. The modified Jones model indicates significance for the profitable group. In the Technology industry, findings are consistent with the alternative hypothesis H-Acc 1 for all groups. As expected, there is a significant difference for accruals between years -1 to +2 and years -2 and +3.

6.3.1.1.4 Construction

In the year before the IPO, companies in the Construction and Manufacturing industries display no accruals management. The results are all negative but insignificant. In the first year after the issue, the accrual model indicates evidence of accruals management for the overall and profitable firms, but not for unprofitable ones. Obviously, profitable firms influence investors by managing accruals upwards, while loss firms do not. This confirms the notion that scrutiny declines after the IPO and profitable firms start using discretion in accounting. The modified Jones model indicates very strong positive significance for the overall and profitable samples. This supports the method of dividing the overall group into subgroups. In the second year after the IPO, the results for earnings are insignificant. The loss group is almost significant (11% level).

The results in the second year before the IPO include only seven companies at most, so the results are not reliable. Nevertheless, some results seem to be worth mentioning. The outcome is insignificant for all groups, showing negative overall and profitable samples while the loss sample includes only two observations (which display a positive result, untabulated). In the third year after going public, there is no systematic accruals management in any group. In the Construction industry, findings are consistent with the alternative hypothesis H-Acc 1 for all groups. As expected, there is a significant difference for accruals between years -1 to +2 and years -2 and +3. However, there are only few significant results overall.

6.3.1.1.5 Wholesale

In the Wholesale industry in the year before the IPO, the outcome indicates no significant discretion only a slight hint at negative accruals management in all groups. In the first year after the issue, the results for accruals management indicate that both subgroups try to influence investors by high accruals which might be due to lower scrutiny compared to the pre-issue year. There is significance (1% or 5% levels) for the overall, profitable, and loss groups. In the second year after the issue, the results indicate that companies use accruals to manage earnings upward in both subgroups. The outcomes indicate positive and significant (5% level) discretion in earnings for all three subgroups.

In the second year before the IPO, there are only seven observations. The results are mostly insignificant with negative amounts. In the third year after the IPO, accruals are very low and confirm that companies do not manage accruals. The outcome for the modified Jones, model is insignificant. In the Wholesale industry, findings are consistent with the alternative hypothesis H-Acc 1 for all groups. As expected, there is a significant difference for accruals between years -1 to +2 and years -2 and +3.

In no industry the companies manage earnings accruals upward in the year before the IPO. However, they are expected to influence other line items to increase the issue price if they do not manage earnings. The outcomes of the employed accruals model supports the argumentation of Ball/Shivakumar (2008) that companies do not manage earnings upward but rather downward due to the scrutiny before an IPO. The results are mainly consistent with prior literature (especially Armstrong et al. (2009) for the same time horizon). Equally to this literature, the results contradict Teoh et al. (1998b) about accruals management behavior in the pre-IPO year. Additionally, the significant negative pre-IPO accruals management was not discovered in prior literature, particularly for Biotech firms. The outcome can be attributed to the fact that few studies considered the differentiation between industries. The insight based on the results helps capital market participants when evaluating companies.

6.3.1.2 Hypotheses Sales 1 and 2

6.3.1.2.1 Biotech

As above, the results are presented by industry (Biotech, Internet, Technology, Construction, and Wholesale) and within them by year group (-1 to +2 versus -2 and +3), for all three groups of companies (overall sample, profitable, and loss groups). The results represent tests for the basic hypothesis and the hypothesis H-S 1: In years -1 to +2 companies use discretion proportionately more frequently in sales than in years -2 and +3 around an IPO.

Table 13 shows results for change in receivables, Table 14 for change in gross receivables, and Table 15 for change in deferred revenue. The change in receivables model for Biotech companies points out that profitable firms use positive sales management in the pre-IPO year. Assumingly, this is the case due to higher scrutiny on earnings before an IPO and managers' intent to influence alternative accounts. The overall and loss groups do not manage receivables. However, the significant results for the deferred revenue model of the overall and loss groups are consistent with the findings of Caylor (2010, 83) concerning earnings surprises and the preference of deferred revenue management over gross receivables management. However, the significant results here exist only for loss firms which build the majority and hence are reflected in the overall group. This could mean that loss firms defer their revenue (and earnings) to the years after the IPO. The outcome is in line with the prior finding that these firms show significant negative accruals.

In the year after the IPO, unprofitable Biotech firms manage their receivables upward while the other groups are insignificant. Connected to the results of earnings this implies that loss companies decrease accruals but increase receivables to inflate the stock price because receivables are important for loss firms. This is coherent with channel stuffing and more lenient credit terms. Furthermore, deferred revenue indicates another possibility of inflating the stock price in the future for the unprofitable (and overall) sample(s). For change in deferred revenue the model is highly significant and positive for the overall and the loss samples. The model for change in gross receivables is insignificant for all groups. This corresponds to the findings of Caylor (2010) who advocates that companies preferably manage deferred revenue rather than gross receivables.[261] The profitable subgroup is insignificant in all models. Similarly, Fedyk et al. (2012) find significantly positive discretionary receivables for IPO firms as well. Yet, they do not differentiate between subgroups in industries to get a deeper insight.[262] Differentiating between profitable and loss groups gives a better understanding of subgroup dissimilarities. Investors need to take diverging outcomes into account.

261 Caylor (2010), p. 93.

262 Fedyk et al. (2012), p. 48. Furthermore, the results are not exactly comparable because they use another revenue model as well as other time intervals and have fewer observations. In the prior version of Singer (2007, 60) the results for the profitable group are the same and the loss group shows negative significance. The comparability issues apply here as well, except concerning the particular model.

Table 13: Discretionary Change in Receivables by Year, Group, and Industry

Year	-2			-1			+1			+2			+3		
	all	*profit.*	*loss*	*all*	*profit.*	*loss*	*all*	*profit.*	*loss*	*all*	*profit.*	*loss*	*all*	*profit.*	*loss*
Biotech															
ΔRec	-.003	--	-.008	.005	.018	.003	.003	-.002	**.004***	-.000	-.001	-.000	-.003	.003	-.003
N	27	4	23	192	29	163	371	55	316	443	62	381	418	51	367
Adj. R^2	.307														
Internet															
ΔRec	-.005	.043	-.034	**.013*****	.011	**.014****	**.016*****	**.012*****	**.020*****	**.004***	.003	.005	-.000	.001	-.001
N	22	8	14	374	145	229	867	446	421	914	381	533	814	322	492
Adj. R^2	.764														
Technology															
ΔRec	-.002	.009	-.015	.004	-.004	**.011*****	**.010*****	**.005****	**.017*****	**.007*****	**.010*****	**.004***	**.004****	**.006****	.002
N	37	19	18	432	179	253	1'117	631	486	1'219	587	632	1'140	513	627
Adj. R^2	.442														
Construction															
ΔRec	.002	--	--	.000	.013	-.023	**.018*****	**.019*****	**.017***	.006	**.011****	-.014	**.009****	.003	**.026*****
N	6	4	2	55	36	19	174	138	36	196	157	39	186	133	53
Adj. R^2	.309														
Wholesale															
ΔRec	-.016	--	--	-.006	-.002	-.020	**.012****	**.012****	.013	**.018*****	**.016*****	**.025****	.003	-.000	.011
N	7	4	3	70	55	15	196	158	38	225	163	62	212	144	68
Adj. R^2	.412														

Notes: *, **, *** represent statistical significance at 10 percent, 5 percent, and 1 percent levels (two-sided), respectively (emphasized by bold type). The results are split by group: overall (all), profitable (profit.), and loss. Results show the means of discretionary change in receivables (ΔRec), the IPO sample size (N), and the mean adjusted R-squared (Adj. R^2) for the whole sample in one year (there are similar results in all years). Two consecutive hyphens (--) denote less than five available observations.

Table 14: Discretionary Change in Gross Receivables by Year, Group, and Industry

Year	-2			-1			+1			+2			+3		
	all	*profit.*	*loss*	*all*	*profit.*	*loss*	*all*	*profit.*	*loss*	*all*	*profit.*	*loss*	*all*	*profit.*	*loss*
Biotech															
ΔGrRec	-.011	--	-.016	.040	.080	.031	-.007	.010	-.012	.007	.012	.005	.003	.014	.000
N	9	1	8	63	11	52	113	27	86	130	28	102	122	31	91
Adj. R^2	.345														
Internet															
ΔGrRec	-.061	.009	-.100	.031	**.106****	-.023	**.080*****	**.054*****	**.114*****	.002	.003	.001	-.007	-.020	.002
N	17	6	11	223	94	129	483	274	209	511	243	268	482	209	273
Adj. R^2	.397														
Technology															
ΔGrRec	-.045	-.025	-.071	**.048****	.014	**.074****	**.050*****	**.035***	**.077*****	**.016***	**.028****	.001	.000	.004	-.002
N	30	17	13	261	115	146	696	444	252	756	428	328	712	362	350
Adj. R^2	.412														
Construction															
ΔGrRec	.018	--	--	.056	.011	.130	**.041****	**.039****	**.052***	.021	.013	.054	.017	.009	**.039***
N	5	4	1	34	21	13	102	85	17	118	96	22	114	85	29
Adj. R^2	.411														
Wholesale															
ΔGrRec	-.045	--	--	.004	.001	.025	.032	-.000	.182	.033	**.053****	-.034	**.037****	.028	**.066****
N	5	3	2	45	39	6	128	105	23	146	113	33	138	105	33
Adj. R^2	.395														

Notes: *, **, *** represent statistical significance at 10 percent, 5 percent, and 1 percent levels (two-sided), respectively (emphasized by bold type). The results are split by group: overall (all), profitable (profit.), and loss. Results show the means of discretionary change in gross receivables (ΔGrRec), the IPO sample size (N), and the mean adjusted R-squared (Adj. R^2) for the whole sample in one year (there are similar results in all years). Two consecutive hyphens (--) denote less than five available observations.

Table 15: Discretionary Change in Deferred Revenue by Year, Group, and Industry

Year	-2			-1			+1			+2			+3		
	all	*profit.*	*loss*	*all*	*profit.*	*loss*	*all*	*profit.*	*loss*	*all*	*profit.*	*loss*	*all*	*profit.*	*loss*
Biotech															
ΔDefRev	.002	--	.003	**.041*****	-.021	**.046*****	**.034*****	.015	**.036*****	.006	-.061	**.013****	-.021	.004	-.024
N	20	2	18	82	7	75	86	11	75	80	7	73	96	10	86
Adj. R^2	.051														
Internet															
ΔDefRev	-.009	.029	-.042	**.120*****	**.076*****	**.168*****	**.078*****	**.065*****	**.115*****	**.018***	.018	.017	-.006	.006	-.018
N	11	5	6	95	49	46	86	63	23	77	54	23	104	48	56
Adj. R^2	.102														
Technology															
ΔDefRev	.000	-.011	.012	**.038*****	**.045*****	**.034****	.007	-.005	.021	**-.010***	-.015	-.005	.002	.000	.003
N	14	7	7	138	49	89	134	66	68	117	58	59	158	55	103
Adj. R^2	.094														
Construction															
ΔDefRev	--	--	--	-.002	-.001	-.004	.000	.000	.001	.004	.001	--	.002	-.000	--
N	4	3	1	15	9	6	19	13	6	16	14	2	22	18	4
Adj. R^2	.018														
Wholesale															
ΔDefRev	--	--	--	.001	.001	--	.000	.001	--	-.002	-.003	--	.004	.004	--
N	3	2	1	18	17	1	21	19	2	19	18	1	22	21	1
Adj. R^2	.083														

Notes: *, **, *** represent statistical significance at 10 percent, 5 percent, and 1 percent levels (two-sided), respectively (emphasized by bold type). The results are split by group: overall (all), profitable (profit.), and loss. Results show the means of discretionary change in deferred revenue (ΔDefRev), the IPO sample size (N), and the mean adjusted R-squared (Adj. R^2) for the whole sample in one year (there are similar results in all years). Two consecutive hyphens (--) denote less than five available observations.

In the second year after the issue, accounts receivable are not managed. The only exceptions are positive deferred revenue for loss companies. The results for change in gross receivables is positive but insignificant for all three (sub-) groups. The outcomes for change in deferred revenue are positive for the overall and loss groups but negative for the profitable subgroup. The result for the loss group is significant (5% level) indicating a further delay of revenues to the future.

In the second year before the issue, the results for accounts receivable and revenues do not show any significance and support the notion that firms do not manage these accounts two years before the IPO. It might not be beneficial to have abnormally high receivables two years before the IPO when investors look at the growth rate of two years before to one year before the issue. The model of change in receivables depicts negative values for the overall and loss samples (the profitable subgroup consists of four observations, only). The result for change in gross receivables is only slightly abnormally negative whereas deferred revenue is slightly positive, both insignificant. This supports the notion that firms do not manage these accounts two years prior to the IPO, but wait for inflation to the next year which results in better share prices.

In the third year after the IPO, the results for change in accounts receivable indicate more strict credit terms and low selling records for loss companies because abnormal sales are negative. This is in contrast to the prior years and indicates that the companies had more incentives to engage in positive sales management in the years around the IPO and perhaps now the reversing effect emerges. The abnormal changes in gross receivables are negative and insignificant for all three groups. Similarly, the discretionary changes in deferred revenue are insignificant. In the Biotech industry, the findings are consistent with the alternative hypothesis H-S 1 for all groups. As expected, there is a significant difference in discretionary sales between years -1 to +2 and the years of -2 and +3.

6.3.1.2.2 Internet

In the Internet industry in the year before the issue, sales management is present, indicating that this line item is important for investors in absence of positive income. While the profitable group is significant for gross receivables and deferred revenue, the loss group is significant in the receivables and the deferred revenue models. The overall sample, as the combination of both, is even significant at the 1% or 5% levels, except for gross receivables. The change in gross receivables indicates that profitable companies accelerate sales from future periods with the risk of cash consequences while the loss group is insignificant. The result for the profitable subgroup is positive and significant at the 10% level, only. Yet, it could indicate that the few profitable companies accelerate sales to show positive earnings before going public. Contrarily, the change in deferred revenue indicates that all groups defer revenues to future periods after the issue. This confirms the notion that companies care about their revenues and the resulting market valuation in the years after the IPO as well or even more than in the year before the issue. The results for the model are similar for all groups since they consistently exhibit a positive and high significance.

The receivables model indicates significant and positive abnormal values for all three groups in the year after the IPO. The findings correspond to the outcomes in Fedyk et al. (2012, 48). These high sales amounts influence investors and hence increase the market price after the issue. Similarly, the change in gross receivables indicates more lenient credit terms for all groups and supports the results for the sales models. Interestingly, the deferred revenue is also significant. This points toward the intention to postpone some sales to future periods or could result from influenced cash flow. All models for change in receivables, change in gross receivables, and change in deferred revenue exhibit high significance in all groups. In year +2, the three models indicate non-existent discretion. Merely the overall samples of the accounts receivable model and the deferred revenue model point out significance at the 10% level, respectively.[263]

In year -2, the results for change in receivables, gross receivables, and deferred revenue are insignificant and negative for the overall and loss groups whilst the profitable groups have positive but also insignificant amounts. Identically, in year +3 the results for sales are insignificant and negative for the overall and loss groups while the profitable groups are insignificant and positive. Only the model for change in gross receivables indicates inverted signs for the subgroups. Accordingly, the three models are insignificant for all groups. In the Internet industry, the combined findings are consistent with the alternative hypothesis H-S 1 for all groups. As expected, there is a significant difference in between years -1 to +2 and the years of -2 and +3. In fact, there are no significant results in years -2 and +3 while the other years find many significant amounts. Again, corresponding to Caylor (2010) the results depict that companies use more discretion in change in deferred revenue than in gross receivables.

263 In the first receivables model, the loss subgroup is significant at the 11% level and the overall sample of the second receivables model is significant at the 12% level.

6.3.1.2.3 Technology

In the Technology industry in year -1, the receivables model displays a strong positive significance for loss firms, but not for the profitable subgroup or the overall sample. In fact, the profitable group indicates a negative sign which leaves the overall sample with a positive but insignificant result because both subgroups make up almost half of the overall sample. This underlines the importance of differentiating between profitable and loss companies. The results of the loss groups confirm the notion that rather sales than earnings are managed due to scrutiny in earnings in the pre-IPO period. Furthermore, investors are interested in sales of loss firms to predict their future benefits. The change in gross accounts receivable is positive and significant (5% level) for the overall and loss groups. This indicates that sales are accelerated but cash has not yet been collected confirming the high accounts receivable and low cash. The deferred revenue is significant (1% or 5% levels) for all three groups. Combined with the aforementioned results this underlines the discretion in sales in the year before the issue.

In the post-IPO year, the changes in accounts receivable confirm the findings of Fedyk et al. (2012) that companies use positive discretion in sales. All three groups are significant (1% or 5% levels) and positive. The results for loss firms have a stronger significance than for profitable ones. Furthermore, gross receivables are influenced by both groups, but again more significantly by unprofitable ones. This is coherent with higher receivables in the aforementioned results. Interestingly, deferred revenue is not abnormal in any group. This indicates that companies do not ease their credit policy to accelerate future sales to the present year. The reason could be that companies either want to show a stringent credit behavior or care about sales growth in the next years.

In year +2, the results for change in accounts receivable indicate that profitable firms strongly influence receivables and gross receivables but not deferred revenue. Loss firms also display significant receivables (yet to a lower extent), but no significant abnormal gross receivables or deferred revenue exist. The overall sample is positively significant in the model of change in receivables and gross receivables, but negatively significant in deferred revenue. These results point to a preference of high sales in the second year instead of the third year after the issue which underlines the notion that venture capitalists in the Technology industry cash in after the lock-up period. Inflated sales confirm the notion to increase value relevant line items. Positive abnormal gross receivables point out that companies try to increase receivables by easing credit policies and accelerate future sales.

In year -2, the results for the change in receivables, gross receivables, and deferred revenue do not demonstrate any significance. While for the overall and loss samples the abnormal amount of receivables is negative, the profitable sample is positive, but all are insignificant. In the third year after the IPO, receivables management is present for the overall and profitable groups. The model displays strong positive significance for both groups. Loss companies do not engage in receivables management. No significance exists for change in gross receivables and change in deferred revenue. In the Technology industry, the findings are consistent with the alternative hypothesis H-S 1 for all groups. As expected, there is a significant difference for sales between years -1 to +2 and the years of -2 and +3. In fact, there are few significant results in years -2 and +3 while in the other years the vast majority of results from all models are significant.

6.3.1.2.4 Construction

In the Construction industry in the pre-IPO year, the results for sales are all insignificant. Probably the results for both line items of earnings and sales are the consequence of increased scrutiny by market participants before the IPO. The receivables model detects no significance for any group. Similarly, the models for change in gross receivables and deferred revenue indicate no significance. In year +1, the receivables are influenced by both subgroups. Companies utilize the decreased scrutiny to influence investors' valuation by increasing accounts receivable. Similarly, the change in gross accounts receivable exhibits discretion for all three groups. Both models for receivables and gross receivables find significant (1% or 5% levels) amounts for the overall and profitable groups, while the amounts for the loss groups are significant at the 10% level, respectively. However, the model for change in deferred revenue detects no significance. In year +2, changes in accounts receivable are significantly positive for the profitable firms. Yet, there is no significance for the overall and loss groups. The models for gross receivables and deferred revenue neither indicate significance for any of the groups.

In year -2, the results for sales models include only up to six observations. Still, the outcomes are reported. The overall sample of receivables is insignificant and the subgroups include less than five observations. Similarly, the models of gross receivables and deferred revenue find no significance. In year +3, only the loss subgroup boosts receivables and gross receivables. Deferred revenue is not significant. The overall sample is only significant in the change in receivables model because of the high significance of the loss group. In the Construction industry, the findings are consistent with the alternative hypothesis H-S 1 for the overall and the large profitable groups but not for the small loss group. As expected, there is a significant difference for sales between years -1 to +2 and the years of -2 and +3 for the two major groups. However, there are two significant results in years +3 for the overall and loss groups while year -2 has too few observations. Year -1 exhibits no significant findings while year +1 is very significant. In sum, the hypothesis is accepted for the majority of companies, but not as clearly as in the three aforementioned industries.

6.3.1.2.5 Wholesale

In the Wholesale industry in the pre-IPO year, the findings for receivables are all negative and insignificant whereas the findings for gross receivables and deferred revenue are all positive and insignificant. In the post-IPO year, the results for receivables confirm that profitable companies influence their sales. Investors should be aware of that. The model finds significance (5% level) for the overall and profitable samples but not for the loss companies. This underlines the importance of dividing the overall sample into subgroups. Yet, the change in gross receivables and change in deferred revenue find no significant behavior. In the second year after the IPO, both subgroups inflate their receivables. The accounts receivable model finds significant (1% or 5% levels) and positive amounts for all three groups. Gross receivables indicate that the profitable companies manage this line item upward and accelerate sales without cash being received. The model displays a significant amount for this subgroup, only. The changes in deferred revenue are unmanaged.

In year -2, the change in accounts receivable, gross receivables, and deferred revenue indicate no significant values for any group for only up to seven observations. Similarly, there is no receivables management in the third year after the IPO. No significant values are present for change in accounts receivable and change in deferred revenue. Yet, the result for change in gross receivables indicates that loss firms mainly accelerate sales to the current year. The model finds a significant positive amount for the overall and loss groups. The findings are consistent with the alternative hypothesis H-S 1 for the Wholesale industry for the overall and large profitable groups. Basically, the small loss group exhibits equally as many significant results in both time periods. As expected, there is a significant difference for (discretionary) sales between years -1 to +2 and the years of -2 and +3 for the overall and profitable groups. The basic hypothesis shows that there are few significant results in years +3 while year -2 has too few observations. Year -1 exhibits no significant finding while year +2 is very significant for all groups, respectively.

6.3.1.2.6 Hypothesis Sales 2

The second hypothesis for sales states that companies do not use significantly negative sales management from years -1 to +2 around an IPO.[264] Outcomes in Table 13, Table 14, and Table 15 already point out the results for the two-sided tests. Therefore, further tables are omitted for clarity.

The Biotech industry exhibits no significant and negative results in all years from -1 to +2, but some are positive and significant. This is similar in all sales models and groups. The outcome for the Internet industry is much more striking. Almost all models and groups in years -1 and +1 are positively significant. Only year +2 finds not all results to be positively significant. Yet, no result is significantly negative. The Technology industry depicts that almost all results in all years are positively significant for all groups and models. Merely the result for deferred revenue is negatively significant for the overall sample.

The outcome for the Construction industry is partly positive (mainly in year +1) and partly insignificant (mainly in year -1), but no negative significance is detected. Similarly, the findings for the Wholesale industry are in part positive (mainly in years +1 and +2) and in part insignificant (mainly in year -1), but no negative significance is detected. The findings are consistent with the alternative hypothesis H-S 2 for all industries and groups. Only the deferred revenue of the overall sample in the Technology industry in year +2 indicates negative significance. As expected, companies do not use significantly negative sales (accounts receivable) in the years around the IPO because sales are important for investors when valuing firms (e.g., they use sales multiples if earnings are negative). This finding is in line with Fedyk et al. (2012) for the post IPO year and three industries. Hence, companies care about their sales figures to influence the share price. Interestingly, this is the case for all industries and subgroups.

6.3.1.3 Hypotheses CfO 1 and 2

6.3.1.3.1 Biotech

The results for the hypotheses are arranged by industry (Biotech, Internet, Technology, Construction, and Wholesale) and within them by year group (-1 to +2 versus -2 and +3), for

[264] The test for this hypothesis is one-sided.

all three groups of companies (overall sample, profitable, and loss groups). The results represent tests for the basic hypothesis and for the main hypothesis CfO 1: In years -1 to +2 companies use discretion proportionately more frequently in CfO than in years -2 and +3 around an IPO.

Table 16 demonstrates the findings for CfO. In the pre-IPO year of the Biotech industry, loss firms show a significant negative cash flow, whereas profitable firms depict an insignificant negative sign. Negative cash flow can result from diverse real activities (besides high costs of IPO preparation). Loss firms might use cash in other business activities because cash flow and earnings are less valued by investors for these companies than other line items. The results for the overall and loss samples are highly significant and negative. In year +1, the results are very similar to the prior year. The loss companies have abnormally low cash flow because they are not as important as other numbers in their reporting. That is why these firms utilize their cash in other line items. The result shows highly significant abnormal cash flow with a negative sign for the overall and loss firms. Profitable companies have a negative sign, too, but insignificant. Two years after the issue, loss companies reverse their cash flow behavior. The results for cash from operations display a high significance for the abnormal positive amount of the overall and loss samples, respectively, while the profitable subgroup has a positive but insignificant value. With high cash flow the companies can prove to investors that their business generates cash and their value is high compared to competitors with similar sales and less cash.

Cash flow is not managed in the overall and loss samples two years before the IPO. However, the profitable companies display significance (5% level) of upward managed cash flow, but only for four observations that are available. In year +3 after the IPO, cash flow from operations shows no discretion and only low abnormal positive values. All signs are positive. In the Biotech industry, the findings are consistent with the alternative hypothesis H-CfO 1 for the overall and loss groups. Actually, the very small profitable subgroup includes only four observations in year -2 where it depicts its only significant figure and therefore, the basic null hypothesis is not rejected for this group. As expected, there is a significant difference for CfO between years -1 to +2 and the years of -2 and +3. In fact, there is only one significant result in years -2 and +3 combined which exists for the very small profitable group. In contrast to these results, the years -1 through +2 each depict significant findings which are present for the overall and loss groups. Interestingly, the negative significance of the overall and loss samples in years -1 and +1 turns into a positive significance in year +2. This is in contrast to the results of R&D as well as SG&A and support the notion of possibly reversing behavior over time. Prior literature mainly suggests that CfO is artificially inflated to improve other line items. But the opposite is shown here.

6.3.1.3.2 Internet

In the Internet industry, the pre-IPO year cash flow indicates that loss firms do not care about abnormally low amounts as other line items are obviously more important. The result for the profitable subgroup is insignificant whereas the other two groups show significant (1% or 5% levels) and negative amounts. In the post-IPO year, the cash flow is abnormally low for loss firms but not for profitable ones. The loss group has abnormally low accruals, high sales, and contemporaneously low cash flow. This indicates sales management by low prices. The model for cash flow shows a strong negative significance for the overall sample while the profitable sample displays no significance.

In year +2, cash flow still seems important for loss firms and is not inflated as in the Biotech industry. Profitable companies do not deflate or inflate this line item. The model evidences high significance for the overall and loss sample but is insignificant for the profitable subgroup. The difference between the subgroups in years -1 to +2 is striking. Profitable firms seem to care about normal cash flow. Alternatively, since the model controls for sales levels, it means that loss firms receive much less cash for similar sales amounts. It could be possible that loss companies sell their products with a relatively low margin compared to well-established companies. The control variables of sales are abnormally high as mentioned before; this is confirmed by the results of the cash flow model.

Table 16: Discretionary Cash Flow from Operations by Year, Group, and Industry

Year	-2			-1			+1			+2			+3		
	all	*profit.*	*loss*	*all*	*profit.*	*loss*	*all*	*profit.*	*loss*	*all*	*profit.*	*loss*	*all*	*profit.*	*loss*
Biotech															
CfO	-.060	--	-.098	**-.069***	-.440	**-.072***	**-.203***	-.015	**-.235***	**.045***	.010	**.051***	.022	.020	.022
N	27	4	23	196	29	167	381	56	325	462	63	399	426	52	374
Adj. R^2	.479														
Internet															
CfO	.004	**.082***	-.041	**-.023**	.002	**-.039***	**-.065***	.004	**-.140***	**-.028***	-.012	**-.039***	-.006	-.006	-.006
N	24	9	15	382	147	235	886	458	428	947	391	556	832	326	506
Adj. R^2	.262														
Technology															
CfO	.006	-.002	.015	**-.035***	-.007	**-.054***	**-.052***	**-.036***	**-.073***	**-.037***	**-.039***	**-.036***	**-.019***	**-.022***	**-.017***
N	37	19	18	439	183	256	1'144	646	498	1'254	601	653	1'172	527	645
Adj. R^2	.257														
Construction															
CfO	.004	-.006	--	.007	.005	.011	**-.020**	**-.017***	**-.031***	**-.018**	**-.015***	**-.032**	-.004	.002	**-.022***
N	7	5	2	56	37	19	181	141	40	201	161	40	191	135	56
Adj. R^2	.192														
Wholesale															
CfO	.042	--	--	.020	.022	.014	**-.035***	**-.031***	**-.053***	**-.036***	**-.035***	**-.036**	-.012	**-.017***	-.001
N	7	4	3	73	58	15	202	162	40	231	168	63	218	147	71
Adj. R^2	.075														

Notes: *, **, *** represent statistical significance at 10 percent, 5 percent, and 1 percent levels (two-sided), respectively (emphasized by bold type). The results are split by group: overall (all), profitable (profit.), and loss. Results show the means of discretionary cash flow from operations (CfO), the IPO sample size (N), and the mean adjusted R-squared (Adj. R^2) for the whole sample in one year (there are similar results in all years). Two consecutive hyphens (--) denote less than five available observations.

In year -2, the model for cash flow finds a significant and positive result for the profitable companies; however, there are only nine firms in this group. No significantly abnormal cash flow exists for the other two groups. In year +3, the cash flow indicates no significantly abnormal expenses for both subgroups and the overall sample. In the Internet industry, the findings are consistent with the alternative hypothesis H-CfO 1 for the overall and loss groups. In fact, the very small profitable subgroup includes only nine observations in year -2 where it depicts its only significant figure. The null hypothesis is not rejected for this group. As expected, there is a significant difference for CfO between years -1 to +2 and years -2 and +3. In fact, there is only one significant result in years -2 and +3 combined. In contrast to these results, years -1 through +2 show significant outcomes each. Interestingly, the positive significance of the very small profitable sample in year -2 could be present in the Biotech industry as well, but there are less than five observations. These groups indicate no further abnormal behavior in cash flow in the following years. The hypothesis holds for loss firms but not for the profitable ones.

6.3.1.3.3 Technology

In the Technology industry in the pre-IPO year, the cash flow from operations displays a negative and high significance for the overall and loss samples. The results confirm the abnormally high (gross) receivables which indicate that although (accelerated) sales are abnormally high the cash is abnormally low. This similarly holds for loss companies, only, which might be due to lower margins than comparable and well-established companies which can result from channel stuffing. In the post-IPO year, the cash flow is significant (5% level) and negative for all three groups. This is in line with abnormally high earnings accruals from above and obviously sales are abnormally high without receiving the corresponding cash. Again, this might be either due to low margins, channel stuffing, or manipulated sales.

In year +2, the findings for cash flow from operations point to a severe influence in cash activities as these are negative with a high significance for all groups. High accruals can emerge from low cash but high sales should deliver increased cash except if sales are built on channel stuffing and other methods of sales acceleration without the corresponding payments. On the other hand, high R&D, SG&A, and advertising influence cash outcomes, too. This underlines the importance of looking into different line items when analyzing the behavior of firms around an IPO and interpreting the findings.

In year -2 in the Technology industry, the results for cash flow do not show any significance. However, in year +3, operating cash flow indicates abnormally negative amounts with a high significance for all three groups. Yet, the loss group does not influence sales and earnings, which means that the results must be traced back to something else such as R&D or SG&A expenses. In the Technology industry, the findings are consistent with the alternative hypothesis H-CfO 1 for all groups. As expected, there is a significant difference for CfO between years -1 to +2 and the years of -2 and +3. Yet, only in year -2 there are no significant results. In years -1 through +2 all groups are significant except the profitable group in year -1.

6.3.1.3.4 Construction

In the Construction industry, cash flow seems unmanaged before the IPO. The model exhibits a positive sign for all three groups but no significance. In year +1, cash flow is abnormally low and indicates its use in other business activities and corresponding line items. For example, increased production and lower margins from sales management (channel stuffing) can lead to these results. The findings for sales are in line with these indications. The CfO model finds (strong) significant and negative amounts for all three groups. In year +2, results for cash flow indicate that both subgroups have abnormally low amounts. The model finds negative significance for all three groups.

In year -2, results are insignificant for only seven observations of the overall sample. Year +3 discovers a slight negative significance (10% level) for the loss group while the other groups are insignificant. In the Construction industry, the findings are consistent with the alternative hypothesis H-CfO 1 for all groups. However, the loss group cannot be calculated in year -2 but is significant in year +3. As expected, there is a significant difference for CfO between years -1 to +2 and the years of -2 and +3. Yet, only in year +3 there is one significant result for the loss group. In years +1 and +2 all groups are significant in contrast to years -1 and -2.

6.3.1.3.5 Wholesale

In the Wholesale industry in year -1, cash flow is not abnormal. This is only comparable to the Construction industry. The findings are consonant with inexistent abnormal results for earnings accruals and sales. In the post-IPO year, operating cash flow indicates abnormally low discretionary amounts for all three groups. This is partly coherent with the findings for accruals management of both groups and abnormally high receivables for the profitable group. In year +2, the operating cash flow is similarly significant (1% or 5% levels) and negative in all three groups. Again, the findings correspond to abnormally high earnings and high sales which indicate discretionary behavior.

In year -2, results for cash flow exhibit no significance for only seven observations. In the third year after the issue, the results for operating cash flow point out a slightly negative amount for the profitable group at the 10% level of significance. The other groups are insignificant. In the Wholesale industry, the findings are consistent with the alternative hypothesis H-CfO 1 for all groups. As expected, there is a significant difference for CfO between years -1 to +2 and the years of -2 and +3. Concerning the basic hypothesis, only in year +3 there is one significant result for the profitable group. In years +1 and +2, all groups are significant in contrast to year -1 and -2. Interestingly, this profitable industry is almost identical to the other profitable industry (Construction), whereas the unprofitable industries find abnormal values for CfO in year -1.

6.3.1.3.6 Hypothesis CfO 2

The second hypothesis for CfO states that companies do not show significantly positive CfO management from years -1 to +2 around an IPO.[265] Outcomes in Table 16 already point out the results for the two-sided tests and indicate no negative significance. Therefore, further tables are omitted for clarity.

The Biotech industry exhibits negative significance for the overall and loss groups in -1 and +1, but significantly positive results in year +2. Obviously, the spending in cash reversed over these periods. The loss group does not show any significance in all years, although the (algebraic) sign is the same as for the other groups. The Internet industry does not depict any positive significance of CfO in all years and groups, but mainly show negative significance. The Technology industry exhibits similar results, only that all results are negatively significant, except one.

Likewise, the outcome for the Construction industry includes mainly negative and significant results except for the pre-IPO year. The findings for the Wholesale industry are almost identical. The findings are consistent with the alternative hypothesis H-CfO 2 for all industries and groups. Only the overall and loss groups of the Biotech industry indicate

---

[265] Tests for this hypothesis are one-sided. Results are equally to two sided tests in terms of overall significance, yet stronger.

positive significance for CfO in year +2, respectively. As expected, companies do not use significantly positive CfO in the years around the IPO because CfO is biased by other line items and can hardly be managed upward by growing companies. Hence, companies care about other important figures than CfO to influence the share price. Interestingly, this is the case for almost all industries and subgroups although CfO valuation models are quite common in practice. Yet, models using multiples (e.g., enterprise value divided by sales) are also typically used in practice, especially by investment banks.

6.3.1.4 Hypothesis R&D 1

6.3.1.4.1 Biotech

The results for the hypotheses are arranged by industry (Biotech, Internet, Technology, Construction, and Wholesale) and within them by year group (-1 to +2 versus -2 and +3), for all three groups of companies (overall sample, profitable, and loss groups). The results represent tests for the basic hypothesis and the hypothesis R&D 1: In years -1 to +2 companies use discretion proportionately more frequently in R&D than in years -2 and +3 around an IPO.

Table 17 shows outcomes for R&D. In the Biotech industry in the pre-IPO year, unprofitable and profitable companies use positive discretion in R&D expenses. These findings support the notion that firms in R&D intensive industries inflate their R&D expenditures prior to the IPO in hope of a better investor valuation. The significantly high R&D is consistent with abnormally low cash flow and negative earnings accruals for loss firms. Obviously, these companies do not have to care for positive results; however, other line items than earnings are of interest. Profitable firms show abnormally high R&D, but lower than the loss group. For investors this could mean the companies care about their profitability and therefore, they do not invest as much in R&D, have no abnormally low cash flow, and do not defer their revenues to the next years but inflate current sales. Cash might be used for investments in R&D. The results from the R&D model partly support this notion and show significance (5% level) for profitable and high significance (1% level) for loss subgroups as well as the overall group.[266] Interestingly, the abnormal negative amount of cash flow almost equals the abnormal positive amount of R&D for all firms.

In year +1, R&D expenses are significantly managed upward by loss companies. These firms are mainly valued by their receivables and R&D investments which are both significantly higher than for comparable companies. The results display that profitable companies do not manage R&D significantly. The model includes 291 observations. It shows highly significant positive values for the overall and loss samples, respectively. The profitable group has an insignificant positive sign. In year +2, R&D expenses are not managed in any groups. An explanation might be that in two years around the IPO the loss companies use discretion in R&D to influence their valuation and stock price, but they cannot keep that level over a long time period. In the reversal process they obviously do not change sharply from significantly positive to negative but by a slower extent and therefore, they exhibit no significance in the second year after the issue and even negative significance in the third year. Likewise, the profitable companies do not manage R&D expenses. All groups exhibit positive results, however, insignificant.

In year -2, loss firms do not manage R&D expenses (17 observations). Equally, profitable firms do not manage R&D expenses (three observations). The reason for inexistent discretion might be that R&D management can only be made in the short-term and will reverse in the following years. The second year before the IPO would be too early to start managing R&D and is not as useful as high R&D in the first year before and after an IPO, because of higher investor valuations in this time horizon. The outcome is consistent with the results of earnings and cash flow above which indicate almost no discretion in accounting. R&D expenses do not show any abnormal significance either. The model displays a slightly negative result for all groups. It includes up to 27 observations.

[266] The abnormal R&D value for unprofitable and all firms is even significant at the 0.02% level.

Table 17: Discretionary R&D by Year, Group, and Industry

Year	-2 *all*	-2 *profit.*	-2 *loss*	-1 *all*	-1 *profit.*	-1 *loss*	+1 *all*	+1 *profit.*	+1 *loss*	+2 *all*	+2 *profit.*	+2 *loss*	+3 *all*	+3 *profit.*	+3 *loss*
Biotech															
R&D	-.015	--	-.003	**.060*****	**.059***	**.060*****	**.053*****	.002	**.061*****	.012	.010	.012	**-.025*****	.007	**-.029*****
N	20	3	17	133	20	113	283	42	241	334	51	283	324	37	287
Adj. R^2	.805														
Internet															
R&D	-.015	-.026	-.088	**.023*****	**.026*****	**.021*****	**.018*****	**.012*****	**.024*****	**.006***	.003	.008	**-.011*****	-.006	**-.015*****
N	21	8	13	285	99	186	641	333	308	674	277	397	603	229	374
Adj. R^2	.764														
Technology															
R&D	.013	.001	**.029***	**.013*****	**.012*****	**.014*****	**.006*****	**.007*****	.004	**.009*****	**.008*****	**.010*****	-.001	.001	-.003
N	21	12	9	330	149	181	871	527	344	969	497	472	930	450	480
Adj. R^2	.798														
Construction															
R&D	--	--	--	**.007***	.008	.005	-.001	.000	-.007	-.002	-.002	-.002	**.003***	**.002****	.004
N	2	2	0	17	11	6	66	53	13	69	56	13	72	53	19
Adj. R^2	.768														
Wholesale															
R&D	--	--	--	.000	-.000	.004	.000	-.000	.002	.000	**.000***	-.000	.000	**.001***	**-.001*****
N	4	2	2	29	24	5	77	62	15	80	64	16	82	55	27
Adj. R^2	.889														

Notes: *, **, *** represent statistical significance at 10 percent, 5 percent, and 1 percent levels (two-sided), respectively (emphasized by bold type). The results are split by group: overall (all), profitable (profit.), and loss. Results show the means of discretionary R&D expenses, the IPO sample size (N), and the mean adjusted R-squared (Adj. R^2) for the whole sample in one year (there are similar results in all years). Two consecutive hyphens (--) denote less than five available observations.

Year +3 shows that loss companies overinvested heavily in R&D in the years around the IPO and have to underinvest in that year to arrive at a normal level of investment and cash results. The outcomes might also indicate that loss companies invest less to make sure the cash from operations is not too low compared with other companies. It might be that after the IPO the cash flow is more important for a high investor evaluation than the R&D expenses. This is contrarily to the two years around the IPO. The results for discretionary R&D in the model exhibits a high significance with a negative sign for the overall and loss samples and a positive but insignificant amount for the profitable subgroup. The reason is probably that few cash is hold in the company and invested in R&D instead of the matched companies. In the Biotech industry, the findings are consistent with the alternative hypothesis H-R&D 1 for all groups. As expected, there is a significant difference for R&D between years -1 to +2 and the years of -2 and +3. Yet, in years -2 and +2 there are no significant results. In years -1 and +1 almost all groups are significant. Interestingly, while there is overinvestment in R&D in the two years around the IPO there is underinvestment in the third year after the IPO for loss firms. This hints at discretionary behavior over time. The Biotech industry seems to be almost identical to the other unprofitable and R&D intensive industry (Internet), while the profitable industries (Construction and Wholesale) mainly differ.

6.3.1.4.2 Internet

In the Internet industry in the pre-IPO year, the results for R&D obviously signal a future benefit to investors. They are influenced by the companies to receive a higher market valuation. The model is highly significant and positive for all groups. The findings contradict prior literature that R&D spending is cut to increase earnings and cash flow. In the post-IPO year, the R&D expenditures are abnormally high for all groups, which supposedly increases the market price. The model for R&D exhibits high significance for all three groups. In year +2, R&D expenses are insignificant for all groups, except for the overall sample which is positive at the 10% level. Obviously, companies do not expect investors to value this line item as much as high earnings or growing earnings after the offering.

In year -2, the results for R&D expenses exhibit no significance in any group. In year +3, however, R&D expenses are significantly low for the overall and loss groups, and indicate low spending in R&D while the profitable companies do not manage R&D costs. The model detects highly significant and negative values for the overall and loss samples while the profitable group is insignificant. In the Internet industry, the findings are consistent with the alternative hypothesis H-R&D 1 for all groups. As expected, there is a significant difference for R&D between years -1 to +2 and the years of -2 and +3. Yet the basic hypothesis shows that in year -2 there are none and in year +2 there is only one significant result. In years -1 and +1, all groups are significant. Interestingly, while there is overinvestment in R&D in the two years around the IPO there is underinvestment in the third year after the IPO for loss firms. This hints at discretionary behavior over time from overinvestment in years -1 and +1, to no abnormal behavior in year +2, to underinvestment in year +3. The Biotech industry seems to be almost identical to these findings, while the profitable industries (Construction and Wholesale) mainly differ.

6.3.1.4.3 Technology

In the Technology industry in the pre-IPO year, the results for R&D indicate that companies inflate their R&D spending. Assumingly, this should convince investors of probable future benefits resulting from R&D investments. Interestingly, there is no difference between the profitable and loss groups. The results show a high significance for all three groups. In the post-IPO year, the R&D expenses are significantly positive for the overall and profitable groups while loss firms are insignificant. The results indicate that profitable companies inflate R&D to receive a higher valuation. The overall sample is highly significant. This supports the notion to divide between the subgroups. In year +2, R&D spending accentuates the notion that companies inflate R&D expenses to signal future benefits to investors. The model exhibits high significance and positive amounts for all groups. This finding can explain the abnormal low cash flow from above.

In year -2, the model detects abnormal positive behavior only for the loss subgroup with nine observations. In year +3, the R&D model indicates no discretion in R&D. In the Technology industry, the findings are consistent with the alternative hypothesis H-R&D 1 for all groups. As expected, there is a significant difference for R&D between years -1 to +2 and the years of -2 and +3. In year -2 there is only one and in year +3 there is no significant result. While in years -1 to +2 all groups are significant except the loss group in year +1. Interestingly, there is again overinvestment in R&D in the two (and even three) years around the IPO. The Technology industry seems to be similar to the Biotech and Internet industries except for years +2 and +3, but not comparable to the profitable industries (Construction and Wholesale). This finding recommends differentiating between firms and industries.

6.3.1.4.4 Construction

In the Construction industry in the pre-IPO year, the results for R&D display discretion only for the overall group at the 10% level of significance, but not for the subgroups. In contrast to the other sectors, COMPUSTAT includes R&D values for only around 30 to 40 percent of the whole sample. This underlines the unimportance of R&D for this industry group and the fact that the firms went public a long time ago when the data for R&D was not collected. In the post-IPO year, the results for R&D are all insignificant and show no systematic pattern. This contradicts prior literature that companies cut R&D expenses to increase earnings and thereby influence investors. In year +2, the model for R&D exhibits no significance but negative amounts for all groups.

In year -2, the results for R&D include only two companies. As aforementioned, this underlines the unimportance of R&D for this industry group and perhaps might result from the fact that the firms went public a long time ago. In year +3, R&D spending is abnormally high for the overall and profitable samples which is rather surprising. It could mean that profitable companies invest more in R&D than their more well-established counterparts (matched approach) because of their young age and need to improve their products. In the Construction industry, the findings do not reject the null hypothesis of H-R&D 1 for all groups.[267] Prior literature mainly expected companies to reduce R&D spending for better earnings and influencing investors. However, as the basic hypothesis already shows, year +3 is significant in two groups while years -1 to +2 are not. Only year -1 finds the overall sample to be abnormally high but no other amount. In year +3, the overall and profitable samples are significant. The Construction industry seems to be very different to the prior three industries (Biotech, Internet, and Technology) in almost all years. Differentiating between industries seems necessary.

6.3.1.4.5 Wholesale

In the Wholesale industry in year -1, the findings for R&D are insignificant and only negative for the profitable sample. This is in line with no significance for CfO. Hence, there are only small hints that profitable firms reduce R&D spending to increase income. In the post-IPO year, R&D spending is insignificant in all groups. In year +2, R&D expenses indicate no abnormal behavior except for the profitable group at the 10% level of significance.

[267] The correct term is that due to the results "the null hypothesis of H-R&D 1 is not rejected", but for reasons of easier and better understating, sometimes the notation "not consistent with the alternative hypothesis" is used in this study.

In year -2, R&D expenses include too few observations (four) for valid results. In year +3, abnormal R&D expenses partly confirm the findings in CfO. The model finds significant positive values for the profitable sample while at the same time exhibits negative discretion for the loss sample directing to an effort to decrease spending in favor of a better (but still negative) net income. These opposing outcomes of subgroups support the notion to differentiate between them. In the Wholesale industry, the findings do not reject the null hypothesis H-R&D 1 for all groups. There is not the expected significant difference and direction in years -1 to +2 and years -2 and +3. Prior literature mainly expected companies to reduce R&D spending for inflated earnings and influencing investors. However, the basic hypothesis shows that the profitable subgroups are significant and positive in years +2 and +3 while one negative and significant amount exists in year +3. The Wholesale industry seems to be very different to the R&D-intensive industries (Biotech, Internet, and Technology) in almost all years. This finding supports to differentiate between industries.

6.3.1.5 Hypothesis SG&A 1

6.3.1.5.1 Biotech

The results for the hypotheses are arranged by industry (Biotech, Internet, Technology, Construction, and Wholesale) and within them by year group (-1 to +2 versus -2 and +3), with all three groups of companies (overall sample, profitable, and loss groups). The results represent tests for the basic hypothesis and the hypothesis SG&A 1: In years -1 to +2 companies use discretion proportionately more frequently in SG&A than in years -2 and +3 around an IPO.

Table 18 illustrates results for SG&A. In the Biotech industry in the pre-IPO year, abnormally high SG&A expenses point at abnormally high expenditures for sales personnel or increased expenses because of the IPO preparation (legal and consulting expenses). The high value can also be the reason for the negative cash flow results. The SG&A model shows significant positive results for all groups. In year +1, SG&A expenses are abnormally high. This implies increased sales activities which are in line with the abnormally high receivables and abnormally low CfO for loss firms. The results are significant (1% or 5% levels) with a positive amount for all groups. In year +2, SG&A expenses are suddenly abnormally low for the overall and loss groups. This might display the intention of managers to invest less in certain business activities and increase CfO which might be more value relevant to investors in this period. Accordingly, this item exhibits an opposing (algebraic) sign after the issue. A similar behavior exists for R&D expenses. The model for SG&A shows negative and significant amounts for the overall and loss samples whereas the profitable subgroup is insignificant.

In year -2, results for SG&A expenses are insignificant. The model displays a positive amount for the overall and loss samples but a negative one for the profitable group. In year +3, SG&A expenses do not exhibit any discretion. The model indicates negative amounts for all groups. In the Biotech industry, findings are consistent with the alternative hypothesis H-SG&A 1 for all groups. In fact, there is a significant difference for CfO between the two year groups. The basic hypothesis shows that especially years -1 and +1 are significant for all groups while years -2 and +3 exhibit no significance at all. Prior literature mainly expected companies to reduce SG&A expenses for higher earnings and influencing investors. However, the results are all positive and significant in the two years around the IPO. The findings are quite analogous to the results for R&D and could indicate that SG&A are similarly used to express future benefits (e.g., brands, customer lists, patents) to investors. Yet, they could also be reduced in the following periods to express an improving organization (e.g., better sales efficiency). These interpretations are dependent on the specific line items which make up SG&A and vary between future investments (patents) and inefficiency (sales force) which can be part of future research. Similar to R&D expenses, the industry seems to be very different to the very profitable industries (Construction and Wholesale) in almost all years around the IPO. This finding suggests differentiating between industries.

6.3.1.5.2 Internet

In the Internet industry in year -1, results for SG&A show high abnormal values which indicate abnormal costs for sales personnel or increased costs because of the IPO preparation (e.g., legal and consulting expenses). Alternatively, this means trying to manipulate investors by signaling future benefits. The model detects high significance and positive amounts for all subgroups. In year +1, results for SG&A indicate high expenses and support the findings of abnormally low CfO. The outcomes are highly significant for all groups. This implies increased sales activities which are in line with the abnormally high receivables and abnormally low CfO for loss firms. In year +2, the model for SG&A expenses exhibits no significant results.

Table 18: Discretionary SG&A by Year, Group, and Industry

Year	-2			-1			+1			+2			+3		
	all	*profit.*	*loss*	*all*	*profit.*	*loss*	*all*	*profit.*	*loss*	*all*	*profit.*	*loss*	*all*	*profit.*	*loss*
Biotech															
SG&A	.036	--	.163	**.169*****	**.112***	**.194*****	**.234*****	**.168*****	**.269*****	**-.054****	-.029	**-.066****	-.018	-.054	-.003
N	11	4	7	80	24	56	133	46	87	164	52	112	128	37	91
Adj. R^2	.453														
Internet															
SG&A	.002	-.016	.013	**.163*****	**.110*****	**.196*****	**.246*****	**.210*****	**.285*****	-.006	.011	-.020	.014	-.030	.003
N	24	9	15	370	141	229	818	428	390	852	366	486	745	300	445
Adj. R^2	.398														
Technology															
SG&A	-.033	-.053	-.011	**.109*****	**.068*****	**.139*****	**.127*****	**.113*****	**.146*****	**.025*****	**.023*****	**.026*****	**.026*****	**.030*****	**.023****
N	35	18	17	408	174	234	1'072	629	443	1'153	582	571	1'092	509	583
Adj. R^2	.466														
Construction															
SG&A	-.005	.014	--	-.021	**-.047*****	.032	-.004	**-.018***	**.045****	-.004	-.006	.007	.013	.012	.015
N	7	5	2	55	37	18	177	139	38	193	156	37	183	133	50
Adj. R^2	.390														
Wholesale															
SG&A	.125	--	--	.031	.004	**.123***	.009	.004	.031	-.009	-.008	-.010	.013	.001	.036
N	7	4	3	75	58	17	194	156	38	229	166	63	211	143	68
Adj. R^2	.179														

Notes: *, **, *** represent statistical significance at 10 percent, 5 percent, and 1 percent levels (two-sided), respectively (emphasized by bold type). The results are split by group: overall (all), profitable (profit.), and loss. Results show the means of discretionary SG&A expenses, the IPO sample size (N), and the mean adjusted R-squared (Adj. R^2) for the whole sample in one year (there are similar results in all years). Two consecutive hyphens (--) denote less than five available observations.

In year -2, results for SG&A expenses confirm this finding and exhibit no significance in any subgroup. In year +3, SG&A expenses seem to be normal and indicate no uncharacteristic behavior in all groups. In the Internet industry, findings are consistent with the alternative hypothesis H-SG&A 1 for all groups. There is a significant difference for CfO between years -1 to +2 and years -2 and +3. Especially, the basic hypothesis shows that years -1 and +1 are significant for all groups, equally to the Biotech industry. In the same way, years -2 and +3 exhibit no significance in both industries. Prior literature mainly expected companies to reduce SG&A expenses in favor of higher earnings to influence investors. However, results are all positive and significant in the two years around the IPO. The findings are quite analogous to the results for R&D and could indicate that SG&A are similarly used to express future benefits (e.g., brands) to investors. Similar to R&D expenses, the industry seems to be very different to the highly profitable industries (Construction and Wholesale) in almost all years around the IPO. This finding should be of interest for investors when examining different kinds of industries.

6.3.1.5.3 Technology

In the Technology industry in year -1, SG&A expenses indicate that the companies have abnormally high costs. The model displays a high significance for all three groups which gives a powerful result. Equally in year +1, SG&A expenses exhibit abnormally high amounts for companies after the issue. The findings indicate highly significant and positive results for all three groups. In year +2, the findings for SG&A are very similar to the prior years. The model detects high significance for all groups. The findings in this year differ from all other industry results. Interestingly, this is equally the case for R&D expenses. The Technology industry seems to differ from the other included industries. This conclusion is in line with prior literature.[268]

In year -2, there exists no significance for SG&A expenses. In year +3, SG&A expenses explain the negative operating cash flow. The results are significant (1% or 5% levels) and positive for all groups. In the Technology industry, findings are consistent with the alternative hypothesis H-SG&A 1 for all groups. There is a significant difference for CfO between the two year groups. Interestingly, all years from -1 to +3 are significant for all groups, except year -2. In the two years around the IPO, the industry is identical with the Biotech and Internet industries (in year -2 all industries are equal). Yet, in years +2 and +3 it differs from

[268] Francis et al. (2012), pp. 261-262; Hsu (2009), pp. 264-265; Sievers/Klobucnik (2012), pp. 1-3.

all other industries. Prior literature mainly expected companies to reduce SG&A expenses for higher earnings. However, the results are all positive and significant in years -1 to +3. The findings are quite analogous to the results for R&D, except for year +3, and could indicate that SG&A are similarly used to express future benefits (such as customer lists) to investors. Again, the industries diverge.

6.3.1.5.4 Construction

In the Construction industry in the pre-IPO year, SG&A expenses are abnormally low for the profitable group, indicating that these companies try to lower their expenses for high cash and earnings. This behavior is in line with prior literature.[269] The profitable group is significant (1% or 5% levels) and negative. The result for the loss group displays a positive sign and is insignificant. The result for the profitable companies might be due to demonstrating an efficient company to investors. The argument of SG&A expenses being investments is not valid here, because these kinds of companies have not equally high intangible assets. In year +1, SG&A expenses indicate deflation by profitable firms and inflation by unprofitable ones. This might be caused by demonstrating efficient structures in the profitable group or reaching profitability (net profit larger than zero). Contrarily, the loss group might be unprofitable due to these high costs which designate their inefficiency in structures, they invest in sales personnel, or loss companies do not care about being even more unprofitable and use SG&A to follow another benefit, for example. While there is significant negative discretion for the profitable subgroup, the loss companies exhibit significant positive discretion. Here, the interesting case occurs that the profitable and loss groups are opposed to each other, leaving the overall sample insignificant. The research design shows that these two groups of companies have to be separated when interpreting results. Prior studies which only analyze the overall sample miss some substantial information. In year +2, results are insignificant.

In years -2 and +3, results indicate no discretionary behavior. In the Construction industry, findings are consistent with the alternative hypothesis H-SG&A 1 for the separate profitable and loss groups. In fact, there is a significant difference for CfO between the two year groups for these categories of companies. Interestingly, the overall group exhibits no significant results while the two subgroups are each significant in year +1. Remarkably, the two subgroups are opposed in their signs and leave the overall group insignificant. This underlines the importance to differentiate between these two groups of companies around IPOs. There

[269] Gunny (2010), pp. 858-859. However, she does not differentiate between industries and notes that SG&A will be reduced in all companies.

are significant results in years -1 and +1, only. All other years are insignificant. The results are not in line with the three prior industries and even opposed for the profitable group in the two years around the IPO but they are in line with Gunny (2010). The findings are only partly analogous to the results for R&D. Again, outcomes for industries fluctuate.

6.3.1.5.5 Wholesale

In the Wholesale industry in the pre-IPO year, results for SG&A expenses indicate that loss firms have abnormally high spending which might point out a reason for their unprofitable bottom line. These costs could result from the efforts of going public, but they are not equally and significantly present for the profitable group, although the (algebraic) sign is also positive. The model indicates positive significance for the loss sample. All results depict a positive sign. In the post-IPO year, results for SG&A do not point out any significant value. Equally, in year +2, SG&A expenses support no discretion as they are insignificant and negative for all groups.

In year -2, SG&A expenses are insignificant and positive for all groups whilst the subgroups have too few observations to calculate results. In year +3, SG&A expenses are unmanaged with insignificant and positive results. In the Wholesale industry, findings are blurred compared to the basic hypothesis, but obviously consistent with the alternative hypothesis H-SG&A 1 for the loss group whereas the null hypothesis is not rejected for the overall and profitable groups. There is only one significant result in year -1 while in year -2 there are too few results for calculation. Findings are not consistent with prior literature proposing SG&A expenses are deflated in favor of earnings. The outcome is only partly analogous to R&D where mainly no discretion is present. Again, this industry differs from other industries.

6.3.1.6 Hypothesis Advertising 1

6.3.1.6.1 Biotech

Results for the hypotheses are arranged by industry (Biotech, Internet, Technology, Construction, and Wholesale) and within them by year group (-1 to +2 versus -2 and +3), with all three groups of companies (overall sample, profitable, and loss groups). The results represent tests for the basic and the hypothesis Adv 1: In years -1 to +2 companies use discretion proportionately more frequently in advertising than in years -2 and +3 around an IPO.

Table 19 presents results for advertising. In the Biotech industry in the pre-IPO year, advertising expenses do not show any significance for the overall and loss samples. The profitable sample cannot be taken into account because of a lack of available data. In the post-IPO year, advertising expenses do not show any significant abnormal value either. While profitable companies decrease advertising costs, the loss subgroup proceeds contrarily. For the latter this might be the case due to an increase of their visibility in the market and because of already unprofitable results which are not value relevant. In year +2, advertising expenses are still insignificant.

In year -2, the model for advertising expenses cannot be calculated due to a lack of data for this time horizon. In year +3, SG&A expenses do not give any hint for discretion. The results do not exhibit any significance. In the Biotech industry, there are too few observations to adequately test the main hypothesis. The basic hypothesis shows no significant result in all years and the number of observations is relatively low compared to other accounting items in the study. For example, the profitable group cannot be calculated for two out of five periods.

6.3.1.6.2 Internet

In the Internet industry in the pre-IPO year, advertising expenses seem to be only marginally influenced. The model finds positive and significant values for the overall and profitable samples (5% and 10% levels, respectively). In the post-IPO year, advertising expenses are coherent with low cash for the loss group. Both subgroups seem to overinvest in advertising to promote the going public process. Especially loss companies seem not to care if earnings are negatively influenced by this measure. As mentioned before, companies with already negative earnings prefer managing other line items. The model identifies high significance for the overall and loss samples, respectively, while the profitable sample is significant at the 5% level. In year +2, advertising expenses are insignificant and positive in all groups. Interestingly, there is an abundance of advertising data relating to the Internet industry.

In year -2, results for advertising expenses exhibit no significance in any subgroup with 12 observations for the overall sample, only. Similarly, in year +3, there are no significant results. Advertising indicates no uncharacteristic behavior in all groups. In the Internet industry, findings are consistent with the alternative hypothesis H-Adv 1 for all groups. There are significant differences in the two year groups. Results in the two years around the IPO indicate the Internet companies spend abnormally high amounts to attract investors and make the company visible to the public.

Table 19: Discretionary Advertising Expenses by Year, Group, and Industry

Year	-2			-1			+1			+2			+3		
	all	*profit.*	*loss*	*all*	*profit.*	*loss*	*all*	*profit.*	*loss*	*all*	*profit.*	*loss*	*all*	*profit.*	*loss*
Biotech															
Adv	--	--	--	-.001	--	--	.005	-.000	.009	.004	-.001	.005	.006	.007	.006
N	1	1	0	7	3	4	28	12	16	31	11	20	24	7	17
Adj. R^2	.162														
Internet															
Adv	.006	--	.012	**.010****	**.010***	.010	**.017*****	**.009****	**.024*****	.003	.007	.001	.000	.000	.000
N	12	4	8	108	46	62	203	99	104	229	79	150	221	72	149
Adj. R^2	.077														
Technology															
Adv	.012	.012	--	**.006****	**.013*****	.001	**.005*****	.003	**.008*****	-.000	-.002	.001	.000	.000	.000
N	10	6	4	78	34	44	231	136	95	234	132	102	198	98	100
Adj. R^2	.093														
Construction															
Adv	--	--	--	--	--	--	-.003	-.001	--	-.015	--	--	-.001	.003	-.005
N	0	0	0	4	4	0	10	8	2	7	4	3	12	6	6
Adj. R^2	.154														
Wholesale															
Adv	--	--	--	-.000	**-.017***	--	.000	-.009	--	-.003	-.006	.000	-.006	-.000	-.013
N	1	1	0	10	8	2	10	8	2	21	12	9	24	12	12
Adj. R^2	.049														

Notes: *, **, *** represent statistical significance at 10 percent, 5 percent, and 1 percent levels (two-sided), respectively (emphasized by bold type). The results are split by group: overall (all), profitable (profit.), and loss. Results show the means of discretionary advertising expenses (Adv), the IPO sample size (N), and the mean adjusted R-squared (Adj. R^2) for the whole sample in one year (there are similar results in all years). Two consecutive hyphens (--) denote less than five available observations.

6.3.1.6.3 Technology

In the Technology industry in the pre-IPO year, advertising costs seem to be valuable for the profitable firms but not for the loss group. The model displays high significance (1% level) of positive abnormal expenses for the profitable group while the loss firms do not exhibit any significant amount. The overall sample is significant (5% level). In the post-IPO year, expenses for advertising are highly significant for the loss and overall samples but not for the profitable group. This indicates that loss companies value current advertising expenses higher than current profits. Obviously, they do not mind being even more unprofitable and do not try being profitable by cutting expenses as prior accounting research expected. In year +2, advertising expenses are insignificant.

In year -2 in the Technology industry, no significance is detected. In year +3, there is no discretion in advertising expenses for any group. In the Technology industry, findings are consistent with the alternative hypothesis H-Adv 1 for all groups. There is a significant difference for advertising between years -1 to +2 and years -2 and +3. However, there are only few observations in year -2. Technology companies seem to value high advertising costs around the IPO more than earnings and cash flow.

6.3.1.6.4 Construction

In the Construction industry in the pre-IPO year, the model for advertising expenses includes only four observations (all profitable) and is not taken into account. In the post-IPO year, results for advertising costs do not indicate any pattern for the ten observations while the loss group includes only two observations. In year +2, advertising expense is negative and insignificant for all groups and seven observations in the overall sample.

In year -2, there are no observations available for this industry. In year +3, there are no significant results for 12 observations. In the Construction industry, there are too few observations to adequately test the main hypothesis. There are many results missing due to the low data availability.[270]

6.3.1.6.5 Wholesale

In the Wholesale industry in the pre-IPO year, the results for advertising costs indicate that profitable firms apply downward discretion to improve their net income. This is similar to the

[270] There are no statistical procedures employed to replace missing data.

findings for R&D. The model finds a negative and significant amount for the profitable sample, only, while the loss group includes too few observations. In the post-IPO year, the results for advertising expenses neither find any significant value while the loss sample has too few observations again. In year +2, advertising expenses are insignificant with a negative amount for the profitable group which could indicate that these firms care about their earnings while loss firms exhibit a positive sign.

In year -2, advertising expenses have too few observations to calculate. In year +3, advertising expenses are unmanaged and indicate no significance. In the Wholesale industry, there are too few observations to adequately test the hypothesis. For the basic hypothesis there is only one significant result for the profitable sample, but there are many results missing in both groups due to the low data availability. The overall sample indicates no significance.

6.3.1.7 Hypothesis Discretionary Expenses 1

6.3.1.7.1 Biotech

The results for the hypotheses are arranged by industry (Biotech, Internet, Technology, Construction, and Wholesale) and within them by year group (-1 to +2 versus -2 and +3), with all three groups of companies (overall sample, profitable, and loss groups). The results represent tests for the basic hypothesis and the hypothesis discretionary expense 1: In years -1 to +2 companies use discretion proportionately more frequently in discretionary expense than in years -2 and +3 around an IPO.

Since discretionary expenses include R&D, SG&A, and advertising expenses, there is a high probability to find significant results as in the prior accounting items. This would mean that overall discretionary expenses are also abnormally high before the IPO. Most prior literature usually used variables of SG&A or discretionary expenses, but not R&D as well. The present procedure sheds more light on firms' behavior, especially when R&D is important for the respective industry.

Table 20 illustrates outcomes for discretionary expenses. In the Biotech industry in the pre-IPO year, the aggregate measure of discretionary expenses indicates that all groups use discretion. This results mainly from high R&D and SG&A expenses. The findings are significant at the 1% and 5% levels. In the post-IPO year, discretionary expenses follow the findings for R&D and SG&A expenses. The expenditures show that firms invest heavily after the IPO and do not try to lower these costs to increase profit. This mainly contradicts prior literature which suggests that all industries are similar.[271] There is high positive significance for all groups. In year +2, discretionary expenses show an opposing influence because they are reduced by loss firms to increase cash flow. Around the lock-up period, cash flow seems to be more value relevant than in the two years before. This might be connected to the presence of venture capitalists.[272] The model finds negative and highly significant values for the overall and profitable samples.

In year -2, the amounts of the results for discretionary expenses indicate no abnormal behavior while the profitable group includes too few observations. Results are consistent with the outcomes for R&D and SG&A. In year +3, discretionary expenses are expected to be abnormal and significant according to R&D results, but they are not. This result is probably caused by a lower level of (required) observations in SG&A than in R&D because of restricted data availability. This underlines the importance of dividing the aggregate measure of discretionary expenses into specific accounts. In the Biotech industry, the findings are consistent with the alternative hypothesis H-DisExp 1 for all groups. There is a significant difference for discretionary expenses between the two year groups. Almost all results in years -1 to +2 around the IPO are significant, except one. However, year -2 is invalid for the profitable group due to a lack of data. Yet, year +3 indicates no significance. Biotech companies seem to prefer expenses in some business activities over positive discretion in earnings and cash in years -1 and +1. Nevertheless, there are negative results in year +2 which indicate that companies either change their preference after the offering or they have to reverse overinvestments.

[271] Teoh et al. (1998c), pp. 175-176.
[272] Wongsunwai (2013).

Table 20: Abnormal Discretionary Expenses by Year, Group, and Industry

Year	-2			-1			+1			+2			+3		
	all	*profit.*	*loss*	*all*	*profit.*	*loss*	*all*	*profit.*	*loss*	*all*	*profit.*	*loss*	*all*	*profit.*	*loss*
Biotech															
DisExp	.043	--	.253	**.267*****	**.197****	**.299*****	**.367*****	**.265*****	**.424*****	**-.104*****	-.027	**-.141*****	-.036	-.110	-.006
N	11	4	7	76	24	52	129	46	83	161	52	109	127	37	90
Adj. R^2	.280														
Internet															
DisExp	.017	-.028	.045	**.332*****	**.230*****	**.396*****	**.423*****	**.391*****	**.458*****	-.026	-.009	-.039	.014	.025	.007
N	24	9	15	364	141	223	813	427	386	847	365	482	743	299	444
Adj. R^2	.237														
Technology															
DisExp	-.028	-.052	-.001	**.199*****	**.135*****	**.247*****	**.212*****	**.206*****	**.220*****	**.052*****	**.057*****	**.047*****	**.048*****	**.061*****	**.037*****
N	34	18	16	406	174	232	1'060	625	435	1'151	581	570	1'090	508	582
Adj. R^2	.348														
Construction															
DisExp	.012	.038	--	-.017	**-.064*****	**.077***	.008	-.015	**.095*****	.010	.007	.025	.010	.003	.028
N	7	5	2	55	37	18	176	138	38	193	156	37	182	132	50
Adj. R^2	.306														
Wholesale															
DisExp	.132	--	--	.050	.016	**.184****	.025	.017	.059	.009	.009	.006	.025	.012	.051
N	7	4	3	73	58	15	194	156	38	226	164	62	211	143	68
Adj. R^2	.152														

Notes: *, **, *** represent statistical significance at 10 percent, 5 percent, and 1 percent levels (two-sided), respectively (emphasized by bold type). The results are split by group: overall (all), profitable (profit.), and loss. Results show the means of abnormal discretionary expenses (DisExp), the IPO sample size (N), and the mean adjusted R-squared (Adj. R^2) for the whole sample in one year (there are similar results in all years). Two consecutive hyphens (--) denote less than five available observations.

6.3.1.7.2 Internet

In the Internet industry in the year before the IPO, results for the aggregate measure of discretionary expenses confirm the findings of R&D and SG&A. The model indicates positive and highly significant discretion in all groups. In the post-IPO year, discretionary expenses support the notion that companies in the Internet industry do not artificially decrease these expenditures to increase earnings but apply other actions which deflate earnings. The results are consistent with the findings in R&D, SG&A, and advertising expenses. The outcomes for cash flow in the profitable group seem not to follow the discretionary expenses but obviously, they are reversed by some other business activities. In year +2, the aggregate measure of discretionary expenses indicates no significant amount.

In year -2, the aggregate measure of discretionary expenses detects no significance in any subgroup. Equally, in year +3, discretionary expenses are insignificant in all groups. The discretion of R&D expenses is not reflected here. This underlines the importance to divide discretionary expenses into more components to check for respective discretion and not only this assembled account. In the Internet industry, findings are consistent with the alternative hypothesis H-DisExp 1 for all groups. There is a significant difference for discretionary expenses between the two year groups for each category. All results in years -1 and +1 around the IPO are highly significant. No other years indicate discretion. Internet companies seem to prefer expenses in some business activities over inflation of profit and cash.

6.3.1.7.3 Technology

In the Technology industry in the year before the IPO, results for discretionary expenses are in line with R&D and SG&A from above. They also exhibit highly significant and positive abnormal amounts for all groups. The companies do not artificially decrease expenses, but perhaps they partly have to increase them because of the costs associated with an IPO and partly they voluntarily inflate R&D and SG&A to signal to outsiders. In year +1, as expected from the aforementioned results, discretionary expenses indicate abnormally high expenditures. The model finds highly significant and positive results for all groups. This outcome points out that contrarily to many studies in prior literature companies do not cut discretionary expenses after the IPO.[273] In year +2, discretionary expenses indicate that companies do not cut the spending in favor of higher cash flow, but invest money for future

[273] Teoh et al. (1998c), pp. 175-176, for example.

benefits. This behavior is probably supported by new investors after the issue. The expenses are abnormal and highly significant in all subgroups.

In year -2, the aggregate measure of discretionary expenses does not show any significance. In year +3, discretionary expenses underline the prior mentioned accounting items. The model finds highly significant results for all groups. In the Technology industry, findings are consistent with the alternative hypothesis H-DisExp 1 for all groups. There is a significant difference for discretionary expenses between both year groups for all categories. All results in years -1 to +3 around the IPO are highly significant and positive while year -2 exhibits no discretion. Technology companies are similar to the Biotech and Internet industries in years -1 and +1, but differ in the following years. This industry is neither comparable to the Construction nor the Wholesale industries. Companies in this industry seem to prefer expenses in some business activities over inflation of profit and cash.

6.3.1.7.4 Construction

In the Construction industry in the pre-IPO year, there is negative discretion of the profitable group while the loss group shows positive discretion, leaving the overall sample with no significance. The results for the two groups are opposed and underline the notion that studies should differentiate between these two clusters of companies. In the post-IPO year, the result indicates a high significance for the positive amount of loss firms. Again, the signs of the subgroups are opposed to each other. Results are in line with the findings for SG&A expenses. In year +2, the aggregate measure of discretionary expenses does not indicate any significance.

In year -2, the calculation includes only seven observations and finds no significance for the overall and profitable groups while the unprofitable group includes too few observations. In year +3, similarly, there are no significant results. This is in line with the results for SG&A but not with R&D. Compared to the Biotech firms, the findings for R&D are not dominating the discretionary expenses results, but here the SG&A outcomes are reflected in this aggregate measure. This is coherent with low R&D expenses in the Construction and Manufacturing industries compared to Biotech firms. In the Construction industry, findings are consistent with the alternative hypothesis H-DisExp 1 for the separate profitable and loss groups. However, the overall group indicates no significance. There is a significant difference for discretionary expenses between both year groups for two categories. Significant results are present in years -1 and +1 around the IPO. All other years are insignificant while year -2 includes too few observations. Construction companies deflate expenses before the IPO, but only, if they are profitable. However, loss companies exhibit positive abnormal amounts. The findings underline the importance of differentiating between the two subgroups, otherwise, wrong conclusions could be drawn. Furthermore, the results support the diverging industries. The Construction industry is closest to the Wholesale industry, but categorically different from the three prior industries, especially in case of profitable companies.

6.3.1.7.5 Wholesale

In the Wholesale industry, the results for the pre-IPO year indicate management of discretionary expenses for the loss subgroup, only. The amount is abnormally positive (5% level). In the post-IPO year, the aggregate measure of discretionary expenses is insignificant for all amounts. In year +2, discretionary expenses mainly support prior findings of R&D and SG&A. There is no significance and all amounts are positive.

In year -2, there are positive and insignificant values for seven observations, only. In year +3, discretionary expenses confirm prior results and indicate no significance. The amounts mainly follow the results for SG&A expenses. In the Wholesale industry, findings are unclear due to missing data. The null hypothesis H-DisExp 1 is not rejected for all groups. There is no significant difference for discretionary expenses between the year groups. Yet, there exists one significant result in year -1 for the loss group. All other years are insignificant while year -2 includes too few observations for the subgroups. Wholesale companies only influence discretionary expenses in the pre-IPO year, but only, if they are unprofitable. The outcomes underline the importance of differentiating between profitable and loss firms. Furthermore, the results support the differences between industries. The Wholesale industry is closest to the Construction industry for all years, but absolutely different from the three other industries in the pre- and post-IPO years.

6.3.1.8 Hypothesis Change in Inventory 1

6.3.1.8.1 Biotech

The results for the hypotheses are arranged by industry (Biotech, Internet, Technology, Construction, and Wholesale) and within them by year group (-1 to +2 versus -2 and +3), with all three groups of companies (overall sample, profitable, and loss groups). The results represent tests for the hypothesis change in inventory 1: In years -1 to +2 companies use discretion proportionately more frequently in change in inventory than in years -2 and +3 around an IPO.

Table 21 points out results for change in inventory. In the Biotech industry, the results for the pre-IPO year inventory model indicates no discretion during the issue and do not deflate this account to increase earnings. In the post-IPO year, results indicate that change in inventories are abnormally high for profitable firms and connote increased production which is supposed to be sold in the future. Producing now and selling in the future shifts costs to the present and increases earnings later or it is caused by emptying stock in the prior year without refilling it appropriately or overproduction to lower COGS. The profitable subgroup shows a significant (5% level) and positive value. Loss firms show a divergent outcome because they are insignificant. The overall sample neither is significant. In year +2, inventories are not managed by the Biotech companies; therefore, they indicate no overproduction.

In year -2, inventories are unmanaged. While the profitable group includes only four observations, the overall and unprofitable groups point out no significance. In year +3, the inventory model exhibits results around zero and does not direct to any discretionary behavior. In the Biotech industry, findings indicate that the null hypothesis H-dInv 1 is not rejected. There is no significant difference for discretionary expenses between the year groups. While the profitable subgroup exhibits one significant result in year +1, year -2 cannot be calculated. Biotech companies have the least amount of significant results for all industries and indicate that these companies do not extensively use discretion in this accounting item. The finding underlines the importance of differentiating between profitable and loss companies as well as distinguishing between industries concerning line items.

Table 21: Discretionary Change in Inventory by Year, Group, and Industry

Year	-2			-1			+1			+2			+3		
	all	*profit.*	*loss*	*all*	*profit.*	*loss*	*all*	*profit.*	*loss*	*all*	*profit.*	*loss*	*all*	*profit.*	*loss*
Biotech															
ΔInv	-.007	--	-.006	-.000	.005	-.001	.000	**.009****	-.001	.000	.000	.000	-.000	.002	-.001
N	27	4	23	196	29	167	381	56	325	461	63	398	426	52	374
Adj. R^2	.118														
Internet															
ΔInv	.000	-.003	.002	**-.001****	**-.002***	-.001	-.000	**-.002*****	.000	**.001****	.000	**.001****	-.000	.000	-.000
N	24	9	15	379	146	233	876	452	424	934	385	549	824	321	503
Adj. R^2	.073														
Technology															
ΔInv	.003	**.017***	-.011	**.005****	.001	**.008****	**.013*****	**.013*****	**.013*****	**.008*****	**.009*****	**.008*****	**.003****	**.007*****	.000
N	37	19	18	438	182	256	1'142	645	497	1'251	600	651	1'168	526	642
Adj. R^2	.217														
Construction															
ΔInv	-.010	-.013	--	.010	.013	.003	.007	**.008***	.002	**.008****	**.009****	.005	-.001	.000	-.006
N	7	5	2	56	37	19	181	141	40	201	161	40	191	135	56
Adj. R^2	.213														
Wholesale															
ΔInv	**-.063*****	--	--	.002	.000	.006	**.031*****	**.034*****	.019	**.012****	.009	**.020***	.003	.006	-.000
N	7	4	3	73	58	15	201	161	40	230	167	63	217	146	71
Adj. R^2	.282														

Notes: *, **, *** represent statistical significance at 10 percent, 5 percent, and 1 percent levels (two-sided), respectively (emphasized by bold type). The results are split by group: overall (all), profitable (profit.), and loss. Results show the means of discretionary change in inventory (ΔInv), the IPO sample size (N), and the mean adjusted R-squared (Adj. R^2) for the whole sample in one year (there are similar results in all years). Two consecutive hyphens (--) denote less than five available observations.

6.3.1.8.2 Internet

In the Internet industry, the results for the pre-IPO year for inventories indicate that profitable companies reduce this account before the IPO to increase income and cash. The overall and profitable groups are negatively significant while there is no significance for the loss companies. These findings underline the importance to differentiate between subgroups. In year +1, inventories support the notion that profitable firms decrease these expenses to increase earnings and cash. The findings are in line with the results of no abnormally negative cash flow and earnings compared to the loss subgroup. However, the high sales indicated high inventories, but the contrary is the case. There is high significance for the profitable sample and no significance for the loss subgroup. The overall group is insignificant because the loss companies exhibit a positive sign. Again, there is a substantial difference between the two groups and this argues in favor of dividing the overall sample in these two clusters. In year +2, the inventory model indicates that loss companies have abnormally high inventories but profitable ones do not. This supports the notion of high levels of goods or raw materials in the stocks. The low cash flow for loss firms is consistent with this result because the acquisition of raw materials or an increased production decreases cash. There are positive and significant (5% level) amounts for the overall and loss groups while the profitable subgroup is insignificant. Again, a differentiation between subgroups is useful.

In year -2, the results for inventories confirm the findings of no sales management and display no significance. In year +3, inventories are not managed significantly for all groups. In the Internet industry, findings are consistent with the alternative hypothesis H-dInv 1 for all groups. There is a significant difference for discretionary expenses between both year groups for all categories of companies. Significant results are only existent in years -1 to +2. The other years are insignificant for all groups. Internet companies are the only ones which display significantly negative values for any company. However, negative discretion for inventories was rather expected for Manufacturing and Trade industries. The findings underline the importance of differentiating between profitable and loss companies. Furthermore, the results back that there are differences between industries.

6.3.1.8.3 Technology

In the Technology industry, the results for the pre-IPO year for inventories indicate that loss firms have abnormally high inventories in the year before the IPO. This might be due to preparing for increased sales. Contrarily, profitable companies do not show any significance and probably intend to keep positive earnings. The overall and loss groups are positive and significant (5% level). In year +1, inventory results support the idea that companies inflate inventories to be prepared for higher sales resulting from lowering prices, more lenient credit terms, or channel stuffing, for example. All three groups indicate highly significant and positive results. In year +2, the findings for inventories give again a clear picture of abnormally high values for all groups. This might point out that the companies intend to produce more goods for sale or storage as well as the acquisition of commodities. All results are highly significant and positive.

In year -2, the results for inventories are mixed. The findings are positive and significant (10% level) for the profitable group whereas the others are insignificant. In year +3, the outcomes for inventories of profitable firms are in line with sales management and cash flow management. These firms have abnormally high inventories and high sales but low cash flow. This is supported by the low COGS which indicate more sold products. The loss group indicates no increased inventory. Profitable firms are highly and positively significant while loss companies do not exhibit any significance. The overall sample is also significant (5% level). These ambiguous findings support the notion to divide the overall group into subgroups. In the Technology industry, the findings are consistent with the alternative hypothesis H-dInv 1 for the overall and loss groups, but not for the profitable group. The latter one depicts significant results in every year except in -1. There is a significant difference for discretionary expenses between both year groups for all three categories. Almost all results in years -1 to +2 around the IPO are significant. However, also years -2 and +3 are missing only few significant results. Technology companies seem to manage inventories more often than any other industry which is rather surprising.

6.3.1.8.4 Construction

In the Construction industry, the pre-IPO year depicts no discretion in inventories. While all groups depict positive amounts, none of these is significant. In year +1, the profitable group exhibits a positive and significant amount (10% level). In year +2, inventories indicate that the profitable group manages this line item upward. This outcome is in line with positive sales management from above. The loss group does not manage sales but neither has abnormal inventories. There is positive significance (5% level) for the overall and profitable groups but insignificance for the loss group.

In year -2, there are only seven observations for the overall sample (insignificant). In year +3, the results for inventories indicate no significant behavior. In the Construction industry, findings are consistent with the alternative hypothesis H-dInv 1 for the overall and profitable groups, but not for the very small loss group. There is a significant difference for discretionary expenses between the year groups in two categories (overall and profitable companies). Significant results are only present in years -1 to +2 while years -2 and +3 are insignificant in every group. However, year -2 has only few observations. Construction companies do not deflate inventories, but rather increase them. The Construction industry has some overlaps with each industry, but none of them is more similar to the Construction industry than the others.

6.3.1.8.5 Wholesale

In the Wholesale industry, the pre-IPO year depicts no discretion in inventories. In the post-IPO year, the findings for inventories systematically indicate that profitable companies in the first year after the IPO exhibit abnormally high discretionary amounts. This is in line with sales management for the profitable group. The results for the overall and profitable groups are highly significant while for the loss group results are insignificant. This is a striking difference between subgroups. In year +2, inventories of the profitable group are insignificant. However, the overall and loss samples depict positive and significant results.

In year -2, inventories exhibit the most striking findings for seven observations. The overall sample is highly significant with negative amounts. This might result from artificially decreasing costs and can explain the positive abnormal cash flow although R&D and SG&A are positive, however, all insignificant. In year +3, as expected, inventories are unmanaged. In the Wholesale industry, the outcomes are unclear. They indicate findings consistent with the alternative hypothesis H-dInv 1 for the overall group but not for the subgroups. As expected, there is a significant difference between years -1 to +2 and the years of -2 and +3, however, in year -2 there are only few observations. Since year -2 includes too few observations, the hypothesis cannot be finally tested for the subgroups, although they exhibit significant results in years +1 and +2. There are no significant results in years -1 and +3. Interestingly, inventories are abnormally high in years +1 and +2 and abnormally low in year -2. Firms do not seem to lower these costs but rather need inventories for higher sales. The Wholesale industry has some overlaps with each industry, but is not more similar to a specific one than to any other.

6.3.1.9 Hypothesis COGS 1

6.3.1.9.1 Biotech

The results for the hypotheses are arranged by industry (Biotech, Internet, Technology, Construction, and Wholesale) and within them by year group (-1 to +2 versus -2 and +3), with all three groups of companies (overall sample, profitable, and loss groups). The results represent tests for the basic hypothesis and hypothesis COGS 1: In years -1 to +2 companies use discretion proportionately more frequently in COGS than in years -2 and +3 around an IPO.

Table 22 demonstrates results for COGS. In the Biotech industry, the results for the pre-IPO year indicate that the COGS model is positively significant for all groups. In the post-IPO year, COGS are abnormally high. This indicates underproduction, price discounts, or that young companies are producing similar sales levels as established companies at higher costs. All these issues have a positive effect on COGS relative to sales. Price discounts could explain abnormally high sales and abnormally low cash flow for loss firms. All groups indicate positive and significant results (1% or 5% levels). In year +2, COGS show significance for the profitable sample at the 10% level. Interestingly, this is the only (non-aggregated) significant value for the profitable group in year +2 for all employed accounting items. Since the profitable sample is quite small in the Biotech industry and the positive significance is present in three consecutive years, this might result from abnormally high costs to produce goods. The reason for loss firms to differ in this account can be traced back to influenced sales in each year which bias COGS.

In year -2, the results for COGS show insignificant amounts. Yet, the profitable group includes only four observations. In year +3, the COGS model detects again a positive and significant amount for the profitable sample (10% level), only. In the Biotech industry, the findings are consistent with the alternative hypothesis H-COGS 1 for the overall and loss groups while the result for the very small profitable group is not and is ambiguous in results for the basic hypothesis. There is a significant difference in COGS between the two year groups for the two categories of companies (overall and loss companies). On the one hand, there are three significant results for the profitable group in years -1 to +2, but there is one significant result in +3 and only four observations in year -2 which leaves that year with no finding. Therefore, the profitable group cannot be classified. As expected, there is a significant difference in COGS between years -1 to +2 and the years of -2 and +3 for the overall and loss groups. In fact, there is only one significant result in years +3 and -2 combined. Contrarily, years -1 and +1 exhibit significant findings for all groups, respectively. Interestingly, the positive significance of the profitable sample holds for years -1 through +3. A further remarking point is the positive significance for COGS which is almost exclusively existent in the Biotech industry while the other industries mainly exhibit no or negative significance.

The adjusted R-squared differs heavily between industries. In the growth industries, the value is relatively high with up to 73%, but even higher in the very profitable industries. Actually, the ratio increases for industries which are more profitable. It seems to be very high for industries selling tangible products.

Table 22: Discretionary COGS by Year, Group, and Industry

Year	-2			-1			+1			+2			+3		
	all	*profit.*	*loss*	*all*	*profit.*	*loss*	*all*	*profit.*	*loss*	*all*	*profit.*	*loss*	*all*	*profit.*	*loss*
Biotech															
COGS	-.018	--	.002	**.088*****	**.101***	**.085****	**.137*****	**.123****	**.140*****	-.008	**.090***	-.023	.008	**.108***	-.005
N	27	4	23	202	29	173	388	57	331	466	63	403	427	52	375
Adj. R^2	.324														
Internet															
COGS	-.025	.028	-.057	**-.115*****	**-.107****	**-.120*****	**-.132*****	**-.213*****	-.045	**-.035****	**-.040***	**-.032***	**-.039*****	**-.050****	**-.032***
N	24	9	15	388	147	241	891	459	432	952	392	560	834	327	507
Adj. R^2	.525														
Technology															
COGS	.043	0.31	.054	**-.041*****	-.029	**-.050****	-.007	**-.038*****	**.031***	**-.030*****	**-.047*****	-.015	**-.013***	**-.040*****	+.008
N	38	19	19	442	183	259	1'157	650	507	1'256	602	654	1'175	528	647
Adj. R^2	.730														
Construction															
COGS	-.092	-.103	--	.000	.016	-.030	-.004	-.004	-.006	.000	.002	-.009	**-.023****	**-.024***	-.023
N	7	5	2	56	37	19	183	142	41	201	161	40	192	136	56
Adj. R^2	.937														
Wholesale															
COGS	-.038	--	--	-.095	-.075	**-.161****	**-.061****	**-.062***	-.060	.009	.001	.030	-.018	-.019	-.017
N	7	4	3	75	58	17	202	162	40	234	170	64	218	147	71
Adj R^2	.948														

Notes: *, **, *** represent statistical significance at 10 percent, 5 percent, and 1 percent levels (two-sided), respectively (emphasized by bold type). The results are split by group: overall (all), profitable (profit.), and loss. Results show the means of discretionary COGS, the IPO sample size (N), and the mean adjusted R-squared (Adj. R^2) for the whole sample in one year (there are similar results in all years). Two consecutive hyphens (--) denote less than five available observations.

6.3.1.9.2 Internet

In the Internet industry, the results for the pre-IPO year indicate that companies overproduce or lower the costs of production. Concerning the first notion, sales are abnormally high for both groups which could trigger a positive effect, but obviously, inventories are increased. In the post-IPO year, COGS indicate overproduction for both subgroups. Low COGS indicate a good profit margin. All groups are negative and significant. In year +2, abnormal COGS are again significantly negative, yet, only at the 10% level in both subgroups. In this period, sales are significant for the overall sample while the subgroups would be significant only at the 11% level or higher.

In year -2, the results for COGS confirm the findings of no sales management and display no significance. In year +3, abnormal COGS are negative and significant for all three groups. In the Internet industry, findings are consistent with the alternative hypothesis H-COGS 1 for all groups. As expected, there is a significant difference in (discretionary) COGS between years -1 to +2 and years -2 and +3. In fact, the only invariably insignificant year is -2. In contrast to other industries, Internet companies depict consistently negative findings in four years for all groups. This underlines the difference to other industries. The additional industries diverge in frequency and sign of significant amounts. The industry that is somewhat likely is the Technology industry.

6.3.1.9.3 Technology

In the Technology industry, the results for the pre-IPO year support the findings above that loss companies overproduce. The results for the COGS model show negative significance for the overall and unprofitable groups. Interestingly, the significant positive inventory and significant negative COGS for loss firms cancel each other out in the summarized value of production costs and therefore, the costs do not show any significance. This underlines the importance of differentiating between line items and split aggregate measures. In the post-IPO year, the results for COGS point out negative significance for the profitable companies and positive significant results for the unprofitable group while the overall sample does not depict any significance. This finding supports the procedure to distinguish between the two subgroups. The abnormal result for the loss group is in line with abnormally high sales in all three measures. In year +2, results are in line with overproduction for profitable firms because COGS are low. The result for the loss group is insignificant.

In year -2, the results for abnormal COGS do not depict any significance. This is in line with no sales management. In year +3, the COGS model finds profitable firms to have abnormally low results while loss firms show no significance, but a positive sign. In the Technology industry, the findings are consistent with the alternative hypothesis H-COGS 1 for all groups. As expected, there is a significant difference in COGS between years -1 to +2 and the years of -2 and +3. There are two significant results in year +3 and none in year -2. In contrast to that finding, years -1 through +2 exhibit significant results each year. Interestingly, in almost all years of abnormal COGS sales management is present. However, low COGS can result from overproduction or manipulation of the inventory account, for example. This underlines the importance to test various accounting items and not only earnings. A further remarking point is that COGS in the Technology industry is hardly comparable to other industries, but the closest one is the Internet industry. The difference in industries is striking.

6.3.1.9.4 Construction

In the Construction industry, the results for the pre-IPO year exhibit no discretion in COGS. In the post-IPO years +1 and +2, COGS depict again no significant amounts. In year -2, the results for abnormal COGS are insignificant for the small overall sample of seven observations and the profitable group (five observations). In year +3, COGS are negative and significant for the overall and profitable samples. In the Construction industry, the findings do not reject the null hypothesis of H-COGS 1 for all groups. There is no significant difference between years -1 to +2 and the years of -2 and +3 because the only significance is present in year +3. Results for abnormal COGS in the Construction industry are hardly comparable to other industries. Company behavior differs between industries.

6.3.1.9.5 Wholesale

In the Wholesale industry, the results for the pre-IPO year are abnormally low for the loss sample. The model indicates significantly negative COGS for loss firms at the 10% level for 17 observations. In the post-IPO year, the COGS model detects an abnormally low amount for the overall and profitable groups. This is in line with the findings of high inventories. Since overproduction can lead to low COGS and high inventory costs. In year +2, abnormal COGS are insignificant.

Two years before the IPO, the results for abnormal COGS are insignificant for the overall sample while both subgroups include less than five observations each. Similarly, in year +3,

COGS indicate no discretion. In the Wholesale industry, the combined findings are consistent with the alternative hypothesis H-COGS 1 for all groups. There is a significant difference in COGS between years -1 to +2 and the years of -2 and +3. In fact, there are significant amounts only in years -1 and +1 while only one result is significant for each (sub-) group. Results for abnormal COGS in the Wholesale industry are not similar to other industries.

6.3.1.10 Hypothesis Production 1

6.3.1.10.1 Biotech

The results for the hypotheses are arranged by industry (Biotech, Internet, Technology, Construction, and Wholesale) and within them by year group (-1 to +2 versus -2 and +3), with all three groups of companies (overall sample, profitable, and loss groups). The results represent tests for the basic hypothesis and hypothesis production costs 1: In years -1 to +2 companies use discretion proportionately more frequently in production costs than in years -2 and +3 around an IPO.

Table 23 illustrates outcomes for production costs. In the Biotech industry in the pre-IPO year, the model includes 196 companies that show a significant positive sign for all three groups. This finding is consistent with the results for COGS and inventories. In the post-IPO year, the results for production costs confirm the findings in inventories and COGS again (and also mainly in operating cash flow[274]). The outcome indicates overproduction with high COGS, perhaps due to an increased demand after the IPO. The model displays a high significance for the overall sample which holds for the loss sample. Profitable firms are significant (5% level), too. In year +2, production costs are not significantly managed, except for the profitable sample. There is an insignificant and negative sign for the overall and loss samples while the profitable subgroup exhibits a positive and significant amount. The result for this group is in line with the finding for COGS and inventories.

The adjusted R-squared for Biotech companies is low while it increases in the other industries. The more profitable ones show higher amounts. However, 33% is already an acceptable amount in the earnings management literature.

[274] The cash flow is negatively influenced by other items such as R&D and SG&A, too.

Table 23: Discretionary Production Costs by Year, Group, and Industry

Year	-2			-1			+1			+2			+3		
	all	*profit.*	*loss*	*all*	*profit.*	*loss*	*all*	*profit.*	*loss*	*all*	*profit.*	*loss*	*all*	*profit.*	*loss*
Biotech															
Prod	-.026	--	-.006	**.093********	**.127***	**.087****	**.143*****	**.119****	**.147*****	-.013	**.082***	-.028	.000	**.092***	-.012
N	27	4	23	196	29	167	381	56	325	461	63	398	426	52	374
Adj. R^2	.339														
Internet															
Prod	-.019	.017	-.041	**-.091*****	**-.092****	**-.090*****	**-.094*****	**-.196*****	.014	-.002	-.017	.007	**-.032****	-.037	**-.029***
N	24	9	15	379	146	233	876	452	424	934	385	549	824	321	503
Adj. R^2	.545														
Technology															
Prod	.057	.048	.068	-.013	-.023	-.005	**.031*****	-.011	**.087*****	-.002	**-.017***	.011	.004	**-.019***	**.024****
N	37	19	18	438	182	256	1'142	645	497	1'251	600	651	1'168	526	642
Adj. R^2	.737														
Construction															
Prod	-.101	-.127	--	.001	.020	-.036	.019	.017	.026	.009	.016	-.018	**-.022***	-.018	-.029
N	7	5	2	56	37	19	181	141	40	201	161	40	191	135	56
Adj. R^2	.939														
Wholesale															
Prod	.011	--	--	-.098	-.085	**-.150***	.009	.010	.003	**.045***	.038	.062	-.008	-.006	-.013
N	7	4	3	73	58	15	201	161	40	230	167	63	217	146	71
Adj. R^2	.950														

Notes: *, **, *** represent statistical significance at 10 percent, 5 percent, and 1 percent levels (two-sided), respectively (emphasized by bold type). The results are split by group: overall (all), profitable (profit.), and loss. Results show the means of discretionary production costs (Prod), the IPO sample size (N), and the mean adjusted R-squared (Adj. R^2) for the whole sample in one year (there are similar results in all years). Two consecutive hyphens (--) denote less than five available observations.

In year -2, the outcomes for abnormal production costs are consistent with the findings of inventories and COGS. This means productions costs are not influenced two years before the IPO, but all results depict a negative sign. The profitable group includes too few observations. In year +3, profitable firms indicate abnormal production costs which are significantly high and for unprofitable ones insignificantly low. Outcomes are in accord with the findings for COGS. In the Biotech industry, the findings are consistent with the alternative hypothesis H-Prod 1 for the overall and loss groups whereas the profitable group cannot be taken into account due to missing observations in year -2. There is a significant difference in (discretionary) production costs between years -1 to +2 and the years of -2 and +3, except for the profitable group. The model discovers significant results in years -1 to +3 and none in year -2. Results for abnormal production costs in the Biotech industry are scarcely comparable to other industries.

6.3.1.10.2 Internet

In the Internet industry, the results for the pre-IPO year show that production costs agree with the results of inventory and COGS. The model supports the negative significance of both subgroups and the overall sample from prior results. In the post-IPO year, the aggregate measure of production costs again supports the findings of the two aforementioned line items and directs to low amounts for the profitable sample and insignificant values for the unprofitable one. There is high significance of negative amounts for the overall and profitable samples but no significance for the unprofitable one. In year +2, the results for production costs are insignificant. Interestingly, the results from the positive inventory and the negative COGS neutralize each other. This underlines the importance to split up measures and not only analyzing the aggregate items.

In year -2, the results for abnormal production costs indicate no discretion. Similarly, in year +3, the result mainly transports the findings for inventory and COGS. The model indicates significant values for the overall and loss groups while the profitable sample is insignificant. Interestingly, COGS were abnormally negative for the profitable group, but insignificant and positive for inventories which results in a negative but not significant amount of production costs. Splitting up the aggregate measure increases the information for investors. In the Internet industry, the findings are consistent with the alternative hypothesis H-Prod 1 for the overall and profitable groups, but not for the loss group. There is a significant difference in production costs between years -1 to +2 and years -2 and +3 for the overall as well as the profitable group, respectively. In fact, there are significant results in years -1, +1, and +3 but none in the others. Results for abnormal production costs in the Internet industry are scarcely comparable to other industries. It is the only industry with many significantly negative results.

6.3.1.10.3 Technology

In the Technology industry, the results for the pre-IPO year exhibit insignificant amounts for all groups. Contrarily to these findings, the outcome for inventory is significantly positive and for COGS significantly negative which result in overall insignificance. This underlines the importance of splitting up production costs into inventories and COGS to get a better insight. In the post-IPO year, the aggregate measure of production costs supports the prior findings for the loss group. These firms do not try to avoid even more negative income as long as sales and R&D are abnormally high which is important for investors. While the overall group is also significant, the profitable group is negative and insignificant. This is due to the fact that the profitable group had opposing results for inventories and COGS, which leaves production costs with the mixture of the findings. Again, splitting up the aggregate measure of production costs helps in interpretation of results. Interestingly, the two subgroups show opposing signs and underline the importance of the procedure to divide the overall sample into subgroups. In year +2, production costs partly confirm the findings of the aforementioned models. The profitable group exhibits highly significant positive results in the inventories and highly significantly negative ones in COGS, resulting in significantly (10% level) positive outcomes. As in the prior year, this finding is interesting for future research. The loss group indicates significantly positive results in inventories but insignificant and negative findings for COGS, resulting in positive insignificant amounts of production costs.

In year -2, the results for abnormal production costs indicate that the combined measure is insignificant. In year +3, the aggregate measure of production costs exhibits interesting results. While there is negative significance for the profitable sample the loss group is positive and significant. For profitable firms this is in line with the notion that negative values for COGS are lower than the positive values for inventories, resulting in negative production costs. Again, it is important to divide aggregate measures into the corresponding line items for a better insight. For loss companies, the positive values of COGS and inventories combined in the production costs find the amount to be positive and significant. In the Technology industry, the findings are consistent with the alternative hypothesis H-Prod 1 for the overall sample, but not for separate profitable and loss groups. There is a significant difference between years -1 to +2 and the years of -2 and +3 for the overall sample, only. In fact, there is only one significant result for the overall sample. Results for abnormal production costs in the Technology industry are scarcely comparable to other industries. It is the only industry with a significantly positive and negative result in the same year.

6.3.1.10.4 Construction

In the Construction industry, the results for the pre-IPO year indicate no discretion. This is in line with the findings of inventory and COGS. In the post-IPO year, the model for production costs neither indicates any systematic pattern. The results for the profitable group cancel each other out by opposing signs. In year +2, the aggregate measure is insignificant for all samples, although inventories are significant.

In year -2, the results for abnormal production costs depict that there are few observations. The model includes only seven observations in the overall sample and five of them in the profitable group. In year +3, the aggregate measure is negative and significant at the 10% level for the overall sample while the subgroups are not. The significant value is in agreement with the COGS model. In the Construction industry, the findings do not reject the null hypothesis of H-Prod 1 for all groups. There is no significant difference between the two year groups. The model depicts only one significant result which is in year +3. In fact, there is a lack of observations in year -2. Results for abnormal production costs in the Construction industry are best comparable to the similarly insignificant Wholesale industry but not to the other groups. In the Construction as well as in the Wholesale industries, the R-squared exhibits extremely high amounts. This accentuates the importance to handle this figure with caution. On the one hand, it gives hints about the fit of the model whereas on the other hand, it can be influenced by economic or statistical factors.[275] Apart from that it is obvious that the model seems much better fitted for the well-established industries than for the others.

6.3.1.10.5 Wholesale

In the Wholesale industry, the results for the pre-IPO year of production costs pick up the opposing results of inventory and COGS. The model indicates a negative and significant amount for the loss group. In the post-IPO year, the aggregate measure points out no discretionary behavior in any model. The model combines the significant positive results from inventories and negative results of COGS for the profitable sample to an insignificant amount. This underlines the importance to split production costs into inventories and COGS to get

[275] Comiskey (1972); Gordon (1972).

more specific hints about the behavior of IPO firms. In year +2, the aggregate measure of production costs mainly supports the prior results. Only the overall group is significant and comparable to the result for inventories.

In year -2, the results for abnormal production costs include only seven observations in the overall and less than five in each subgroup. In year +3, the aggregate measure is consistent with findings for inventory and COGS which designate that no discretionary behavior is present in any group. In the Wholesale industry, the findings indicate consistency with the alternative hypothesis H-Prod 1 for the overall group, but not for the profitable and loss groups. There is a significant difference between the year groups for the overall group, only. However, the model depicts merely one significant result in year -1 and year +2, respectively. Furthermore, there are too few observations in year -2 for the subgroups. Interesting findings are the opposing results of inventory and COGS in year +1 which lead to an insignificant mixture of production costs. Again, the importance of splitting up the aggregate measure is visible. Results for abnormal production costs in the Wholesale industry are best comparable to the similarly insignificant Construction industry.

6.3.1.11 Hypothesis GAS 1

6.3.1.11.1 Biotech

The results for the hypotheses are arranged by industry (Biotech, Internet, Technology, Construction, and Wholesale) and within them by year group (-1 to +2 versus -2 and +3), with all three groups of companies (overall sample, profitable, and loss groups). The results represent tests for the basic hypothesis and the hypothesis gain on asset sales 1: In years -1 to +2 companies use discretion proportionately more frequently in gain on asset sales than in years -2 and +3 around an IPO.

Table 24 shows results for gain on asset sales. In the Biotech industry, the results for the pre-IPO year indicate that gains from assets sales are not of any interest for Biotech-based firms. Since they are not well-established yet, they probably do not possess enough property and investments for sale. The results are insignificant. In the post-IPO year, abnormal gain on asset sales is again very low. In year +2, companies similarly rather sell abnormally fewer of their assets, depicting an insignificant and negative sign. This might be the case due to the buildup of the young companies which are still growing and cannot afford to sell invested assets.

Table 24: Discretionary Gain on Asset Sales by Year, Group, and Industry

Year	-2			-1			+1			+2			+3		
	all	*profit.*	*loss*	*all*	*profit.*	*loss*	*all*	*profit.*	*loss*	*all*	*profit.*	*loss*	*all*	*profit.*	*loss*
Biotech															
GAS	.000	--	-.000	-.000	-.000	-.000	.000	-.000	.000	-.000	-.000	-.000	**-.000*****	.000	**-.000*****
N	18	4	14	107	14	93	250	35	215	279	39	240	273	30	243
Adj. R^2	.157														
Internet															
GAS	-.000	-.000	.000	.000	.000	.000	**.000****	-.000	**.000*****	**-.000*****	**-.000****	**-.000****	-.000	-.000	-.000
N	18	7	11	254	87	167	541	276	265	546	224	322	489	193	296
Adj. R^2	.040														
Technology															
GAS	.000	.000	.000	**-.000***	-.000	-.000	**-.000****	-.000	-.000	**-.000***	-.000	**-.000***	-.000	-.000	-.000
N	22	13	9	291	130	161	724	424	300	813	412	401	779	377	402
Adj. R^2	.073														
Construction															
GAS	--	--	--	**.001***	.001	--	.000	.000	.000	**-.000****	-.000	**-.001***	-.000	-.000	.000
N	0	0	0	12	8	4	46	37	9	45	35	10	47	35	12
Adj. R^2	.013														
Wholesale															
GAS	--	--	--	.000	-.000	--	.000	-.000	.000	-.000	-.000	-.000	-.000	.000	**-.000****
N	2	1	1	22	19	3	59	49	10	62	46	16	64	42	22
Adj. R^2	.264														

Notes: *, **, *** represent statistical significance at 10 percent, 5 percent, and 1 percent levels (two-sided), respectively (emphasized by bold type). The results are split by group: overall (all), profitable (profit.), and loss. Results show the means of discretionary gain on asset sales (GAS), the IPO sample size (N), and the mean adjusted R-squared (Adj. R^2) for the whole sample in one year (there are similar results in all years). Two consecutive hyphens (--) denote less than five available observations.

In year -2, the results for abnormal GAS point out that no discretion takes place. This was expected because of the young age of the Biotech companies. In fact, the result of the model is very close to zero and insignificant. Year +3 finds that loss companies avoid selling assets. This might be due to the growth phase of these companies where they cannot afford to sell assets and rather invest. The model displays a negative sign and significance (5% level) for the loss sample. The signs for the profitable sample are positive and insignificant. In the Biotech industry, the findings do not reject the null hypothesis of H-GAS 1 for all groups. There is no significant difference between the year groups for any group of companies. While no result is significant for years -1 to +2, the only significant result exists in year +3. Biotech companies usually are very young and rarely sell assets at this early stage of establishing the company. Interestingly, prior literature expected companies to influence results by managing GAS. However, this is not the case for the Biotech industry. Results for abnormal GAS in the Biotech industry are best comparable to the similarly insignificant Wholesale industry.

6.3.1.11.2 Internet

In the Internet industry, the results for the pre-IPO year indicate no significant results for GAS. However, results are positive and point out an abnormal high value of selling assets which is not present in the Biotech industry. In the post-IPO year, GAS support the notion of loss firms selling assets to increase earnings or have more cash available for investments in R&D and SG&A. Since earnings accruals are still abnormally low, but R&D and SG&A are abnormally high, the latter explanation is favored. The model finds positive and significant (1% or 5% levels) amounts for the overall and loss groups, only. In year +2, results for abnormal GAS indicate that Internet companies sell significantly fewer assets. This is especially coherent with the prior year findings for the loss companies, which sell abnormally many assets and now have to return and sell abnormally fewer assets. Furthermore, in the current year no abnormal R&D and SG&A are present which support the prior interpretation. This outcome might be due to the young age of companies that go public and do not have many assets yet to sell for cash or earnings increases. The model finds strong negative significance for all three groups.

In year -2, the results for abnormal GAS point out that no discretion is present. Equally, year +3 finds insignificant results. In the Internet industry, the findings are consistent with the alternative hypothesis H-GAS 1 for all groups. There is a significant difference between years -1 to +2 and years -2 and +3. Interestingly, prior literature expected companies to influence results by managing GAS upward. However, this is not the case for the Internet industry. Results for abnormal GAS in this industry are especially high in year +1 and low in the following year. This suggests that after one year of discretion by selling assets, the amount has to reverse in the short-term and depicts abnormally few gains for loss firms. Furthermore, loss firms seem to spend this extra cash for investments in R&D and SG&A. The Internet industry is hardly comparable to any other industry. This difference to the other industries backs the procedure to distinguish between sectors.

6.3.1.11.3 Technology

In the Technology industry, the results for the pre-IPO year indicate that GAS is not systematically influenced in the subgroups, but in the overall group. The model finds a negative significance (10% level) for the overall sample while both subgroups are insignificant. Obviously, firms do not sell assets to inflate earnings but they are rather busy with establishing the company and do not have assets to sell yet. In the post-IPO year, the outcomes for GAS indicate again that growing firms do not yet have enough assets to sell for short-term income increase. In fact, abnormal GAS is significantly low for the overall sample but insignificantly for the subgroups. In year +2, GAS displays that loss firms have abnormally low amounts which indicates that these companies are growing and they are not able to sell as much assets as their comparable counterparts.

In year -2, the results for abnormal GAS point out that no discretion is present. Equally, in year +3, the model for GAS finds no significant behavior. In the Technology industry, the findings are consistent with the alternative hypothesis H-GAS 1 for the overall and loss groups, but not for the profitable group. There is a significant difference in discretionary GAS between years -1 to +2 and years -2 and +3, except for the profitable group. In fact, the only significant results are present in the first time interval. Interestingly, prior literature expected companies to manage GAS upward to influence earnings. However, this is not the case for the Technology industry. Results for abnormal GAS in this industry are rather abnormally low. This suggests that companies are young, growing, and still establish the company with few assets available for sale. The Technology industry is hardly comparable to any other industry, except that there are only a few significant results.

6.3.1.11.4 Construction

In the Construction industry, the results for the pre-IPO year indicate systematic discretion in the behavior of firms for the overall sample only, because the sample size is quite small. However, all results are positive. The significance of the overall sample is at the 10% level. In the post-IPO year, the findings are positive again, but point out that companies do not manage this line item. In year +2, the findings are abnormally low for the overall and loss groups. The outcomes indicate that companies from both groups sell assets rather conservatively. This might result from the two prior years, where the abnormal findings were positive and have to reverse now, when incentives decline.

In year -2, results for abnormal GAS are not analyzed due to missing observations. In year +3, GAS indicates no discretionary behavior for this industry. In the Construction industry, the findings are consistent with the alternative hypothesis H-GAS 1 for the overall group, but not for the two subgroups. There is a significant difference between years -1 to +2 and years -2 and +3 in the overall group. In fact, the only significant results exist in years -1 and +2 while year -2 includes no observations. Interestingly, prior literature expected companies to manage GAS upward to influence earnings. This could not be proven, but a slight tendency in favor of this argument exists. Remarkably, as expected, this was detected in the Construction industry, where tangible assets play the most important role of all included industries. Results for abnormal GAS in this industry are rather not comparable to any other, except that there are only a few significant results.

6.3.1.11.5 Wholesale

In the Wholesale industry, the results for the pre-IPO year point out that there is no discretion for the overall and profitable groups while the unprofitable one includes too few observations. In the post-IPO year, results for GAS indicate no discretionary behavior and find no significant amounts. In year +2, GAS is unmanaged.

In year -2, results for abnormal GAS cannot be analyzed due to missing observations. Finally, in year +3, results seem to be abnormally low for the loss firms. This indicates that loss companies probably sold too many assets around the IPO when findings were abnormally positive and reverse now. In the Wholesale industry, the findings do not reject the null hypothesis of H-GAS 1 for all groups. There is a significant difference between years -1 to +2 and years -2 and +3. In fact, the only significant results occur in year +3. Interestingly, while

GAS is abnormally positive for loss firms, yet not significant in the two years around the IPO, they are negatively significant when incentives decline. This suggests that companies use discretion to a certain level around the IPO. Prior literature expected companies to manage GAS upward to influence earnings. This could not be proved, but a slight tendency in favor of this argument is present. Results for abnormal GAS in this industry are best comparable to the Biotech industry, but both include almost no significant result. This variation in industries supports the procedure to distinguish between them.

6.3.2 Results for Specific Industries

6.3.2.1 High-Growth vs. Well-Established Industries

6.3.2.1.1 Hypothesis R&D 2

The results for the group specific hypotheses are ordered as above. Table 25 shows the summary of the following outcomes while single amounts are reported in the subsequent tables.[276] During IPOs, there can be a differentiation between high-growth and well-established industries and companies.[277] High-growth companies (mainly in unprofitable industries around IPOs) use R&D as a signal to investors to point out future benefits rather than currently increasing income. On the other hand, well-established companies (mainly in profitable industries around IPOs) are dependent on positive earnings to a larger extent. A corresponding hypothesis (H-R&D 2) is that companies in high-growth industries (Biotech, Internet, and Technology) use positive discretion in R&D proportionately more frequently in years -1 to +2 than companies in well-established industries (Construction and Wholesale).

[276] It is important to note that the rejection or non-rejection of hypotheses is decided as follows: For example, if in the Biotech industry the overall group is significant compared to the established industries, then the null hypotheses is rejected. However, too few observations in the profitable industries lead to no result and the null hypothesis cannot be rejected although growth industries may have 100% significant results. Like in hypothesis set one, this is a conservative approach within this study.

[277] The differentiation of industries into growth and profitability is dependent on the years around the IPO and is not the designation for the industry in general.

Table 25: Summary for Hypotheses Concerning the Growth of Industries

	R&D 2	SG&A 2	Adv 2	DisExp 2
Biotech				
All	+	+	0	+
Profitable	0	+	0	+
Loss	+	+	0	+
Internet				
All	+	+	+	+
Profitable	+	+	--	+
Loss	+	+	--	+
Technology				
All	+	+	+	+
Profitable	+	+	--	+
Loss	+	+	--	+

Notes: 0 = the results do not reject the null hypothesis of no discretionary behavior. + = null hypothesis is rejected, meaning that discretionary behavior exists. -- = two consecutive hyphens (--) denote too few available observations. R&D 2, SG&A 2, Adv 2, or DisExp 2 = hypothesis R&D 2, SG&A 2, Adv 2, or DisExp 2, respectively.

The outcomes support the findings in the finance literature and give a new insight into accounting behavior around IPOs.[278] Prior accounting studies mainly expected R&D being deflated to reach earnings targets. However, growing companies use R&D around IPOs as a signal for future benefits to investors.

Table 26 illustrates outcomes for the industry comparison. The results for Biotech companies indicate that most groups and all three years are significant, except for the profitable groups in years +1 and +2. These results indicate that overinvestment in R&D is not equally important as for unprofitable companies. It is probable that for the profitable companies R&D is not biased to arrive at a positive net income. This is coherent with the high percentage of profitable firms in year +1 and conservative R&D spending. The outcome for Internet companies is systematic, too. All results are significantly positive in all years and groups, except for the profitable group in year +2. This designates that the Internet industry uses discretion in R&D to demonstrate future benefits. Again, profitable companies seem to overinvest less. The Technology industry also depicts mainly significant and positive outcomes for all groups in all three years, except for the unprofitable group in year +1. In contrast to these results, the findings for the Construction and Wholesale industries point out only rare significant amounts. Actually, in the Construction industry the only significant

[278] Lévesque et al. (2012); Fedyk et al. (2012).

results exist in the pre-IPO year for the overall and the profitable groups (10% level) for 17 and 11 observations, respectively. Similarly, the Wholesale industry exhibits only two significant results. The findings are consistent with the alternative hypothesis H-R&D 2 that all (sub-) groups of companies in high-growth industries (Biotech, Internet, and Technology) use positive discretion in R&D proportionately more frequently in years -1 to +2 compared to the more established industries (Construction and Wholesale). There is a significant difference in discretionary R&D between the two groups of companies. The result supports the notion that industries diverge and should be handled differently around the IPO.

Table 26: Discretionary R&D: Industry Comparison

Year	-1			+1			+2		
	all	*profit.*	*loss*	*all*	*profit.*	*loss*	*all*	*profit.*	*loss*
Biotech									
R&D	**.060*****	**.059****	**.060*****	**.053*****	.002	**.061*****	**.012***	.010	**.012***
N	133	20	113	283	42	241	334	51	283
Adj. R^2	.805								
Internet									
R&D	**.023*****	**.026*****	**.021*****	**.018*****	**.012*****	**.024*****	**.006****	.003	**.008***
N	285	99	186	641	333	308	674	277	397
Adj. R^2	.764								
Technology									
R&D	**.013*****	**.012*****	**.014*****	**.006*****	**.007*****	.004	**.009*****	**.008*****	**.010*****
N	330	149	181	871	527	344	969	497	472
Adj. R^2	.798								
Construction									
R&D	**.007****	**.008***	.005	-.001	.000	-.007	-.002	-.002	-.002
N	17	11	6	66	53	13	69	56	13
Adj. R^2	.768								
Wholesale									
R&D	.000	-.000	.004	.000	-.000	**.002***	.000	**.000****	-.000
N	29	24	5	77	62	15	80	64	16
Adj. R^2	.889								

Notes: *, **, *** represent statistical significance at 10 percent, 5 percent, and 1 percent levels (two-sided), respectively (emphasized by bold type). The results are split by group: overall (all), profitable (profit.), and loss. Results show the means of discretionary R&D expenses, the IPO sample size (N), and the mean adjusted R-squared (Adj. R^2) for the whole sample in one year (there are similar results in all years).

6.3.2.1.2 Hypothesis SG&A 2

A similar issue as for R&D is present for SG&A expenses. There can be a differentiation between high-growth and well-established (slower growth) companies in industries around IPOs. While prior accounting literature suggests the notion that managers cut SG&A to increase earnings and cash flow,[279] the finance literature postulates that high-growth companies (in mainly unprofitable industries) use SG&A as a signal to investors to point out future revenue growth.[280] The resulting hypothesis (H-SG&A 2) states that in years -1 to +2 companies in high-growth industries (Biotech, Internet, and Technology) use positive discretion in SG&A proportionately more frequently than companies in well-established industries (Construction and Wholesale). The corresponding outcomes support the findings in the finance literature and give a new insight into accounting behavior of issuers around IPOs.

Table 27 depicts outcomes of discretionary SG&A for the comparison of industries. The results for the Biotech companies are systematically positive for all groups in the first two years while year +2 indicates no significance. In the pre-IPO year, the model of SG&A finds significance (at least at the 5% level) for all groups. In the post-IPO year, all results are highly significant at the 1% level in favor of the alternative hypothesis which means more positive discretion is present. However, year +2 exhibits no positive significance. The outcome for Internet companies is even more significant. In all three groups and the first two years (years -1 and +1) the abnormal amounts are highly significant (1% level). However, year +2 indicates no significance. The findings for the last growth industry, including Technology companies, are equal to the Internet industry in the first two years. Additionally, in year +2, results are again significant for all groups.

As expected from the theory and hypotheses, R-squared is higher for growth companies than for well-established industries. This emphasizes the importance of SG&A for specific groups of companies and points out that discretion in certain line is meaningful to particular companies, only.

---

[279] Gunny (2010), p. 857.
[280] Lévesque et al. (2012), pp. 47-48.

Table 27: Discretionary SG&A: Industry Comparison

Year	-1			+1			+2		
	all	*profit.*	*loss*	*all*	*profit.*	*loss*	*all*	*profit.*	*loss*
Biotech									
SG&A	**.169*****	**.112****	**.194*****	**.234*****	**.168*****	**.269*****	-.054	-.029	-.066
N	80	24	56	133	46	87	164	52	112
Adj. R^2	.453								
Internet									
SG&A	**.163*****	**.110*****	**.196*****	**.246*****	**.210*****	**.285*****	-.006	.011	-.020
N	370	141	229	818	428	390	852	366	486
Adj. R^2	.398								
Technology									
SG&A	**.109*****	**.068*****	**.139*****	**.127*****	**.113*****	**.146*****	**.025*****	**.023*****	**.026*****
N	408	174	234	1'072	629	443	1'153	582	571
Adj. R^2	.466								
Construction									
SG&A	-.021	-.047	.032	-.004	-.018	**.045*****	-.004	-.006	.007
N	55	37	18	177	139	38	193	156	37
Adj. R^2	.390								
Wholesale									
SG&A	.031	.004	**.123****	.009	.004	.031	-.009	-.008	-.010
N	75	58	17	194	156	38	229	166	63
Adj. R^2	.179								

Notes: *, **, *** represent statistical significance at 10 percent, 5 percent, and 1 percent levels (two-sided), respectively (emphasized by bold type). The results are split by group: overall (all), profitable (profit.), and loss. Results show the means of discretionary SG&A expenses, the IPO sample size (N), and the mean adjusted R-squared (Adj. R^2) for the whole sample in one year.

The outcome for the rather established companies in the Construction industry gives an interesting insight. While the profitable group is insignificant and negative in all years, the loss group seems to prefer the strengthening of growth indicators over inflation of earnings and cash flow. Obviously, profitable and loss companies apply opposed influence in SG&A around the IPO (in years -1 to +2). This supports the notion that further research has to differentiate between these two groups of companies in that specific accounting item. Evidently, loss companies expect investors to value other line items than earnings and cash flow. Therefore, they partly influence the respective accounting items that presumably bring future benefits.

The second industry with established companies is the Wholesale industry. The results are more similar to the Construction industry than to the aforementioned industries, but not equal. On the one hand, profitable companies are insignificant, but exhibit mainly positive amounts.

On the other hand, the results for loss companies are also positive in the first two years and even significant in year -1. Again, this supports the notion that profitable and loss groups diverge or even depict opposing significant results. Loss companies seem to prefer slight overinvestments in SG&A rather than positively influencing earnings and cash flow for a better investor valuation.

The findings are consistent with the alternative hypothesis H-SG&A 2 that all (sub-) groups of companies in high-growth industries (Biotech, Internet, and Technology) use proportionately more frequently positive discretion in SG&A in years -1 to +2 than companies in well-established industries (Construction and Wholesale). There is a significant difference between the two groups of companies. The result supports the notion that industries diverge and should be handled differently around the IPO. Additionally, the subgroups of profitable versus loss companies differ in using discretion in well-established industries but not in growth industries. This finding supports further research for specific accounting items depending on industry and the (algebraic) sign of companies' income. Furthermore, the results indicate a slight difference of discretion in the R&D versus SG&A accounts while prior accounting literature mainly aggregated both in the discretionary expense model.

6.3.2.1.3 Hypothesis Advertising 2

Besides R&D and SG&A, advertising is the third part of discretionary expenses. It is rarely employed as a single measure in prior empirical literature, although managers emphasize the importance of this accounting item to influence investors.[281] Hypothesis (H-Adv 2) states that in years -1 to +2 companies in high-growth industries (Biotech, Internet, and Technology) use proportionately more frequently positive discretion in advertising than companies in well-established industries (Construction and Wholesale). Results of the present study confirm this behavior in most cases.

Table 28 points out the findings of advertising expenses for industry comparisons. The outcome for Biotech companies in the pre-IPO year includes only seven observations in the overall sample. In the following two years, there are still no significant results for around 30 observations. However, the Internet industry exhibits many significant amounts in the time interval. Only the loss group in year -1 and the three groups in year +2 are insignificant. The results for the Technology industry are mainly significant in the pre-IPO year and even

[281] Graham et al. (2005), p. 32.

stronger in the post-IPO year (for two groups, respectively) whilst year +2 indicates no significance (like in the Internet industry).

Table 28: Discretionary Advertising: Industry Comparison

Year	-1			+1			+2		
	all	*profit.*	*loss*	*all*	*profit.*	*loss*	*all*	*profit.*	*loss*
Biotech									
Adv	-.001	--	--	.005	-.000	.009	.004	-.001	.005
N	7	3	4	28	12	16	31	11	20
Adj. R^2	.162								
Internet									
Adv	**.010****	**.010****	**.010***	**.017*****	**.009****	**.024*****	.003	.007	.001
N	108	46	62	203	99	104	229	79	150
Adj. R^2	.077								
Technology									
Adv	**.006*****	**.013*****	.001	**.005*****	**.003***	**.008*****	-.000	-.002	.001
N	78	34	44	231	136	95	234	132	102
Adj. R^2	.093								
Construction									
Adv	--	--	--	-.003	-.001	--	-.015	--	--
N	4	4	0	10	8	2	7	4	3
Adj. R^2	.154								
Wholesale									
Adv	-.000	-.017	--	.000	-.009	--	-.003	-.006	.000
N	10	8	2	10	8	2	21	12	9
Adj. R^2	.049								

Notes: *, **, *** represent statistical significance at 10 percent, 5 percent, and 1 percent levels (one-sided), respectively (emphasized by bold type). The results are split by group: overall (all), profitable (profit.), and loss. Results show the means of discretionary advertising expenses (Adv), the IPO sample size (N), and the mean adjusted R-squared (Adj. R^2) for the whole sample in one year. Two consecutive hyphens (--) denote less than five available observations.

Construction companies indicate no significant results in any year and the findings are entirely negative. Yet, the time interval includes a small number of observations. Similarly, the Wholesale industry exhibits only one significant amount in all years and two unavailable values. Moreover, there are mainly negative abnormal amounts.

The findings are predominantly consistent with the alternative hypothesis H-Adv 2 that all (sub-) groups of companies in high-growth industries use proportionately more frequently positive discretion in advertising in years -1 to +2 than companies in well-established industries. There is a significant difference between the two groups of companies. This does not hold for the Biotech industry alone. Furthermore, the two subgroups of both profitable industries include too few observations for comparison. The result supports the notion that industries diverge and investors should be aware of that. Additionally, the subgroups of profitable versus loss companies differ in using discretion. This finding is corresponding to other research for specific accounting items depending on industry and sign of income. Furthermore, the results indicate a difference of discretion in advertising, R&D, and SG&A accounts while prior accounting literature mainly included all three in the discretionary expense model. Yet, cutting advertising can have a more immediate impact on sales than decreasing or increasing R&D or SG&A. In contrast to prior accounting literature, companies do not mainly cut spending in advertising to lower cash outflows and increase earnings, but increase this line item to influence capital market participants.

The results for R-squared show relatively low amounts compared to the other items, but still acceptable regarding the value for accruals. It has no specific industry group tendencies.

6.3.2.1.4 Hypothesis Discretionary Expenses 2

The aggregate measure of the three aforementioned accounting items is discretionary expense. Therefore, this account should have similar dimensions around IPOs as R&D, SG&A, and advertising combined. The corresponding hypothesis (H-DisExp 2) expects that in years -1 to +2 companies in high-growth industries (Biotech, Internet, and Technology) use proportionately more frequently positive influence in discretionary expenses than companies in well-established industries (Construction and Wholesale). Results of the present study confirm this behavior in almost all cases.

Table 29 illustrates results of discretionary expenses for the industry comparison. The Biotech industry exhibits significant amounts (at least at the 5% level) in the pre-IPO year in all three groups. The post-IPO year depicts very similar results with even high significance for all results. Year +2 indicates no positive significance. The Internet industry shows even stronger significant outcomes in years -1 and +1 and also no positive significance in year +2. The Technology industry even exhibits highly significant results for all amounts in all three years. Established industries differ from growth sectors.

Table 29: Abnormal Discretionary Expenses: Industry Comparison

Year	-1			+1			+2		
	all	*profit.*	*loss*	*all*	*profit.*	*loss*	*all*	*profit.*	*loss*
Biotech									
DisExp	**.267*****	**.197****	**.299*****	**.367*****	**.265*****	**.424*****	-.104	-.027	-.141
N	76	24	52	129	46	83	161	52	109
Adj. R^2	.280								
Internet									
DisExp	**.332*****	**.230*****	**.396*****	**.423*****	**.391*****	**.458*****	-.026	-.009	-.039
N	364	141	223	813	427	386	847	365	482
Adj. R^2	.237								
Technology									
DisExp	**.199*****	**.135*****	**.247*****	**.212*****	**.206*****	**.220*****	**.052*****	**.057*****	**.047*****
N	406	174	232	1'060	625	435	1'151	581	570
Adj. R^2	.348								
Construction									
DisExp	-.017	-.064	**.077****	.008	-.015	**.095*****	.010	.007	.025
N	55	37	18	176	138	38	193	156	37
Adj. R^2	.306								
Wholesale									
DisExp	**.050***	.016	**.184****	.025	.017	**.059***	.009	.009	.006
N	73	58	15	194	156	38	226	164	62
Adj. R^2	.152								

Notes: *, **, *** represent statistical significance at 10 percent, 5 percent, and 1 percent levels (one-sided), respectively (emphasized by bold type). The results are split by group: overall (all), profitable (profit.), and loss. Results show the means of abnormal discretionary expenses (DisExp), the IPO sample size (N), and the mean adjusted R-squared (Adj. R^2) for the whole sample in one year.

The Construction industry comprises two significant results for the loss group in years -1 and +1. The Wholesale industry exhibits similarly weak results. Three out of six amounts are significant, while the profitable group is insignificant in all years. The findings are consistent with the alternative hypothesis H-DisExp 2 that all (sub-) groups of companies in high-growth industries (Biotech, Internet, and Technology) use proportionately more frequently positive influence in discretionary expense in years -1 to +2 than companies in well-established industries (Construction and Wholesale). There is a significant difference between the two groups of companies. This does not hold for the loss subgroups. The results underline the difference between industries and the challenge for investors in evaluating companies. Additionally, the findings confirm the above notion that loss companies in well-established industries use overinvestment in future growth rather than cutting these expenses to increase income and cash flow. Future research should also address the difference in discretion in advertising, R&D, and SG&A accounts while prior accounting literature mainly included all three in the discretionary expense model. In sum, opposed to prior accounting literature, companies mainly do not cut spending in discretionary expense to lower cash outflows and increase income, but rather increase this line item to influence capital market participants.

6.3.2.2 Profitable vs. Unprofitable Industries

6.3.2.2.1 Hypothesis Earnings Accruals 2

The next hypothesis (H-Acc 2) concerns the profitable industries. It states that companies in profitable industries (Construction and Wholesale) show no earnings accruals management in year -1, but use positive discretion in year +1. The results are in line with prior literature that utilized post-IPO financial reports. However, studies that used pre-IPO reports find diverging results (no or conservative accruals management). This is also coherent with the presented findings for year -1. These analogous results dissolve the confusion of some prior studies regarding their different results when using dissimilar years.

As mentioned above, earnings accruals are the only line item that changes signs which are significant, from pre- to post-IPO years. This can explain the varying findings in prior literature. The outcomes are presented in Table 30. The results for the Construction industry exhibit no significance in the pre-IPO year. However, in the post-IPO year the modified Jones model is significantly positive for all groups. The overall and profitable groups are even highly significant. The Wholesale industry exhibits similar results. In the pre-IPO year, there are no significantly positive results. Findings for the post-IPO year point out significantly positive results for all groups (at least at the 5% level). Hence, the findings are consistent with the alternative hypothesis H-Acc 2 for all groups that companies in profitable industries (Construction and Wholesale) do not use discretion in the pre-IPO year, but use positive discretion in the post-IPO year. This is in line with many prior studies about positive earnings accruals management after or at IPOs, but the outcome contradicts some studies which argue for positive discretion before the listing. Therefore, the results dissolve misunderstandings between prior articles in separating specific years of examination. Interestingly, the results are very similar in the Technology industry. They are also mainly positive in the post-IPO year and not in the pre-IPO year. Increasing accruals can result in significantly positive accruals and finally in profitable companies to impress capital market participants and influence investors. These notions are in line with the presented outcomes.

Table 30: Discretionary Earnings Accruals: Profitable Industries

	Year	-1			+1		
		all	*profit.*	*loss*	*all*	*profit.*	*loss*
Construction							
	D.Acc	-.013	-.007	-.025	**.026*** **	**.024*** **	**.032***
	N	56	37	19	181	141	40
	Adj. R^2	.040					
Wholesale							
	D.Acc	-.022	-.016	-.046	**.032*** **	**.028*** **	**.044** **
	N	73	58	15	202	162	40
	Adj. R^2	.124					

Notes: *, **, *** represent statistical significance at 10 percent, 5 percent, and 1 percent levels (one-sided), respectively (emphasized by bold type). The results are split by group: overall (all), profitable (profit.), and loss. Results show the means of discretionary earnings accruals (D.Acc), the IPO sample size (N), and the mean adjusted R-squared (Adj. R^2) for the whole sample in one year.

6.3.2.2.2 Hypothesis Earnings Accruals 3

Other than growth versus well-established industries, there can be a differentiation of profitable versus unprofitable industries. The accruals-specific hypothesis (H-Acc 3) states that loss companies in unprofitable industries (Biotech and Internet) show negative earnings accruals in years -1 and +1, but positive accruals in year +2.

Table 31 illustrates outcomes for earnings accruals of unprofitable industries. Additionally to the findings of loss companies, the overall outcomes are presented, too, since they are very similar due to the large ratio of loss companies in these industries. For Biotech companies the results indicate that in the pre-IPO year there are very strong and significant amounts for the loss group. This is equally true for the post-IPO year while in both years the profitable group exhibits no significance (also for the one-sided test). In year +2, the loss group in the Biotech industry exhibits significant positive amounts. The results for the Internet industry are very similar. While in the pre-IPO year unprofitable Internet companies exhibit high significance (1% level) for the negative amounts, the post-IPO year indicates somewhat less significance. In year +2, the reversing effect is very strong and the abnormal positive amount is highly significant. The findings are consistent with the alternative hypothesis H-Acc 3 that only loss companies in unprofitable industries (Biotech and Internet) do not influence earnings accruals positively in the post-IPO year, but depict significantly negative amounts in the two years around the IPO and a reversing effect in year +2. The finding is coherent with Joos/Plesko

(2005) which indicates that on the one hand, subgroups of companies differ and on the other hand, companies (and investors) value other accounting items more when earnings are negative. If income is already negative, the dimension of the amount seems to be unimportant. This supports the low accruals which can result from deflating current accruals for future accruals inflation, for example. The future inflation exists in year +2 where it improves the valuation by investors. They are expected to evaluate firms more on earnings the longer the company is publicly traded. Furthermore, the results support Lévesque et al. (2012) that R&D spending is high for growth firms if earnings are negative because the examined industries are also included in the category of high-growth industries.[282] Since these industries include many observations, results seem reliable. Due to unprofitability of these industries other measures than accruals seem valuable because the R-squared is quite low.

Table 31: Discretionary Earnings Accruals: Unprofitable Industries

	Year	-1		+1		+2	
		all	*loss*	*all*	*loss*	*all*	*loss*
Biotech							
	D.Acc	**-.050*****	**-.058*****	**-.057*****	**-.066*****	**.011***	**.010***
	N	195	166	380	324	454	391
	Adj. R^2	.055					
Internet							
	D.Acc	**-.029*****	**-.037*****	-.006	**-.015***	**.020*****	**.027*****
	N	382	235	886	428	947	556
	Adj. R^2	.053					

Notes: *, **, *** represent statistical significance at 10 percent, 5 percent, and 1 percent levels (one-sided), respectively (emphasized by bold type). The results are split by group: overall (all) and loss. Results show the means of discretionary earnings accruals (D.Acc), the IPO sample size (N), and the mean adjusted R-squared (Adj. R^2) for the whole sample in one year.

6.3.3 Summary of Results

Chapters 6.3.1 and 6.3.2 outline the detailed findings of this study for both sets of hypotheses. Due to the large amount of single results, the summarized version is presented in this chapter. The hypotheses add further aspects and the outcomes fill gaps in prior literature.

The first set of hypotheses focuses on several aspects and answers specific disputes in current literature. First, it solves the disagreement if discretionary behavior is present around IPOs or

[282] See also Joos/Plesko (2005).

not. The question of existence has been receiving a lot of attention for a long time, but studies use primarily AM models. The authors found divergent outcomes. To shed light on this issue, this thesis additionally includes RAM and not only AM models (13 accounting items overall). Furthermore, the study adds the aspects of different time periods (five years), different industries (five sectors), and groups of profitability (three groups) which have not been examined in this context yet, although these characteristics give substantial insight in this research topic. The outcomes for the first question generally show that discretionary behavior around IPOs exists. This holds for accruals as well as for most accounting items of real activity management. Real activity models play an important role when firms use discretion. Accordingly, capital markets participants may not see through this behavior if they focus on earnings accruals management.

The second aspect is directly involved in these findings. It concentrates on discretionary behavior and the characteristic differences between IPO and non-IPO years. The finding of existing discretionary influence around IPOs demands the follow-up question if discretion in years around the IPO differs. The outcomes are quite clear. First of all, there is frequently more discretion in years -1 to +2 than in years -2 and +3 around IPOs. This holds for most industries, subgroups, and accounting items. The outcome emphasizes the notion that the setting of an IPO includes incentives which make insiders use discretionary behavior to maximize their benefits. Additionally, the findings offer valuable clues to opposing results in prior studies. Incentives in the years before and the years after the IPO differ. The results confirm this notion.

Most models, industries, years, and subgroups comply with the aforementioned set of hypotheses. Except, some results in year -2 could not be calculated due to missing observations in the database. This makes hypotheses testing difficult. In addition, some industries exhibit insignificant results in their smaller profitability group. This means, industries can differ within groups of companies while prior literature mainly focused on one overall group.

Concerning earnings accruals management solely, there exists a similar pattern in all industries. There is systematically no inflation of accruals in the pre-IPO year. On the contrary, in that year only negative amounts which are either significant or insignificant exist. A special circumstance exists for companies in profitable industries. These firms are mainly valued by their profit; therefore, they do not deflate earnings accruals significantly. However, capital market scrutiny is too high to inflate earnings in the pre-IPO year. This is in line with prior literature (see chapter 3.3.2). On the other hand, loss companies in unprofitable industries seem not to care about earnings and show negative significance in accruals for loss firms.

Since scrutiny declines after the IPO, earnings inflation takes place in the post-IPO year in profitable industries. In the year after the lock-up period, incentives for some shareholders to maximize their benefit exist. The outcome underlines the idea that companies try to influence investors with high earnings. This is in line with the earnings fixation hypothesis. It is important to note that there is a striking difference between specific industries.

Correspondingly, unprofitable industries even exhibit negatively significant results in years -1 and +1 whereas year +2 shows an opposing positive sign. This might be caused by reversals of accruals and the presence of venture capitalists in these industries, as prior literature argues. It underlines the intuition that unprofitable industries do not care as much for earnings as for other accounting items. Assumingly, investors value other accounting data than negative profit and aim at indicators of potential future benefits. These might be sales, R&D, or SG&A, for example.

The above outcomes are mainly consistent with prior literature where results exist. For example, Singer (2007) includes fewer specific industries, focuses on one year and finds similar results. Likewise for other cross-sectional studies, the findings of Ball/Shivakumar (2008) and Armstrong et al. (2009) postulate conservative results in the pre-IPO year as above and contradict Teoh et al. (1998b). Furthermore, results after the IPO point to decreasing scrutiny and indicate earnings inflation. This finding is mainly in line with prior studies using post-IPO data.[283] Prior literature neither points out negative earnings management for specific industries nor does it find significant amounts that reverse in terms of (algebraic) signs from negative in periods before to positive in periods after the IPO.

The second set of hypotheses focuses on the difference in industry sectors. Correspondingly to the results for unprofitable industries, high-growth companies exhibit proportionately more frequently positive discretion in expense accounts than companies in well-established industries. These accounts include R&D, SG&A, advertising, and the aggregate measure of discretionary expenses. There are only few exceptions concerning the hypotheses of these accounts. The outcome in this thesis supports findings in the finance literature of increased

[283] Katz (2006); Morsfield/Tan (2006); Wongsunwai (2013), for example.

R&D and SG&A for valuation purposes.[284] Whereas prior accounting literature mainly expects (and finds) deflated R&D and SG&A to lower cash outflows and increase their profit. Interestingly, these findings exist for certain events such as benchmark beating or reaching earnings targets.[285] Obviously, the setting of an IPO delivers a new aspect of accounting behavior in these line items.

The conventional conception of significantly decreasing expense accounts holds only for the profitable group in the Construction industry. The outcome accentuates the importance of splitting up the two subgroups of profitability.

In opposition to the findings for the Construction industry, growing companies use positive R&D management around IPOs to signal future profits to investors. Obviously, SG&A are similarly inflated to express future benefits (e.g., intangible assets) to investors. These outcomes give a new and important insight into accounting behavior around IPOs. Furthermore, outcomes support the concept that high-growth versus well-established industries diverge in using discretion around IPOs. This finding should help investors when examining different industries.

Evidently, results for operating cash flow are driven by the expense accounts and show negative signs for almost all industries. This confirms the findings within the study of increased expenses which lead to abnormally low cash flow. Furthermore, it means that cash flow is not inflated around the issue of stock. Apparently, companies care about other important figures to influence investors.

Special circumstances exist for sales. Interestingly, all industries almost consistently use sales inflation in the years around the IPO. In contrast to this outcome, earnings accruals are not positively influenced. Obviously, firms prefer sales management over earnings accruals management before the IPO when scrutiny is high. Another aspect concerns loss companies and their possibilities. While accruals management is not in their focus, sales management might be more useful to receive a good valuation. The outcomes are in line with Caylor (2010) and Cecchini et al. (2012) concerning revenue management.[286] Furthermore, Fedyk et al. (2012) analogously evidence significant positive abnormal receivables for specific IPO firms after the issue.

---

[284] Lévesque et al. (2012), for example.
[285] Gunny (2010), for example.
[286] Both concentrate on the overall group. Caylor (2010, 83) examines earnings surprises.

Usually, there are strongly diverging results for the adjusted R-squared in the separate industries. This means the fit of models varies between industries. This outcome can be associated with profitability, industry, or other factors. Studies that present the average R-squared for all industries and groups can draw biased conclusions, especially around IPOs when companies are young, growing, and undergo structural changes.

6.4 Robustness Analyses

6.4.1 Tests for Regression Assumptions

This study employs regression models using ordinary least squares. The models use subsamples of the overall sample and estimate betas that appear in the population. The betas are used in computing expected accruals which are used to calculate discretionary accruals. Therefore, the properties of subsample betas have to be unbiased. There are several assumptions which are usually employed to ensure statistical unbiasedness of regression models.[287] If the assumptions are not met, the inferences may be misleading.

First, single observations which substantially differ from others can make a large difference in the results of a regression analysis. Especially, if there exist only few observations in total. A typical example is an outlier. As in prior literature, the included data in this study is winsorized by 1% at the top and bottom of each continuous variable to avoid influence from extreme values.[288] Nevertheless, the industry samples are tested to confirm non-substantial outliers. A common test is Cook's D. This procedure combines the studentized residuals and the leverage (impact) of observations. It can result in a lowest value of zero while values higher than one should be clearly analyzed. The tests for this study indicate no observations which point out a Cook's D value larger than one (e.g., the highest Cook's D value in the Construction industry is 0.02).

Second, the normality of residuals is tested to assure that the p-values for the t-tests and F-test of regressions are valid.[289] However, it is not required to achieve unbiased estimates of the regression coefficients themselves. These coefficients are used in this study while the t-tests

---

[287] Wooldridge (2002), pp. 46-57. All presented tests are used selectively on the regressions. There are 13 regression models for the main accounting items which are applied to each industry and year combination. This results in an enormous amount of regressions. Therefore, selective application is appropriate.

[288] For example, see Gunny (2010, 867) for accruals and Wooldridge (2002, 300-301) for the general idea. Additionally, the discretionary amounts are winsorized by 1% at the top and bottom.

[289] UCLA (2013). Note that the term "residual" does not comply with the final discretionary amounts used in this study due to the matching procedure.

for the coefficients and F-test for the regression are not presented and neither employed in the presented research design. Furthermore, from 600 observations onwards there should be no distortion. Nevertheless, a test is employed to make sure the normality of residuals is present in the overall sample. The test of inter-quartile range does not indicate any resilient misspecification.

Interestingly, an inaccuracy in the normality of residuals results in a biased intercept. The intercept is not of interest in this study and would not cause any harm. Yet, other earnings management studies use regressions without an intercept and run danger of misspecified regressions when residuals are not expected to have a zero mean and the assumption is erroneous.

Third, the homogeneity of the variance of residuals must be given and equal a constant variance (homoscedasticity). This means that if the residuals are plotted alongside the fitted values, the model is well-fitted if there is no systematic. However, if there is a pattern, then the residual variance is heteroscedastic and the variance is dependent on the independent variables. Heteroscedasticity does not necessarily lead to biases in the estimated coefficients which are used in this study. Still, to avoid heteroscedasticity, the earnings management models which are employed here include a deflator of lagged total assets for the continuous variables (except for sales growth), as mentioned above. Nonetheless, the test for homoscedasticity of Breusch-Pagan and Cook-Weisberg are employed. It tests the null hypothesis of a constant variance. The results point out that the p-values are not small enough to reject the null hypothesis of homoscedasticity and hence the alternative hypothesis of a heteroscedastic variance is neither accepted nor present.

Fourth, high correlation between two or more of the independent variables is called collinearity or multicollinearity, respectively.[290] It means that regressors can be described as (exact) linear combinations of the remaining regressors in the respective model. If the degree of correlation increases, the coefficient estimates turn unstable and their standard errors can be inflated. A typical procedure to correct multicollinearity is to drop independent variables gradually. However, a valid variable that belongs to the model should not be dropped. Running a Pearson correlation is not enough to recognize multicollinearity because a combination of more than two independent variables could be correlated.[291] To check if a high correlation is present, the variance inflation factor (VIF) has to be calculated. Typically, a

[290] Wooldridge (2002), pp. 94-95.
[291] Gujarati (2004), pp. 341-349.

variable with a VIF greater than ten should trigger further investigation. Here, all tested variables consistently result in values less than two for the earnings management models.[292] Exemplarily, the result for the modified Jones model in the Biotech industry is presented in Table 32. Since the accrual models are employed over a long time this is no surprise. Most of the real activity models include only few independent variables and these are usually not correlated; hence, the probability of collinearity is low and could be confirmed by the employed tests.

Table 32: Test of Multicollinearity for the Modified Jones Model

Variable	VIF
PPE	1.07
1/A	1.04
ΔSales-ΔRec	1.03
Mean VIF	1.05

Notes: VIF = variance inflation factor (which is higher than ten if multicollinearity is present). PPE = property, plant, and equipment. A = total assets. ΔSales-ΔRec = change in sales minus change in accounts receivables. The continuous variables are deflated by lagged assets. Calculations are from the post-IPO year.

Fifth, the model must be specified correctly. On the one hand, this is the case if no relevant variables are omitted. Otherwise, the calculation assigns some of the common variance of the omitted and included variables to the latter ones which results in an inflation of the residuals. On the other hand, the model may not include irrelevant variables because this attributes the common variance to these unrelated variables. The misspecifications from these two errors can substantially affect the estimate of regression coefficients. There are several tests to detect specification errors.[293] The results for the chosen models all indicate that the models are not misspecified because the p-values in these test results are not small enough to reject the null hypothesis of no omitted variables.

Sixth, the error terms of observations are assumed to be independent of each other in several different surroundings. Using panel data would introduce another challenge for independence if observations are correlated over time. The test for undesirable autocorrelation can make sense for earnings management studies if regressions are employed by year and industry. The observations and their residuals could be clustered systematically. Using the Huber-White

[292] This is also true for the McNichols model, although it includes several variables that might have been expected to correlate.

[293] See Wooldridge (2002, 281-283) for the regression specification-error test (RESET) of Ramsey (1969). In STATA the commands "ovtest" and "linktest" can be used.

clustered standard errors as in Petersen (2009) increases some residuals, which is expected due to specifics in industries and years. Petersen (2009) finds that almost half of the finance papers from 2001 to 2004 do not adjust for correlation even in panel data. The remaining papers proceed by using the Fama-MacBeth (1973) method or include indicator variables for each cluster of fixed effects or within estimation. Another procedure is to use an OLS regression and report standard errors adjusted for the correlation within a firm or industry cluster. Since the other assumptions are met, no further results are presented.

Finally, checking for linearity in simple regressions is straightforward, but for multiple regression models each of the predictor variables has to be plotted against the standardized residuals. No hint for non-linearity could be discovered in the chosen tests. Summing up all tested assumptions, the employed regression models are not (stoutly) misspecified and can be used as valid estimators of discretionary behavior around IPOs.

6.4.2 Further Models

6.4.2.1 Model Development

6.4.2.1.1 Earnings Accruals Models

Prior studies use diverging models for the same accounting items but usually only one model per study. To expand comparability to a larger amount of prior literature and to test for the sensitivity of the employed models, additional regression analyses are calculated here. Due to the length of monographic theses, robustness tests can be explained in greater detail than in journal articles. This thesis employs various models and compares them to each other whereas prior studies usually include only one model per accounting item. For reasons of clarity only one model for each line item is presented in the main section (see models in chapter 5.2). This chapter offers alternative models as sensitivity tests. There are no numeric tables included for the sake of clarity.

The modified Jones model is employed in the main section and the other four accruals models are examined here. The models are specified as follows. Healy (1985) introduced the basic accrual model with no control items for non-discretionary accruals. Accordingly, the model interprets all accruals (differences) as discretionary.

$$\frac{TAcc_{i,t}}{A_{i,t-1}} = \alpha_t + \beta_{1,t}\frac{1}{A_{i,t-1}} + \varepsilon_{i,t} \qquad \text{(Acc2)}$$

where

TAcc = total accruals from cash flow;
A = total assets.[294]

The Jones model (1991) includes change in sales (ΔSales) and property, plant, and equipment (PPE) as control variables for accruals.[295]

$$\frac{TAcc_{i,t}}{A_{i,t-1}} = \alpha_t + \beta_{1,t}\frac{1}{A_{i,t-1}} + \beta_{2,t}\frac{\Delta Sales_{i,t}}{A_{i,t-1}} + \beta_{3,t}\frac{PPE_{i,t}}{A_{i,t-1}} + \varepsilon_{i,t} \qquad \text{(Acc3)}$$

where
ΔSales = sales $_t$ – sales $_{t-1}$;
PPE = gross property, plant, and equipment.

The fourth model is originally from Dechow/Dichev (2002). It includes cash flow from operations in t-1, t, and t+1 (CfO_{t-1}, CfO_t, and CfO_{t+1}) as control variables because they make the argument that accruals in t are connected to these cash flows. The authors consider the matching function of accruals to cash flow as essential. Since accruals anticipate future cash payments and reverse when cash is paid which was previously recognized in accruals. Therefore, they model accruals as a function of past, current, and future cash flow.

$$\frac{TAcc_{i,t}}{A_{i,t-1}} = \alpha_t + \beta_{1,t}\frac{1}{A_{i,t-1}} + \beta_{2,t}CfO_{i,t-1} + \beta_{3,t}CfO_{i,t} + \beta_{4,t}CfO_{i,t+1} + \varepsilon_{i,t} \qquad \text{(Acc4)}$$

where
CfO = cash flow from operations.

McNichols (2002) finds that the Dechow/Dichev model is missing sales while the Jones model is missing cash flow for better specification, respectively. The idea of including cash flow in the Jones model might reduce the correlation of omitted variables of sample firms' economic fundamentals. However, including sales and PPE adds a specification check on the

294 The subscripts are "i" for the company and "t" for the time period.
295 If ROA is included as an additional regressor in the Jones and modified Jones models, the specification improves only marginally, see Kothari et al. (2005a, 186).

extent of measurement error in the cash flow variables. The combination of the aforementioned models is formed by McNichols (2002) and hence includes cash flow in t-1, t, and t+1 to control for performance. Additionally, it includes change in sales as well as gross property, plant, and equipment from the Jones model.[296]

$$\frac{TAcc_{i,t}}{A_{i,t-1}} = \alpha_t + \beta_{1,t}\frac{1}{A_{i,t-1}} + \beta_{2,t}\frac{\Delta Sales_{i,t}}{A_{i,t-1}} + \beta_{3,t}\frac{PPE_{i,t}}{A_{i,t-1}} + \beta_{4,t}CfO_{i,t-1} + \beta_{5,t}CfO_{i,t} + \beta_{6,t}CfO_{i,t+1} + \varepsilon_{i,t}. \qquad \text{(Acc5)}$$

The models demonstrate that various methods in prior studies would lead to an overview of differences in results. Similarly, this is true for using total accruals from the statement of cash flow instead of working capital accruals to compare these measures of accruals. The circumstance that prior studies do not compare possible procedures can also be a reason for diverging results.

6.4.2.1.2 Sales Model

For sales there is one alternative model which is employed in prior studies. It is very similar to the first one but excludes the variable funds.[297] This model similarly detects, for example, more lenient credit requirements which lead to an increase in receivables relative to sales, but does not control for the companies' financial resources. This means that the difference between specific companies would not be considered. However, it equally takes into account all kinds of revenue management.

$$\frac{\Delta Rec_{i,t}}{A_{i,t-1}} = \alpha_t + \beta_{1,t}\frac{1}{A_{i,t-1}} + \beta_{2,t}\frac{\Delta Sales_{i,t}}{A_{i,t-1}} + \varepsilon_{i,t}. \qquad (\Delta\text{Rec2})$$

6.4.2.1.3 Various Real Activity Models

Additionally to the first R&D model there are three other models. To maintain comparability, they are included in this study. The second R&D model (which means number one of robustness models) is equal to the first model which is used in the main chapters except that

---

296 The model uses the change in reported revenues rather than the change in cash revenues (ΔSales-ΔRec) to avoid biased estimates of discretion for growth firms; see also Stubben (2006), p. 34.

297 Roychowdhury (2006), p. 352; Stubben (2006), p. 14; Stubben (2010), p. 700. The model uses the change in reported revenues instead of the change in cash revenues to avoid biased estimates of discretion for growth firms; see Stubben (2006), p. 34.

sales growth (SalesGR2) is calculated with two years of changes in growth.[298] The results from these very similar models are expected to be parallel in years when sufficient observations are available.

$$\frac{RD_{i,t}}{A_{i,t-1}} = \alpha_t + \beta_{1,t}\frac{1}{A_{i,t-1}} + \beta_{2,t}\frac{RD_{i,t-1}}{A_{i,t-1}} + \beta_{3,g,t}\frac{AvChe_{i,t}}{A_{i,t-1}} + \beta_{4,t}SalesGR2_{i,t} + \varepsilon_{i,t} \qquad \text{(RD2)}$$

where

SalesGR2 = sales growth within two years.[299]

Other models for discretionary R&D are derived by using the models of Dechow et al. (1998) and Roychowdhury (2006) who deploy diverging models for RAM. Dechow et al. (1998) express expenses as a linear function of contemporaneous sales. This model attributes that R&D expenses are only dependent on the sales of the company. Following their model and including an intercept normal R&D is estimated as:

$$\frac{RD_{i,t}}{A_{i,t-1}} = \alpha_t + \beta_{1,t}\frac{1}{A_{i,t-1}} + \beta_{2,t}\frac{Sales_{i,t}}{A_{i,t-1}} + \varepsilon_{i,t}. \qquad \text{(RD3)}$$

Very similar to the first SG&A model from the above analysis, Roychowdhury (2006) uses prior year sales instead of current sales to explain discretionary expenses. They argue that the simplifying assumptions of Dechow et al. (1998) would induce a problem if companies use positive discretion in sales that could result in unusually low residuals, although companies do not use negative discretion.[300] To avoid this problem they recommend using lagged sales.[301] However, if companies use discretion in consecutive years, for example around the IPO, this maintains the problem. Hence, their model might make sense in their research setting, but it is biased for IPOs if sales are managed in sequential years. Additionally, for the pre-IPO years there are few observations left if lagged sales would be used. Accordingly, this model is taken as the fourth model in case there is no discretion over several years and for comparison reasons. The corresponding model is:

---

298 Using past revenue instead of future revenue means that R&D is used according to present information instead of information that is not available to managers when deciding about these expenses. Furthermore, there is no possibility to use Tobin's Q in pre-IPO years as one model in Fedyk et al. (2012, 40). The corresponding authors mention no diverging results of the model with sales growth instead of Tobin's Q.

299 Note that "change in sales" is deflated by total assets while "sales growth" is deflated by sales.

300 Roychowdhury (2006), p. 345.

301 The results are still biased if the aforementioned hypotheses hold and sales are managed in several years around the issue.

$$\frac{RD_{i,t}}{A_{i,t-1}} = \alpha_t + \beta_{1,t}\frac{1}{A_{i,t-1}} + \beta_{2,t}\frac{Sales_{i,t-1}}{A_{i,t-1}} + \varepsilon_{i,t}. \quad \text{(RD4)}$$

Similar to the previous model, Roychowdhury (2006) uses prior year sales instead of current sales to explain discretionary SG&A expenses. The same arguments as above are valid here. The corresponding model is:

$$\frac{SGA_{i,t}}{A_{i,t-1}} = \alpha_t + \beta_{1,t}\frac{1}{A_{i,t-1}} + \beta_{2,t}\frac{Sales_{i,t-1}}{A_{i,t-1}} + \varepsilon_{i,t}. \quad \text{(SG\&A2)}$$

The third model is based on Gunny (2010) and adapted to the present research setting to estimate the normal level of SG&A. Since pre-IPO years cannot include stock market data, the corresponding variables have to be replaced. Instead of market value, sales are used to control for size. According to prior studies, Tobin's Q can be replaced by sales growth to proxy for future marginal benefits from additional marginal costs of investments.[302] Furthermore, the model includes controls for sticky cost behavior. Basically, sticky costs describe how managers wait with certain maintenance investments of unutilized resources in times of weak demand until demand increases and adjustment costs are due.[303] During IPOs this can be the case in both directions, depending if the firm is in a high-growth period or if it saves costs to influence income. To control for a sticky cost behavior, the model uses the change in sales times an indicator variable equal to one when sales revenue decreases between t-1 and t. The exclusion of this variable might cause under- or overestimation of costs when sales change. A reason for using this model as the third one is that the adaptions are not used in prior studies; hence, best comparability is given for the two aforementioned models. The normal level of SG&A is estimated using the described model:

$$\frac{SGA_{i,t}}{A_{i,t-1}} = \alpha_t + \beta_{1,t}\frac{1}{A_{i,t-1}} + \beta_{2,t}\frac{IntFu_{i,t}}{A_{i,t-1}} + \beta_{3,t}\frac{Sales_{i,t}}{A_{i,t-1}} + \beta_{4,t}SalesGR_{i,t} + \beta_{5,t}\frac{\Delta Sales_{i,t}}{A_{i,t-1}} + \beta_{6,t}\frac{\Delta Sales_{i,t}}{A_{i,t-1}} * DD + \varepsilon_{i,t} \quad \text{(SG\&A3)}$$

where

DD = indicator variable equal to 1 when total sales decrease between t_{-1} and t_0, 0 otherwise.

R&D and SG&A are tested sometimes in prior literature but advertising expenses usually not

302 Singer (2007), p. 24.

303 Anderson et al. (2003), pp. 48-49.

when examining RAM.[304] However, advertising expenses can be important in this research area and for companies around issues. The second model is equal to the model for SG&A and is based on Roychowdhury (2006) and Dechow et al. (1998) using contemporaneous sales as control variable. This leads to fewer observations before the IPO. The second model to calculate normal advertising expenses is:

$$\frac{Adv_{i,t}}{A_{i,t-1}} = \alpha_t + \beta_{1,t}\frac{1}{A_{i,t-1}} + \beta_{2,t}\frac{Sales_{i,t}}{A_{i,t-1}} + \varepsilon_{i,t}. \qquad \text{(Adv2)}$$

Discretionary expenses are usually employed when examining RAM measures. A notable fact is that some prior studies request SG&A expenses to be existent for the calculation of the model. This means that only if SG&A are available, the model is run because it is seen as the most important figure.[305] Another possibility would be to require all variables to be existent for the calculation because it would eliminate cases where any of the accounts is not collected by COMPUSTAT and reduce bias. However, this results in even less available observations. Nevertheless, this approach is taken into account, as well. Accordingly, the first model from the main calculation – employing lagged sales as control – is also the third model with the requirement that all three variables are available. Additionally, as in SG&A, the second model to calculate normal discretionary expenses is a linear function of contemporaneous sales.[306] Again, this model can be calculated with an obligatorily available value in SG&A or with all three values as requirement. Hence, the second – and at the same time the fourth – models are:[307]

$$\frac{DisExp_{i,t}}{A_{i,t-1}} = \alpha_t + \beta_{1,t}\frac{1}{A_{i,t-1}} + \beta_{2,t}\frac{Sales_{i,t}}{A_{i,t-1}} + \varepsilon_{i,t}. \qquad \text{(DisExp2\&4)}$$

Models two and three for change in inventories are presented here. The second model is based on Dechow et al. (1998) and used by Roychowdhury (2006). It includes change in sales and prior year change in sales. This means that sales from two years prior to t_0 are required and results in a loss of many observations before the IPO. Nevertheless, this model is used for

[304] For an exemption see Cohen et al. (2009, 1-2).
[305] If R&D and advertising are non-existent in COMPUSTAT, both are presumed as zero.
[306] Dechow et al. (1998); Roychowdhury (2006), p. 345.
[307] Since both approaches of mandatory SG&A as well as mandatory R&D, SG&A, and advertising are used, the first model is also used as model three but with a different data basis. Equally, the second and fourth models only differ by the approach of data prerequisites.

comparability reasons to prior studies. To estimate normal inventory change the subsequent regression is used:[308]

$$\frac{\Delta Inv_{i,t}}{A_{i,t-1}} = \alpha_t + \beta_{1,t}\frac{1}{A_{i,t-1}} + \beta_{2,t}\frac{\Delta Sales_{i,t}}{A_{i,t-1}} + \beta_{3,t}\frac{\Delta Sales_{i,t-1}}{A_{i,t-1}} + \varepsilon_{i,t}. \quad (\Delta\text{Inv2})$$

Furthermore, Aaker/Gjesdal (2010) use a cash flow inventory model which is based on the working capital accruals models of Jones (1991) and Dechow/Dichev (2002) with the further adaption of Pae (2005).[309] It introduces cash flow as additional explanatory variables and is in line with many similar linear cash flow models.[310]

$$\frac{\Delta Inv_{i,t}}{A_{i,t-1}} = \alpha_t + \beta_{1,t}\frac{1}{A_{i,t-1}} + \beta_{2,t}\frac{\Delta Sales_{i,t}}{A_{i,t-1}} + \beta_{3,t}\frac{CfO_{i,t}}{A_{i,t-1}} + \beta_{4,t}\frac{CfO_{i,t-1}}{A_{i,t-1}} + \varepsilon_{i,t}. \quad (\Delta\text{Inv3})$$

There is one alternative model for COGS which is based on discretionary expenses in Roychowdhury (2006) and includes lagged sales as a control variable. However, lagged sales only partly influence COGS in the current year, therefore it is not presented here. A further alternative would be to include current sales and change in sales. Untabulated results indicate that the outcomes are very similar to the first model.

The aggregate measure of production costs is the sum of change in inventories and COGS. The second model to estimate normal production costs regresses this account on sales, change in sales, and prior year change in sales.[311] Since this model requires sales from two years before the IPO or the respective examined year, there will be few observations available; hence, it is employed as a robustness check, only.

$$\frac{Prod_{i,t}}{A_{i,t-1}} = \alpha_t + \beta_{1,t}\frac{1}{A_{i,t-1}} + \beta_{2,t}\frac{Sales_{i,t}}{A_{i,t-1}} + \beta_{3,t}\frac{\Delta Sales_{i,t}}{A_{i,t-1}} + \beta_{4,t}\frac{\Delta Sales_{i,t-1}}{A_{i,t-1}} + \varepsilon_{i,t}. \quad (\text{Prod2})$$

---

308 Roychowdhury (2006), p. 345. See also Dechow et al. (1998), but differently in Aaker/Gjesdal (2010, 11).
309 Dechow/Dichev (2002), pp. 40-41; Pae (2005), p. 9.
310 Aaker/Gjesdal (2010), pp. 8-10. Although it outperforms other models in this category it is only used in the robustness section due to a loss of observations when using lagged CfO.
311 Roychowdhury (2006), p. 346.

6.4.2.2 Results for Periods around IPO

6.4.2.2.1 Earnings Accruals

Biotech

The results are presented by industry (Biotech, Internet, Technology, Construction, and Wholesale) and within them by year group (-1 to +2 versus -2 and +3), for all three groups of companies (overall sample, profitable, and loss groups).[312]

The following results include the analysis of discretionary reporting around IPOs for the Healy, Jones, Dechow/Dichev, and McNichols models compared to the modified Jones model from the main chapter. The outcomes in the year before the IPO show highly significant negative earnings accruals management in all five accrual models simultaneously for the overall and loss samples.[313] These parallel results manifest the reliability of the findings. The five models do not show any significant pattern for profitable companies, but insignificant and negative results. In the year after the IPO the overall and loss samples still have significantly low discretionary earnings accruals in all five models. Yet, the profitable companies do not show any significance and have positive values in four out of five models. The results are consistent with Singer (2007).[314] In the second year after the IPO the results are significant in only two out of five models for the overall and loss samples. Interestingly, amounts for all results are positive in contrast to prior years. The models find very similar results in these three years; yet, in year +2 their outcomes differ with a certain degree. While three models show no significance for any group, the two models of Healy and Dechow/Dichev display significance for the overall and loss samples.[315] The high abnormal value of cash flow can be a reason for a significant Dechow/Dichev model.

In the second year before the IPO, results reveal that firms do not manage earnings significantly. The five earnings accruals models display very similar results. The amount of

---

312 For the sake of clarity numerical tables are omitted.

313 It is important to note that the interpretation concerns the abnormal part of accounting items since the models estimate results for the significance of the discretionary parts. However, the discretionary part is also included in the sum of the actual amount (i.e., regular accruals plus discretionary accruals equal the reported accruals) and this affects the overall amount.

314 Singer (2007), p. 58. Fedyk et al. (2012) do not evaluate the two subgroups within one industry, but only within the overall sample which is insignificant. The outcomes of the overall groups are not exactly comparable because of the slightly different research design and Fedyk et al. (2012) use 30% fewer observations. The different design includes, for example, average total assets instead of total assets as a deflator which decreases amounts.

315 The Jones and modified Jones models display positive significance at the 17% level for loss firms, respectively.

the results two years before the IPO is almost exactly the contrary to one year before the IPO. The absolute magnitude is similar for all models. This might support the notion that companies use the second year before the IPO as a preparation year for IPO discretionary behavior. In the third year after the IPO, all models depict insignificant but positive results for discretionary accruals. Only the overall samples of Healy and Dechow/Dichev as well as the profitable group of the latter model are significant.

Especially the Jones and McNichols models are basically in line with the modified Jones model. The Healy and Dechow/Dichev models are similar, but comparable to a lesser extent.

Internet

In the year before the IPO, the Internet industry seems to use negative accruals management or is forced to report conservatively because of increased scrutiny of market participants. Especially, the loss companies and the overall sample display highly significant and negative results in all models while the profitable group exhibits significant values in the Jones, Dechow/Dichev, and McNichols models, but not in the crucial modified Jones model. In the first year after the IPO earnings seem to be managed downward again for the loss group in four out of five models. The profitable companies exhibit no abnormal behavior while the overall sample is negative and significant in three out of five models. In the second year after the IPO, Internet companies exhibit significant and positive accruals for the overall sample in all five models. The loss subgroup is significant in four models and the profitable companies in only two models (excluding the modified Jones model). This indicates that especially loss companies are expected to exhibit positive discretionary earnings to investors. Profitable firms still do not inflate earnings. The results for the five models are not identical. Interestingly, all five models find significance (5% level) for the overall sample which is usually presented in prior studies. Yet, the results for the subgroups differ.

For the Internet group the accruals models do not find any significance in the second year before the IPO. Almost all results display negative amounts for the 24 observations. In the third year after the IPO, the five models for accruals management do not find any significance in any group. All models are basically similar in this industry whereas the modified Jones model indicates the fewest significant results.

Technology

In the Technology industry, the accruals models display no systematic results in the year before the IPO. The overall sample has a positive significant result in the Dechow/Dichev model and a negative one in the Jones model. While the Healy and Dechow/Dichev models find significant positive results for the loss sample (10% level), the Jones and modified Jones models find (strong) significance of negative results for the profitable subgroup. Consistently with Ball/Shivakumar (2008), (profitable) firms manage earnings downward in the year before the IPO and they are rather conservative. This could also mean they postpone accruals for the upcoming years because of their short time reversal. In the year after going public, management of earnings is present in profitable companies. All five models consistently find significance (1% or 5% levels) for the profitable groups and insignificant results for the loss groups. The overall sample is significant in the Healy, modified Jones, and Dechow/Dichev models. In the second year after the issue, Technology firms exhibit a systematic pattern in managing earnings upward. All five models display highly significant (1% level) and positive amounts of accruals management for all three subgroups. Since scrutiny decreases after the IPO to a common level, the companies influence the line items which are most important for investors.

In the second year before the IPO, the models for accruals do not show any significance, except for the profitable group in the Dechow/Dichev model which finds a positive significance. This indicates that cash flow cannot explain the high accruals. In all five models the profitable groups have an insignificant amount and positive sign while the loss subgroup has a negative one except for the Dechow/Dichev model. In the third year after the IPO, the findings for accruals indicate that loss companies do not apply discretion while profitable companies still manage earnings. This finding can result from a reduced intention of the management to influence the share price after many insiders have sold their shares. In sum, the ambiguity in the findings of the earnings models underlines the differences in the two years after the IPO, when all models find very similar results. Only the Healy and Dechow/Dichev models find highly significant and positive accruals for the overall and profitable groups, while the loss group is only significant in the Dechow/Dichev model. The modified Jones model supports the significance of the profitable group while the Jones and McNichols models find no significance for any group. As in the other industries, all models are quite similar in their results.

Construction

In the year before the IPO, the companies in the Construction and Manufacturing industry display no accruals management. The five models are very similar in their results. The Healy, Jones, and modified Jones models are identical in their signs for the groups which are all negative but insignificant. The Dechow/Dichev and McNichols models are identical and find a positive sign but insignificant amount for the loss group. In the first year after the issue, the accrual models find evidence for accruals management of profitable firms, but not for unprofitable ones. Obviously, profitable firms influence investors by managing accruals upwards, while loss firms do not. This confirms the notion that scrutiny declines after the IPO and profitable firms start using discretion in accounting additionally to RAM. The three models of Healy, Jones, and modified Jones find very strong positive significance for the overall and profitable samples. This supports the method of dividing the overall group. However, the Dechow/Dichev and McNichols models find no accruals management. This might be the case due to cash flow management. In the second year after the IPO, the results for earnings are not systematic, but indicate that profitable and overall groups do not use accruals management while loss firms show indications of negative accruals management. While the Healy model finds positive significance at the 10% level for the profitable firms, the Dechow/Dichev model even finds high significance. Yet, all other models find no significance for this group. The loss group is significantly negative (10% level) in the Jones and McNichols models and almost in the modified Jones model (11% level), but not in the Healy and Dechow/Dichev models.

The results in the second year before the IPO include only up to seven companies, so the outcomes are not reliable. Nevertheless, some results seem to be worth mentioning. First, the models for accruals management are all identical in their results of signs and insignificance for all groups. In all models, the overall sample has a negative sign as well as the profitable sample which has five observations while the loss sample with two observations displays a positive result. In the third year after going public, there is no systematic accruals management in any group. Again, the models of Healy, Jones, and modified Jones are identical in terms of signs and find no significant values. The Dechow/Dichev and McNichols models find negative significance for the profitable subgroup, but not for the other two groups. While the Jones model is equal to the modified Jones model in practically all years and groups, the other models diverge in certain aspects.

Wholesale

In the year before the IPO in the Wholesale industry, accruals models indicate no systematic and significant discretion for all models and only slightly hint at negative accruals management of the unprofitable and overall groups. The five models mainly find negative abnormal amounts, but only the Jones and McNichols models are significant for the overall and loss samples. In the first year after the issue, the results for accruals management indicate that both subgroups try to influence investors by high earnings which might be due to lower scrutiny compared to the pre-issue year. Four out of five models find high significance for the overall and profitable groups, while the loss subgroup is significant in three models. Only the McNichols model finds no significance for any group. If the study would only apply the McNichols model, it would find diverging results compared to studies using any of the other four models. This underlines the importance of comparing various models when studies should be linked to each other. In the second year after the issue, the results for earnings indicate that companies use accruals to manage earnings upward in both subgroups. Four out of five models find positive and significant discretion in earnings for all three subgroups. Again, only the McNichols model discovers no significance except for the overall group, while both subgroups would be significant at the 14% and 12% level, respectively.

In the second year before the IPO, there are only seven observations which are quite few for reliable results. Yet, the results are presented here. Accruals models predominantly find insignificant and negative amounts, but only the loss group exhibits significant values for only three observations. This finding is rather a trend. In the third year after the IPO, accruals rarely exist and confirm that companies do not manage accruals. While the Jones, modified Jones, and McNichols models are all insignificant, the Healy and Dechow/Dichev models find significant positive values for the overall and profitable samples.

Again, the Jones and modified Jones models are practically equal while the other models diverge only in specific years and groups. Over all industries, the models are quite similar but diverge in certain years and subgroups. The Jones model is closest to the results of the modified Jones model.

6.4.2.2.2 Sales

The results are presented by industry (Biotech, Internet, Technology, Construction, and Wholesale) and within them by year group (-1 to +2 versus -2 and +3), for all three groups of companies (overall sample, profitable, and loss groups).

Biotech

The two models for change in receivables are equal for Biotech companies and find that profitable firms use positive sales management in the pre-IPO year.[316] The overall and loss groups do not manage receivables. The two receivables models show almost exactly the same results even in terms of amounts. In the year after the IPO, unprofitable Biotech firms manage their receivables upward in both accounts receivable models while the other groups are insignificant. Similarly, Fedyk et al. (2012) find significant positive discretionary receivables for IPO firms as well, but only examine the overall group. In year +2, there is no significance in any of the two models.

In the second year before the issue the results for accounts receivable and revenues do not show any significance and are equal again. Both models of change in receivables depict a negative value for the overall and loss samples while the profitable one consists of four observations, only. In the third year after the IPO, the results for both models indicate abnormally low sales for loss companies and insignificant amounts for the others. Both models are equal in terms of significance in all years and subgroups.

Internet

In the Internet industry in the year before the issue, sales management is present for the loss sample while the profitable sample displays no significance, but exhibits positive amounts. The overall sample is significant at the 1% level for model one and at the 5% level for model two. In the year after the IPO, the receivables models equally indicate highly significant and positive abnormal values for all three groups. The findings are in accord with the outcomes in Fedyk et al. (2012).[317] In year +2, the models for change in accounts receivable differ slightly.

---

316 Since the accounts receivable models are mainly the same throughout the study, they are only reported separately if they diverge.

317 Fedyk et al. (2012), p. 48.

While model one points at discretion in the overall group, the second model indicates no significance.[318]

In year -2, the results for both change in receivables models are insignificant and negative for the overall and loss groups while the profitable groups have positive but also insignificant amounts. Identically, in year +3, the results for the models are insignificant and negative for the overall and loss groups while the profitable groups are insignificant and positive. Both models are equal in terms of significance in all years and subgroups, except for year +2 and the overall group.

Technology

In the Technology industry in year -1, both receivables models equally display strong positive significance for loss firms, but not for the profitable subgroup or the overall sample. Actually, the profitable group has a negative sign in both models resulting in a positive but insignificant overall sample because both subgroups make up almost half of the observations. In the post-IPO year, the changes in both accounts receivable models are consistent with the findings of Fedyk et al. (2012) that companies use positive discretion in sales. All three groups are (very strongly) significant and positive. The results for loss groups have a higher significance than for profitable ones. Only in model two there is significance at the 10% level for the profitable group. In year +2, the results for models one and two for changes in accounts receivable indicate that profitable firms strongly influence receivables. Loss firms also display significant receivables (yet to a lower extent). The overall sample is positively significant in the models of change in receivables. These results point to a preference of high sales in the second year instead of the third year after the issue. Inflated sales confirm the notion to increase value relevant line items. Positive abnormal gross receivables point out that companies try to increase receivables by easing credit policies and accelerating future sales.

In year -2, the results for the two models in change in receivables do not exhibit any significance. All results are insignificant. In the third year after the IPO, model one and two indicate receivables management for the overall and profitable groups, only. The two models display strong positive significance for both groups. Both models are equal in terms of significance in all years and subgroups.

[318] In the first receivables model the loss subgroup is significant at the 11% level and the overall sample of the second receivables model is significant at the 12% level.

Construction

In the Construction industry in the pre-IPO year, the results for both models are insignificant. The two receivables models are equal in their findings. In year +1, the receivables are boosted in both subgroups resulting in an inflated overall outcome. Both models detect highly significant amounts for the overall and profitable groups while the amounts for the loss groups are significant at the 10% level, respectively. In the second year after the offering, the two models for changes in accounts receivable indicate inflated receivables for the profitable groups, only.

In year -2, the results for sales models include only up to seven observations for the overall groups, both insignificant. In year +3, there is the first difference which is worth mentioning. The overall sample is only significant in the first receivables model because of the very strong and positive significance of the loss group while the second model finds low positive significance for loss companies and no significance in the overall group. Both models are equal in terms of significance in all years and subgroups, except for the overall group in year +3.

Wholesale

In the Wholesale industry in the pre-IPO year, there are only insignificant findings for receivables which are all negative. In the post-IPO year, both models identically find strongly and significant overall and profitable groups. In year +2 after the IPO, all groups are equally significant.

In year -2, the two models for change in accounts receivable indicate no significant values for any group for only up to seven observations in the overall samples. Similarly, there is no receivables management in the third year after the IPO. Both receivables models are equal in terms of significance in all years and subgroups. There are no additional models employed for abnormal cash flow from operations.

6.4.2.2.3 R&D

Biotech

In the Biotech industry in the pre-IPO year, the second R&D model includes only 21 firms and the results are not significant. The third R&D model is consistent with the first one, displaying (very strong) significance for all groups, but with higher amounts of R&D management. This is similar to the fourth model. In year +1, models one and two are very similar although the number of observations is 291 in model one and 130 in model two. Both show highly significant positive values for the overall and the loss samples, respectively. While the profitable group has an insignificant positive sign in model one it has a negative sign in model two. Model numbers three and four are also highly significant for the overall samples, but at a higher amount and both subgroups are highly significant, respectively.

In year +2, the results for R&D are very similar in models one and two where all groups have positive results, however insignificant. Only models three and four display a negative value for the overall and loss samples which are significant, while the profitable group shows a positive abnormal and insignificant amount.

In year -2, the first model displays a slightly negative result for all groups while the third and fourth models find a positive amount for the overall sample and the loss subgroup, respectively. The fourth model includes only four observations. The other models consist of up to 27 observations. The second model comprises less than five observations and is not taken into account.[319]

In year +3, the results for discretionary R&D in the first two models are very similar, displaying a high significance with a negative sign for the overall and loss samples, respectively, and a positive but insignificant amount for the profitable subgroup. The third and fourth models differ and depict a negative sign and insignificant value for the overall and loss samples, while the profitable group has a positive and significant (1% or 5% levels) amount. Since the third model does not take cash into account, as the first two models, it finds R&D to be higher for profitable firms than the sales level expects it to be. The reason is probably that less cash is held in the company and invested in R&D instead of the matched companies.

[319] This results from the control variable of sales growth from two years.

Internet

In the Internet industry in the pre-IPO year, models one, three, and four are highly significant and positive for all groups while the second model does not find any significance (only at the 12% level for 23 observations). In the post-IPO year, all four models for R&D exhibit high significance for all three groups. In year +2, R&D expenses are insignificant for all groups, except for the overall sample in the first model.

In year -2, the results for R&D expenses in all models exhibit no significance in any group. In year +3, the first two models are not in line with the others. While model one and two find highly significant and negative values for the overall and loss samples, the profitable group is insignificant. The third and fourth models find significance (5% level) for the profitable sample but no significance for the loss companies.

Technology

In the Technology industry in the pre-IPO year, the results show a high significance for all three groups in the first, third, and fourth models, respectively. The second model finds no significance, which might be due to the low data availability. In the post-IPO year, the R&D expenses are significantly positive for profitable firms in three out of four models, yet, not for loss firms in the first and second models. The overall samples are (strongly) significant in all models. In year +2, all four models exhibit significance (1% or 5% levels) and positive amounts for all subgroups. This finding can explain the abnormal low cash flow from above.

In year -2, all four models for R&D mainly display no significance except for model one and the loss subgroup with nine observations. In year +3, the R&D models find ambiguous results but indicate no discretion in R&D in the third year after the issue. The first model does not find any discretion in R&D. The second model is significant for the loss sample at the 10% level with a negative amount. The third and fourth models are positive and significant (5% level) for all three groups.

Construction

In the Construction industry in the pre-IPO year, the results for R&D display discretion only for the overall group in model one at the 10% level of significance, but not for the subgroups. All four models consistently exhibit no significance for all other results. In the post-IPO year, the results for R&D are all insignificant and show no systematic pattern in all models. In year +2, the models for R&D exhibit no significance but negative amounts for nearly all groups.

In year -2, the results for R&D include only two companies. In year +3, the first two R&D models find positive significance for the overall and profitable groups while models three and four do not. The loss companies are insignificant in any model.

Wholesale

In the Wholesale industry in year -1, the findings for R&D are negative and significant for the overall and profitable groups in models three and four while the other models are insignificant. In the post-IPO year, R&D spending is insignificant in all models and groups. In year +2, R&D expenses indicate no abnormal behavior in any model except for the profitable group in model one at the 10% level.

In year -2, R&D expenses include too few observations (four) for valid results. In year +3, models one and two of R&D expenses find significant positive values for the profitable samples. The first model also exhibits negative discretion for the loss sample. Models three and four are insignificant for all subgroups.

6.4.2.2.4 SG&A

Biotech

There are two alternative models for SG&A management. In the Biotech industry in the pre-IPO year, the first SG&A model shows significant positive results for all groups. Similarly, the second model even finds significant (1% or 5% levels) positive results for all samples. The third model is also significant in the overall and loss groups, but not in the profitable one. In the year +1, the results for all three models are significant (1% or 5% levels) with a positive amount for all groups. In year +2, models one and two for SG&A expenses are very similar in their results and show negative and significant amounts for the overall and loss samples while the third model finds a significant result for the overall sample, only. The profitable subgroup is insignificant in all groups.

In year -2, the results of the three models for SG&A expenses are insignificant. All models display a positive amount for the overall and loss samples and a negative one for the profitable group. In year +3, all three models exhibit negative and insignificant amounts for the overall and profitable samples while the loss sample has a positive sign in models two and three.

Internet

In the Internet industry in year -1, all three models find high significance and positive amounts for all subgroups. In year +1, all models display highly significant amounts for all groups. In year +2, the first model for the SG&A expenses exhibits no significant results, while the second model finds a negative amount for the loss group at the 10% level. The third model similarly indicates negative discretion for the overall and loss groups.

In year -2, there is no significance in any subgroup for any model. In year +3, SG&A expenses indicate no significant amount in any group for models one and two. Only model three points out positive significance at the 10% level for the overall sample.

Technology

In the Technology industry in year -1, all three models display a high significance for all three groups. Equally, in year +1 all models find highly significant and positive results for all three groups. In year +2, models one and two find high significance for all groups while the third model also exhibits positive amounts but only significant (5% level) in the overall and profitable groups.

In year -2, there exists no significance for SG&A expenses in any model. In year +3, models one and two are significant (1% or 5% levels) and positive for all groups, while the third model is equal except for an insignificant loss group.

Construction

In the Construction industry in the pre-IPO year, the profitable group is significant (1% or 5% levels) and negative in all models. The result for the loss group is not systematic. It is significant only in the second model and displays a positive sign. In year +1, all three models differ. While the first one finds significant negative discretion for the profitable subgroup, the loss companies exhibit significant positive discretion, leaving the overall sample insignificant. The second model finds positive significant abnormal amounts for the loss sample, only, while the third model indicates no discretion. In year +2, the results for all models are insignificant.

In year -2, the results for all models indicate no discretionary behavior. In year +3, the models find no significant behavior as well, except for model three and the loss group.

Wholesale

In the Wholesale industry in the pre-IPO year, models two and three find significant positive amounts for the overall samples while models one and two also indicate positive significance for the loss samples. All results have a positive sign. In the post-IPO year, results in all models are insignificant. Equally, in year +2, the SG&A expenses are insignificant for all groups in all three models.

In year -2, there are only insignificant and positive amounts for all groups and models. In year +3, SG&A expenses are unmanaged in all models.

6.4.2.2.5 Advertising Expenses

Biotech

There is one alternative model for advertising expenses. In the Biotech industry in the pre-IPO year, advertising expenses do not show any significance in both models. In the post-IPO year, advertising expenses are insignificant in both models, too, and again the signs for the subgroups are equal. In year +2, these expenses are still insignificant in the models and differ only in the (algebraic) sign for the profitable group.

In year -2, both models for advertising expenses cannot be calculated because of a lack of data. In year +3, the results for the two advertising models are very similar, except for an opposing sign of the profitable groups and do not exhibit any significance. Overall, there is no significant result in all years for both models, but the number of observations is low compared to other accounting items in the study.

Internet

In the Internet industry in the pre-IPO year, the two models differ for the overall and profitable samples. The second model finds positive and significant values for the profitable and overall samples (10% and 5% levels, respectively) while the first one indicates no abnormal amounts. In the post-IPO year, the two models are identical for the overall and loss samples with high significance, respectively. However, the profitable sample is significant

(5% level) in the first model, only. In year +2, the advertising expenses are insignificant in all groups in both models.

In year -2, the results for advertising expenses are equal in both models, except for the sign of the profitable group. Similarly, in year +3 there are no significant results and the (algebraic) signs of the overall and unprofitable groups differ. Overall, there are five significant results in two years around the IPO for model one and only two significant results for model two.

Technology

In the Technology industry in the pre-IPO year, both models display significance (1% or 5% levels) of positive abnormal expenses for the profitable groups while the unprofitable ones do not exhibit any significance. The overall sample is significant (5% level) in the first model, only. In the post-IPO year, the expenses for advertising are significant and positive for the unprofitable and overall samples but not for the profitable groups in both models. While model one finds significance at the 1% level, model two is significant at the 5% level. In year +2, advertising expenses are only significant for the second model in the profitable group. Cutting advertising directs to preferring earnings and cash flow to be high.

In year -2, the second advertising model has a positive significance for the profitable group, however, including only six observations. No other significance is detected. In year +3, there is no discretion in any model.

Construction

In the Construction industry in the pre-IPO year, the two models for advertising expenses include only four observations (all profitable). In the post-IPO year, both models are almost identical. In year +2, there is a negative and significant (10% level) amount for the overall sample for seven observations in the second model while the first one is insignificant.

In year -2, there are no observations available for this industry. In year +3, there are no significant results. Overall, there is only one significant result for the overall sample, but many results are missing due to the low data availability.

Wholesale

In the Wholesale industry in the pre-IPO year, both advertising models indicate negative and significant amounts for the profitable samples, only, while the loss groups include too few observations. In the post-IPO year, neither model indicates any significant value while the loss sample again has too few observations. In year +2, only model two exhibits a significant amount for the profitable firms.

In year -2, for both models there are too few observations. In year +3, advertising expenses are unmanaged in the two models. Overall, there are only three significant results for the profitable sample in both models while many amounts are missing due to the low data availability.

6.4.2.2.6 Discretionary Expenses

There are three additional models for discretionary expenses. In sum, there are four variations. The existence of SG&A is mandatory for models one and two of discretionary expenses, while the existence of SG&A, R&D, and advertising values are mandatory for models three and four. This explains the differences in data availability.

Biotech

In the Biotech industry in the pre-IPO year, models one and two indicate abnormally high amounts for all groups. Models three and four include only five observations due to the few advertising results.[320] The overall amounts are similarly significant as in the first two models. In the post-IPO year, the results for the first and second models are very similar. Both find high significance for all groups. While model three indicates significance for the overall and unprofitable groups, the fourth model only finds significance for the overall sample. In year +2, models one and two find negative significant values for the overall and profitable samples. Models three and four detect no abnormal behavior.

In year -2, models one and two are similar while models three and four are not available due to data limitations. In year +3, there is no significance in any model. Overall, interestingly, models one and two do not differ in significant results in all years (also if sales are unmanaged). However, Roychowdhury (2006) differentiated between the models to overcome sales management. Models three and four consist of few available results, only.

[320] Discretionary expenses are calculated if R&D, SG&A, and advertising data are available.

Internet

In the Internet industry in the year before the IPO, all four models indicate positive and highly significant discretion in all groups. In the post-IPO year, all models find positive and high significance again for all groups. In year +2, only model three exhibits significance at the 10% level for the profitable sample.

In year -2, there is no significance in any model. Equally, in year +3, all results are insignificant in all four models and the signs are all positive. Interestingly, as above, models one and two do not differ in significant results in all years.

Technology

In the Technology industry in the year before the IPO, all four models exhibit significant (1% or 5% levels) and positive abnormal amounts for all four models and all groups. In year +1, all four models find highly significant and positive results for all groups. In year +2, the expenses are abnormal and highly significant in all subgroups for models one and two, while the models with all three required line items (R&D, SG&A, and advertising) are less significant and even insignificant for the profitable group in the fourth model.

In year -2, there is no significance in any of the models while the signs are almost all equal and negative. In year +3, models one and two indicate highly significant results for all groups while models three and four exhibit significance (5% level) for the overall and profitable samples, only. Again models one and two do not differ in any year.

Construction

In the Construction industry in the pre-IPO year, the first and second models indicate negative discretion for the profitable groups. Additionally, the first model indicates positive discretion for the loss group, leaving the overall sample with insignificant outcomes. The third and fourth discretionary expense models do not have enough data available to calculate results. In the post-IPO year, models one and two indicate a high significance for the positive amount of loss firms. Additionally, model two finds negative significance for the profitable group. Again, results of the subgroups are opposed to each other. Models three and four include only five observations and indicate no significance. Results are in line with the findings for SG&A expenses. In year +2, the aggregate measure of discretionary expenses does not find any significance in any model.

In year -2, model two includes only eight insignificant observations while models one and three indicate positive significance for the profitable groups. The signs in all three models are equal. In year +3, all three models for inventories find profitable firms to be highly and positively significant while loss companies do not exhibit any abnormal behavior. The overall sample is significant (5% level) in all models, too. Overall, models one and three are almost identical in terms of significance while model two differs in years -2 and -1.

Construction

In the Construction industry, the pre-IPO year finds all models with positive amounts for the three groups, none of which are significant, except the overall sample of seven observations in model two. In year +1, only model two exhibits a positive and significant amount (10% level) for the profitable group while all other results are insignificant. In year +2, all three inventory models consistently find positive significance (1% and 5% levels) for the overall and profitable groups but insignificant amounts for the loss group.

In year -2, the inventory models include only up to seven observations and none of them is significant. In year +3, the results for inventories indicate no significant behavior for all three models. Overall, the three models differ in years -1 and +2 in one significant result each.

Wholesale

In the Wholesale industry in the pre-IPO year, all three models have identical signs and none of them is significant. In the post-IPO year, the results for the overall and profitable groups are highly significant and for the loss group findings are consistently insignificant in all three models. This is a striking difference between subgroups. In year +2, inventories of the profitable group are insignificant in all models. However, the loss group depicts ambiguous results. While model two finds no significance, models one and three are abnormally high for the overall and loss samples.

In year -2, model two includes too few observations; models one and three find the overall samples to be significant in their negative amounts. In year +3, all three models are very similar in signs and find no significant results. Overall, model two only finds significant results in year +1. Interestingly, models one and three are equally significant in years +1, +2 and -2. In years -1 and +3, no significance exists for all models.

6.4.2.2.8 Production Costs

There is one alternative model for production costs. The models are based on Roychowdhury (2006). While the second model includes sales, change in sales, and change in sales from the prior year as control variables, the first model drops sales in change from the prior year. This makes sense due to the low data availability in the years before the IPO.

Biotech

In the Biotech industry in the pre-IPO year, results for the first model show a significant positive sign for all three groups while the second model is insignificant, but the profitable sample includes only two observations. In the post-IPO year, both models depict the same significance levels in all groups while the first model includes almost twice as much observations. In year +2, only the profitable sample in model one is significant but the second one depicts no abnormal behavior.

In year -2, the first model is insignificant for all subgroups while the second model cannot be calculated due to missing observations. In year +3, both production cost models indicate a systematic behavior. For profitable firms the abnormal production costs are significantly high and for unprofitable ones insignificantly low. Overall, the findings for the second model differ in year -1 and year +2. In fact, for the second model results are difficult to interpret due to low data availability.

Internet

In the Internet industry in the pre-IPO year, the first model is negatively significant for all three groups while the second model indicates no significance for less than one tenth of observations. In the post-IPO year, both models are identical in terms of significance. In year +2, only model two finds a significant and negative amount for the profitable sample whereas all other groups and model one are insignificant.

In year -2, the second model has too few observations for calculation while the first one points out insignificant results. However, in year +3, both models find significant values for the overall and loss groups and an insignificant profitable sample. Overall, as in the Biotech industry, the findings for the second model differ in year -1 and year +2 while they are identical in years +1 and +3.

Technology

In the Technology industry, the results for the pre-IPO year exhibit insignificant amounts for both production cost models. In the post-IPO year, the loss group is significant and positive in both models. However, the profitable group is negative and only significant in the second model. This leaves the overall sample with a positive significance in model one and an insignificance in model two. Interestingly, the two subgroups show opposing signs in both models. In year +2, there are ambiguous results for both models. While the profitable group is negatively significant for the first model, it exhibits a positive and insignificant sign for the second one. The loss group exhibits a significant and positive result in the second model, but an insignificant and positive sign in the first one.

In year -2, model one is insignificant and model two can only be calculated for the overall group due to a lack of observations. In year +3, there is positive significance for the loss group in both models while model one is additionally negatively significant for the profitable group. Overall, the second model differs from the first one in three years and has a lack of observations in year -2.

Construction

In the Construction industry, the results for the pre-IPO year indicate no discretion for both models. However, model one includes only seven and five observations in the overall and profitable samples, respectively. In the post-IPO year, the models for production costs neither find any systematic pattern. In year +2, in model two only the profitable group is positive and significant.

In year -2, there are too few observations. Model one includes only seven companies in the overall sample and five in the profitable group while model two includes only four companies. In year +3, only model one finds one negative and significant amount at the 10% level for the overall sample. The significant value is in agreement with the COGS model. Overall, models one and two differ in years +2 and +3 while years -2 and -1 include too few observations. Model one exhibits only one significant result in year +3. In fact, both models lack observations in year -2 and model two in year -1.

Wholesale

In the Wholesale industry, model one indicates a negative and significant amount for the loss group while model two finds no significant results for nine observations. In the post-IPO year, there are no significant amounts in both models but they include opposing signs for all subgroups. In year +2, only model one depicts one significant result for the overall group, but all signs for both models are equal.

In year -2, there are only up to seven observations for model one and three observations for model two. In year +3, no discretionary behavior is present in any group. Overall, while model two exhibits no significant result in any year, model one depicts significance in year -1 and year +2. In fact, both models have to handle few observations in year -2 and additionally model one in year -1.

There are no additional models for gain on asset sales employed here. Actually, the models for GAS proved to be negligible for companies around the IPO. Obviously, established companies use this feature as prior literature points out while companies that go public abandon this instrument.

6.4.2.3 Results for Specific Industries

6.4.2.3.1 High-Growth vs. Well-Established Industries

The differentiation in industries concerning growth versus established and profitable versus unprofitable industries are presented in this chapter. The results for the group specifics are ordered as in the previous and main chapters.

R&D

The results for Biotech companies indicate that almost all models are significant in all groups and all three years, except for the first two models and the profitable groups in years +1 and +2. These results indicate that overinvestment in R&D is not equally important as for unprofitable companies. It is probable that for these companies R&D is not biased to arrive at a positive net income. This is coherent with the high percentage of profitable firms in year +1 and conservative R&D spending. The outcome for Internet companies is systematic, too. All results are significantly positive in all years and groups, except for model two and the profitable group (ten observations, only) as well as mixed results in year +2. This designates that the Internet industry uses discretion in R&D to demonstrate future benefits. Again, profitable companies seem to overinvest less than unprofitable firms. The Technology industry also depicts mainly significant and positive outcomes for all groups in all three years, except for the unprofitable group in year +1. Only model two exhibits few insignificant results, but the number of observations is quite low in year -1.

In contrast to these results, the findings for the Construction and Wholesale industries point out only rare significant amounts. Actually, in the Construction industry, the only significant results exist in the pre-IPO year in model one for the overall and the profitable groups (10% level) for 17 and 11 observations, respectively. Similarly, the Wholesale industry exhibits only two significant results in both models and years.

SG&A

The outcomes for SG&A support the findings in the finance literature and enhance the view on accounting behavior of issuers around IPOs. The results for the Biotech companies are systematically positive for all groups of companies in the first two years while year +2 indicates no significance. In the pre-IPO year, all three models of SG&A find at least significance (5% level) for all groups, except for the profitable group in model three for only 14 observations. However, in the post-IPO year all results are highly significant at least at the 1% level in favor of the alternative hypothesis. Year +2 exhibits consistently no positive significance. The outcome for Internet companies is even more significant. In all three models, three groups and the first two years the abnormal amounts are highly significant (1% level). However, year +2 indicates no significance. The findings for the last growth industry, including Technology companies, are equal to the Internet industry in the first two years. Again, in all three models, three groups, and both years the abnormal amounts are highly significant (1% level). Yet, in year +2, results are still significant for all models and groups.

The outcome for the rather established companies in the Construction industry gives an interesting insight. While the profitable group is insignificant and negative in all three models in all years, the loss group seems to prefer the strengthening of growth indicators over inflation of earnings and cash flow. Obviously, profitable and loss companies apply opposed influence in SG&A around the IPO (in years -1 to +2). This supports the notion that further research has to differentiate between these two groups of companies in that specific accounting item. Evidently, loss companies expect investors to value other line items than earnings and cash flow; therefore, they partly influence the respective accounting items that presumably bring future benefits.

The second industry with established companies is the Wholesale industry. The results are more similar to the Construction industry than to the aforementioned industries, but not equal. On the one hand, profitable companies are insignificant, but exhibit mainly positive amounts. On the other hand, the results for loss companies are positively significant in two out of three models in the first two years. Again, this supports the notion that profitable and loss groups diverge or even depict opposing results. Loss companies seem to prefer slight overinvestments in SG&A rather than positively influencing earnings and cash flow for a better investor valuation.

Overall, the result supports the notion that industries diverge around the IPO. Additionally, the subgroups of profitable versus loss companies differ in using discretion in well-established industries but not in growth industries.

Advertising

The outcome for Biotech companies in the pre-IPO year includes only eight and seven observations in the overall samples, respectively. In the following two years, there are still no significant results for around 30 observations. However, the Internet industry exhibits many significant amounts in this time interval. The profitable group for the Dechow et al. (1998) model is insignificant in year +1. This might result from abnormally high sales for this group in the current year. The other advertising model includes prior year sales which are less inflated for this subgroup. This could be the reason why the other model is significant. The results for the Technology industry are mainly significant in the pre-IPO year and even more in the post-IPO year while year +2 indicates no significance.

In the Construction industry, there are no significant results in any year or model and the outcomes are entirely negative. Yet, the time interval includes a small number of observations. Similarly, the Wholesale industry exhibits only two significant amounts in all years. Moreover, there are mainly negative abnormal amounts.

Discretionary Expenses

The Biotech industry exhibits significant amounts (at least 5% level) in the pre-IPO year in all three groups for models three and four while models one and two include insufficient observations. The post-IPO year depicts very similar results with even high significance for models three and four while models one and two include 18 observations overall with four significant results out of six. Year +2 indicates no significance. The Internet industry shows even stronger significant results. Actually, all four models consistently find high significance in all four models, three groups and years -1 and +1 while year +2 indicates mixed results for the models. The Technology industry even exhibits significant results for all amounts. Again, most outcomes are significant at the 1% level.

The established industries differ. The Construction industry depicts some significant results for the loss group, only, while models one and two include too few observations for calculation. The Wholesale industry exhibits similarly weak results. Three out of six amounts for the loss group are significant while all profitable groups indicate insignificance in all models. Models one and two include only few observations.

6.4.2.3.2 Profitable vs. Unprofitable Industries

For Biotech companies, the results indicate that in the pre-IPO year all five accrual models find very strong and significant amounts for the loss group. Equally this is true for the post-IPO year while in both years the profitable group exhibits no significance (also for the one-sided test). In year +2, the loss group in the Biotech industry exhibits significant positive amounts in four out of five models, except for McNichols. The results for the Internet industry are very similar. While in the pre-IPO year unprofitable Internet companies exhibit high significance at the 1% level for the negative amounts in all five models, the post-IPO year indicates somewhat less significance, but still all models find significant discretion. In year +2, the reversing effect is very strong with a significance level of 1% in most models. Hence, the loss group is very strongly positive in year +2.

The examination is based on profitable industries. The results for the Construction industry exhibit no significance in any of the five accruals models in the pre-IPO year. However, in the post-IPO year, three out of five models are significantly positive for all groups, respectively. The Healy, Jones, and modified Jones models are very similar in their results. All find high significance for the overall and profitable groups and slight significance for the loss group. The Dechow/Dichev and McNichols models indicate no significance.

The Wholesale industry exhibits similar results. In the pre-IPO year, there are no significant results in three out of five models. The Healy, modified Jones, and Dechow/Dichev models are insignificant for all groups while the other two models find few significant amounts at a mainly low level in two out of six groups. In the post-IPO year, all models exhibit significant positive results for all groups, except in the McNichols model for the loss group. The Healy, Jones, and modified Jones models find significance (at least at the 5% level) for both subgroups and the overall sample, respectively.

7. Conclusion

7.1 Summary

When companies go public, many players are involved in this important event. The management of the company prepares the financial reports and could be tempted to follow the incentives which are present around IPOs. Financial results are managed in different ways depending on various factors such as differences in time horizons, accounting items, industry specifics, and profitability of companies. The purpose of this thesis is to shed light on the obscurity of discretionary reporting in the years around IPOs in particular industries and in individual accounting items. This is achieved by examining specific aspects of earnings management when companies go public and provide investors with a better understanding of financial reports around IPOs. By informing capital market participants about discretionary behavior (and incentives) information asymmetry is reduced.

Time Period

Despite the fact that prior literature sometimes mixes financial reports of pre- and post-IPO years into one sample, the differentiation between these years is important and gives substantial insight because the incentives and possibilities vary. The results illustrate that earnings management differs from two years before to three years after the IPO. More precisely, in most industries, groups, and accounting items, there is more discretion in the time frame of years -1, +1, and +2 than in the two specific years -2 and +3 around this window. This outcome is consistent with the notion that incentives in the periods closer to the IPO are stronger. Overall, IPO companies are divergent in many cases from non-IPO companies. Investors have to take this aspect into account when valuing companies. No similar tests for AM and RAM and comparisons of years around IPOs exist in prior studies.

The important aspect of differentiating between time periods around the IPO results from the varying incentives and restrictions. In particular, in both years around the IPO (years -1 and +1), the respective groups of shareholders prefer a high share price. Original shareholders want to cash in on going public while new shareholders also want to profit from an increasing share price after the IPO. However, some prior studies argue that conservative accruals around IPOs exist due to increased scrutiny whereas other authors evidence positive accruals management.[321] The results of this thesis concretize these findings and dissolve the confusion. In general, pre-IPO earnings accruals in year -1 are either negative or insignificant while post-IPO accruals in year +1 are either positive or insignificant. This supports the hypothesis that increased scrutiny before the IPO makes it difficult to influence earnings whereas the strong incentive after the IPO (when the lock-up period ends) to realize a high market value of the firm leads to AM and RAM. Correspondingly, earnings accruals are the only line item that systematically differs in algebraic signs with significant amounts between pre- and post-IPO years, being negative when high market scrutiny is present and positive when scrutiny declines. This outcome supports the earnings fixation theory for the post-IPO years whereas in the pre-IPO year companies rather follow the signaling theory by influencing other accounting items.

Accruals and Real Activity Management

Prior earnings management literature concentrates on accruals when testing for discretionary behavior around IPOs and unearths diverging results. However, there are other accounting items which are also of interest depending on firm and industry specifics which influence investors in pricing decisions. Hence, these aspects also affect financial reporting behavior and have to be taken into account in order to shed light on the current research of IPOs. A comprehensive test for RAM around IPOs does not yet exist, but the findings in this study indicate that RAM around this event is present.

Particularly around IPOs, boosting earnings is more eye-catching than inflating other accounting items which investors also value. Only sales are similarly the focus of such scrutiny. Managing earnings and sales by real activities is less likely to be uncovered as influential behavior than using accruals would. Consistently, the findings for RAM indicate discretionary amounts that positively influence investors in the time frame around the IPO. For example, sales are never negatively influenced in any of the accounts examined. This emphasizes their importance for companies in all industries.

Prior accounting literature mainly focused on real activities managements as a means to an end to increase profit. This myopic view is disproved by the finance literature that allocates a positive meaning to higher expense accounts in certain settings which can influence investors. The presented results extend earnings management literature, because expense accounts seem inflated for valuation purposes in certain industries if incentives are present.

321 Ball/Shivakumar (2008); Teoh et al. (1998b).

Furthermore, the results indicate that earnings are not always in line with the expected incentives; however, RAM mainly follows expectations. The outcome that RAM can be a substitute for AM confirms prior literature.[322]

Authors of prior studies apply varying RAM models when examining financial reports. For reasons of comparability and robustness, several models are included in this study. These models mainly show clear results. While some models are very similar, others diverge from models with the same accounting item as the dependent variable. Additionally, the study examines some line items which are not well analyzed in prior literature and finds valuable results. The influence of factors like industry sector and profitability especially has to be taken into account.

Industry Differences

There are differences in specific industries dependent on growth and profitability. This makes evaluating and interpreting financial results a challenge for investors and researchers. The outcomes indicate that in specific industry groups, AM and RAM follow a systematic pattern before and after IPOs. Accordingly, prior studies can be biased depending on the composition of the industries they have included. In general, if diverging industries are mixed within one sample, the outcome is essentially influenced and the results may give an unclear picture. Therefore, a differentiation between industries with specific characteristics is preferable for an analysis.

The results presented confirm the findings of previous finance studies and extend the current earnings management research. In finance, the valuation literature already finds (high) R&D and SG&A expenses to be value relevant for growth firms and industries. Abnormally high R&D or SG&A are considered as being of future benefit for growth companies. Nevertheless, earnings management literature mainly depicts R&D and SG&A as accounting items which are deflated to increase earnings and cash flow. While the earnings fixation hypothesis is predominant in earnings management literature, the findings presented support the signaling theory. This theory indicates that companies signal value to investors by several accounts. Hence, interpreting the results for R&D and SG&A without taking the finance literature into account is difficult. Evidently, growth companies are interested in long-term goals and not in short-term (earnings) performance.

---

[322] Cohen et al. (2008); Graham et al. (2005); Zang (2012).

Furthermore, besides differences between industries, there can be discrepancies within one industry dependent on the profitability of companies (i.e., profitable or loss companies). Results indicate that loss companies prefer managing accounts other than earnings. Beyond that, some companies deflate earnings and cash flow for the benefit of other items which can signal value to investors. However, there are accounts which are similarly influenced in all industries and companies (e.g., sales). If accounts differ depending on subgroup (profitable vs. loss) within one industry and studies do not differentiate between them, but pool both groups in the overall sample, the results are biased. The influence can either result in findings in line with the larger group which means an erroneous interpretation for the smaller group, or the influence can end with no significant outcomes, although one or both of the groups would be significant, for example. In summation, it is important to note that specific groups can show divergent findings which would be mixed up if pooled together in one overall sample. Therefore, differentiation in terms of growth and profitability is useful.

Discretion in accounting around IPOs is a well-examined topic for earnings accruals. However, to the best of my knowledge there is no study that systematically examines AM and diverse RAMs around IPOs in specific industries and certain groups of companies. This gap is filled by this thesis presented. It gives a comprehensive understanding of several accounting items and their interconnection around IPOs in different industries. On the one hand, this substantially extends current research and on the other, it is useful for analysts, investors, and regulators; all of whom are involved in IPOs.

7.2 Limitations

Although the dissertation gives important insights into discretionary behavior around IPOs in specific industries, it has several caveats similar to literature undertaken before. Some are discussed in the following section. First, the annual reports are included in the time periods of -2 to +3 by financial year-end. However, the complete post-IPO reports are made public around three months later and in the past even six months which means they are finally published in the next time interval. For example, if the first financial year after the IPO ends ten months after the issue, then the results are included in period +1; however, the publication of these results occurs in period +2. Therefore, the influence of annual reports on share prices and the intention to influence investors has its limitations. Yet, some numbers and estimates are already made public before the issue of the full report and quarterly reports can also influence investors. The sum of the quarterly financial results is included in annual statements. Additionally, the IPO prospectus is a very important document anyway when setting the market price because usually, no financials are available for companies prior to the IPO. Since it is difficult to include the final publication date for all companies from other databases and the arguments above hold in favor of the procedure, the employed calculation seems appropriate.

A further limitation is that AM and RAM can be affected by specific circumstances which occur around IPOs or for specifics of young and growing companies (endogeneity). Since many agents and corresponding incentives are present in this time period, the true intention of managers' decisions is difficult to identify. However, even if the results were not willingly influenced by incentive driven managers, the findings help increase investors' awareness of existing differences between IPOs and comparable companies.

Outcomes may originate from omitted variables or something other than intentional behavior. For example, the results of increased R&D, SG&A, and advertising in the years around the IPO are interpreted as discretionary signals to investors that the company invests heavily in order to increase the future profitability. However, one could argue that the result indicates that the companies are growing even more than matched companies in the same industry and it is normal for them to invest heavily in these accounts.

Yet, there are several reasons why abnormal amounts are based on discretionary behavior rather than typically high investments for this kind of company. First, comparable high-growth companies in these industries exhibit lower investments by sales than IPOs although they similarly depend on these investments. Second, while they especially exhibit abnormal amounts in years -1 to +2 there is no discretion in years -2 and +3. Therefore, not all time periods are affected by there being an IPO. Third, these accounts are not the only indicator of existent incentives, but other accounting items such as sales are also found to be discretionary and support the notion of incentives around IPOs to influence investors. If studies examine earnings accruals management alone, no supporting accounts are involved. Finally, the setting of an IPO event in this study is very likely for managers to engage in discretionary behavior.

The models employed are not free from any bias. Hence, implications drawn from the tests can be imperfect. Prior literature shows that practically every model of earnings management has limitations under specific circumstances.[323] This is one reason why current literature does not agree on one model. The models could be employed according to the best results. To counter this problem, several alternative models are applied as robustness checks. Still, if, for example, sales are found to be abnormally high, then other models and results are influenced by this circumstance. Since the models in this study find abnormally high sales and other accounting amounts, which are still abnormally high (such as R&D), the sales influence seems to be too low for these accounts to show abnormally low amounts. However, if there are accounts that seem to be unmanaged because sales are abnormally high, then they might be managed if other explanatory variables could be used.

There are several aspects within the models which influence the outcome. For example, prior literature discusses whether to include an intercept or not (see chapter 6), using lagged assets or average assets as a deflator and also, whether or not to use the matching procedure. When the matching procedure is employed, results are dependent on the comparable companies and their corresponding abnormal values. The fewer IPO firms are available, the more dependent the results are on companies with the same SIC, year, and closest ROA. Furthermore, the findings determine only the part of discretion that is higher for IPOs than for comparable companies. This means if comparable companies already use earnings management, the sample firm has to apply even more discretion in order to show abnormal values. Hence, research would need information about the correct level of accruals which has to be compared with the sample firms. One possibility that could be employed in the short term would be to use an average covering several comparable companies instead of one firm alone. This helps especially if there are few observations and the influence of outliers can be considerable.

The study of this long time horizon includes the fact that all years and agents exhibit comparable specifics over the years and therefore, they are treated equally. However, an IPO in 1990 might differ from one in 2010 in terms of circumstances for the agents, accounting rules, and market condition. Hence, concentrating on specific time intervals might be helpful. However, since the data availability is substantial for the models, the amount of observations also plays a key role.

[323] Kothari et al. (2005a) test several accrual models for their specifics while Cohen et al. (2013) test RAM models. Cohen et al. (2013) discuss additional caveats of earnings management research.

7.3 Research Perspectives

The models and procedure in this thesis are state-of-the art and help investors as well as future researchers by providing explicit insight in the choice of alternative earnings management measures. However, there are still some aspects which are not addressed. Future research should examine the specific circumstances of IPOs (e.g., motivation) and the resulting abnormal values of particular accounting items. For example, the real intentions of managers are not included in the models but interpreted in the aftermath. As chapter 0 illustrated, motivations for going public are varied; hence, incentives and the resulting influences on financial statements are changeable, too. A mere number based study always falls short in several aspects. Including non-financial information (of the prospectus) or even conducting a survey would add to the understanding of IPO intentions of issuers as well as of agents. A study that contains behavioral aspects will substantially advance research in this field.

The differentiation in years is helpful in understanding changing incentives and corresponding behaviors. However, distinguishing the time periods is user-defined. Comparing several quarterly and annual time periods that are differently defined could provide a better picture of discretionary behavior around IPOs. Additionally, year -2 (and year -3) is still insufficiently examined and could be analyzed by using a database with information available or by collecting these financial statements by hand.

By splitting up combined measures such as the discretionary expense model into its constituents of advertising, R&D, and SG&A gives further insight and understanding of earnings management behavior. For other accounts there is the possibility of delving into their specifics for a better understanding. A broader view of the accounting items shows patterns of behavior that cannot possibly be drawn from one measure alone. Beyond this, using various models or methods for the same accounting item adds to an understanding of the complete picture. This would be a kind of scenario analysis for earnings management research.

The separation of groups showed specific patterns for the included industries. However, the interpretation of reasons for this outcome is vague. Concentrating on a similar group and digging deeper into its particularities and circumstances could give a comprehensive picture of discretionary behavior. It is important to address the question of which accounting items are valued by investors. This would make the interpretation of the results more informed. Connected to this question, an analysis of underpricing and the stock value development would also be helpful.

While this thesis suggests that groups of firms differ in discretionary behavior, other specifics of groups can also be helpful in identifying discretionary behavior. For example, the size or age of companies, shareholder patterns, amount of equity issued, or governance structures can influence behavior around the IPO. This thesis should inspire further research to examine IPOs and help investors as well as researchers to understand discretionary reporting around the issue as well as in other contexts and therefore reduce information asymmetry.

Appendix

Hypotheses

Basic Hypothesis: Companies use discretionary behavior around an IPO.

1) Hypotheses for Specific Periods

Main Hypothesis Periods: In years -1 to +2 companies use discretion in certain accounting items proportionately more frequently than in years -2 and +3 around an IPO.

Hypothesis Earnings Acc 1 (H-Acc 1): In years -1 to +2 companies use discretion in earnings accruals proportionately more frequently than in years -2 and +3 around an IPO.

Hypothesis Sales 1 (H-S 1): In years -1 to +2 companies use discretion in sales proportionately more frequently than in years -2 and +3 around an IPO.

Hypothesis Sales 2 (H-S 2): Companies do not show significantly negative discretion in sales in years -1 to +2 around an IPO.

Hypothesis CfO 1: In years -1 to +2 companies use discretion in CfO proportionately more frequently than in years -2 and +3 around an IPO.

Hypothesis CfO 2: Companies do not show significantly positive discretion in CfO in years -1 to +2 around an IPO.

Hypothesis R&D 1: In years -1 to +2 companies use discretion in R&D proportionately more frequently than in years -2 and +3 around an IPO.

Hypothesis SG&A 1: In years -1 to +2 companies use discretion in SG&A proportionately more frequently than in years -2 and +3 around an IPO.

Hypothesis Adv 1: In years -1 to +2 companies use discretion in advertising expenses proportionately more frequently than in years -2 and +3 around an IPO.

Hypothesis DisExp 1: In years -1 to +2 companies use discretion in discretionary expense proportionately more frequently than in years -2 and +3 around an IPO.

Hypothesis ΔInv 1: In years -1 to +2 companies use discretion in inventory change proportionately more frequently than in years -2 and +3 around an IPO.

Hypothesis COGS 1: In years -1 to +2 companies use discretion in COGS proportionately more frequently than in years -2 and +3 around an IPO.

Hypothesis Prod 1: In years -1 to +2 companies use discretion in production costs proportionately more frequently than in years -2 and +3 around an IPO.

Hypothesis GAS 1: In years -1 to +2 companies use discretion in gain on asset sales proportionately more frequently than in years -2 and +3 around an IPO.

2) *Hypotheses for Specific Industries*

Hypothesis R&D 2: In years -1 to +2 companies in high growth industries (Biotech, Internet, and Technology) use positive discretion in R&D proportionately more frequently than companies in well-established industries (Construction and Wholesale).

Hypothesis SG&A 2: In years -1 to +2 companies in high growth industries (Biotech, Internet, and Technology) use positive discretion in SG&A proportionately more frequently than companies in well-established industries (Construction and Wholesale) industries.

Hypothesis Adv 2: In years -1 to +2 companies in high growth industries (Biotech, Internet, and Technology) use positive discretion in advertising proportionately more frequently than companies in well-established industries (Construction and Wholesale).

Hypothesis DisExp 2: In years -1 to +2 companies in high growth industries (Biotech, Internet, and Technology) use positive influence in discretionary expenses proportionately more frequently than companies in well-established (Construction and Wholesale) industries.

Hypothesis Accruals profitable industries (H-Acc 2): Companies in profitable industries (Construction and Wholesale) exhibit no positive earnings accruals management in year -1, but use positive discretion in year +1.

Hypothesis Accruals of loss firms in unprofitable industries (H-Acc 3): Loss companies in unprofitable industries (Biotech and Internet) exhibit negative earnings accruals in years -1 and +1, but use positive accruals in year +2.

References

Aaker, Harald/Gjesdal, Frøystein (2010): Do Models of Discretionary Accruals Detect Actual Earnings Management via Inventory? A Comparison of General and Specific Models. Working paper, Bodø University College, Norway.

Aggarwal, Rajesh/Bhagat, Sanjai/Rangan, Srinivasan (2009): The Impact of Fundamentals on IPO Valuation, in: *Financial Management*, Vol. 38, No. 2, pp. 253-284.

Aharony, Joseph/Lin, Chan-Jane/Loeb, Martin (1993): Initial public offerings, accounting choices, and earnings management, in: *Contemporary Accounting Research*, Vol. 10, No. 1, pp. 61-81.

Ahearne, Michael J./Chapman, Craig J./Boichuk, Jeffrey P./Steenburgh, Thomas J. (2012): Real Earnings Management in Sales, the Interaction with Finance and Appearance in Financial Reports. Working paper, Kellogg School of Management.

Akerlof, George A. (1970): The market for "lemons": Quality uncertainty and the market mechanism, in: *Quarterly Journal of Economics*, Vol. 84, No. 3, pp. 488-500.

Amir, Eli/Lev, Baruch (1996): Value-relevance of nonfinancial information: The wireless communications industry, in: *Journal of Accounting and Economics*, Vol. 22, pp. 3-30.

Anderson, Mark C./Banker, Rajiv D./Janakiraman, Surya N. (2003): Are selling, general, and administrative costs "sticky"?, in: *Journal of Accounting Research*, Vol. 41, No. 1, pp. 47-63.

Armstrong, Christopher/Foster, George/Taylor, Daniel (2009): Earnings Management around Initial Public Offerings: A Re-Examination. Working paper, University of Pennsylvania.

Arthurs, Jonathan D./Hoskisson, Robert E./Busenitz Lowell W./Johnson, Richard A. (2008): Managerial agents watching other agents: Multiple agency conflicts regarding underpricing in IPO firms, in: *Academy of Management Journal*, Vol. 51, No. 2, pp. 277-294.

Baber, William/Fairfield, Patricia/Haggard, James (1991): The effect of concern about reported income on discretionary spending decisions: the case of research and development, in: *The Accounting Review*, Vol. 66, No. 4, pp. 818-829.

Baber, William R./Kang, Sok-Hyon/Li, Ying (2011): Modeling Discretionary Accrual Reversal and the Balance Sheet as an Earnings Management Constraint, in: *The Accounting Review*, Vol. 86, No. 4, pp. 1189-1212.

Baetge, Jörg/Kirsch, Hand-Jürgen/Thiele, Stefan (2004): Bilanzanalyse, 2nd edition, Düsseldorf, Germany: IDW-Verlag GmbH.

Baik, Bok/Cho, Kwanghee/Kang, Jun-Koo (2010): Information Asymmetry and Earnings Management: Evidence from Cross-Border Mergers. Working paper, Seoul National University.

Ball, Ray/Bartov, Eli (1996): How naive is the stock market's use of earnings information?, in: *Journal of Accounting and Economics*, Vol. 11, No. 3, pp. 319-337.

Ball, Ray/Shivakumar, Lakshmanan (2008): Earnings quality at initial public offerings, in: *Journal of Accounting and Economics*, Vol. 45, No. 2-3, pp. 324-349.

Ball, Ray/Shivakumar, Lakshmanan (2006): The Role of Accruals in Asymmetrically Timely Gain and Loss Recognition, in: *Journal of Accounting Research*, Vol. 44, No. 2, pp. 207-242.

Barber, Brad/Lyon, John (1996): Detecting abnormal operating performance: The empirical power and specification of test statistics, in: *Journal of Financial Economics*, Vol. 41, No. 3, pp. 359-399.

Barth, Mary/Kallapur, Sanjay (1996): The effects of cross-sectional scale differences on regression results in empirical accounting research, in: *Contemporary Accounting Research*, Vol. 13, pp. 527-567.

Bartov, Eli/Mohanram, Partha/Seethamraju, Chandrakanth (2002): Valuation of Internet Stocks – An IPO Perspective, in: *Journal of Accounting Research*, Vol. 40, No. 2, pp. 321-346.

Bassioni, S./Price, T./Hassan, M. (2004): Performance Measurement in Construction, in: *Journal of Management in Engineering*, Vol. 20, No. 2, pp. 42-50.

Basu, Sudipta (1997): The Conservatism Principle and the Asymmetric Timeliness of Earnings, in: *Journal of Accounting and Economics*, Vol. 24, No. 1, pp. 3-37.

Baxter, Nevins (1967): Leverage, Risk of Ruin and the Cost of Capital, in: *The Journal of Finance*, Vol. 22, No. 3, pp. 395-403.

Beaver, William/Engel, Ellen (1996): Discretionary behavior with respect to allowances for loan losses and the behavior of security prices, in: Journal of Accounting and Economics, Vol. 22, No. 1, pp. 177-206.

Bédard, Jean/Coulombe, Daniel/Courteau, Lucie (2008): Audit Committee, Underpricing of IPOs, and Accuracy of Management Earnings Forecasts, in: *Corporate Governance: An International Review*, Vol. 16, No. 6, pp. 519-535.

Beneish, Messod D. (1998): Discussion of Are Accruals during Initial Public Offerings Opportunistic?, in: *Review of Accounting Studies*, Vol. 3, No.1, pp. 209-221.

Bens, Daniel/Nagar, Venky/Wong, Franco (2002): Real investment implications of employee stock option exercises, in: *Journal of Accounting Research*, Vol. 40, pp. 359-393.

Benveniste, Lawrence M./Spindt, Paul A. (1989): How investment bankers determine the offer price and allocation of new issues, in: *Journal of Financial Economics*, Vol. 24, No. 2, pp. 343-361.

Berger, Philipp (1993): Explicit and Implicit Tax Effects of the R&D Tax Credit, in: *Journal of Accounting Research*, Vol. 31, No. 2, pp. 131-171.

Bernard, Viktor L./Skinner, Douglas J. (1996): What motivates managers choice of discretionary accruals, in: *Journal of Accounting and Economics*, Vol. 22, No. 1-3, pp. 313-325.

Bhattacharya, Utpal/Daouk, Hazem/Welker, Michael (2003): The world price of earnings opacity, in: *The Accounting Review*, Vol. 78, pp. 641-678.

Bhojraj, Sanjeev/Hribar, Paul/Picconi, Marc/McInnis, John (2009): Making Sense of Cents: An Examination of Firms That Marginally Miss or Beat Analyst Forecasts, in: *The Journal of Finance*, Vol. 64, No. 5. pp. 2361-2388.

Black, Bernard/Gilson, Ronald (1998): Venture Capital and the Structure of Capital Markets: Banks Versus Stock Markets, in: *Journal of Financial Economics*, Vol. 47, No. 3, pp. 243-278.

Block, Stanley B. (1999): A Study of Financial Analysts: Practice and Theory, in: *Financial Analysts Journal*, Vol. 55, No. 4, pp. 86-95.

Bode-Greuel, Kerstin/Greuel, Joachim (2010): Bewertung von Biotech-Unternehmen, in: Drukarczyk, Jochen/Ernst, Dietmar (Eds.): Branchenorientierte Unternehmensbewertung, 3rd edition, pp. 293-307.

Bowen, Robert/Davis, Angela/Rajgopal, Shivaram (2002): Determinants of revenue-reporting practices for Internet firms, in: *Contemporary Accounting Research*, Vol. 19, No. 4, pp. 523-562.

Bradley, Daniel/Jordan, Bradford/Roten, Ivan/Yi, Ha-Chin (2001): Venture capital and IPO lockup expiration: An empirical analysis, in: *Journal of Financial Research*, Vol. 24, pp. 465-492.

Brau, James (2010): Why do firms go public? Working paper, Brigham Young University. *Forthcoming* in: Cumming, Douglas (Ed.), The Oxford Handbook of Entrepreneurial Finance, Oxford University Press.

Brau, James/Fawcett, Stanley E. (2006): Initial Public Offerings: An Analysis of Theory and Practice, in: *The Journal of Finance*, Vol. 61, No. 1, pp. 399-436.

Brau, James/Sutton, Ninon/Hatch, Nile (2010): Dual-Track Versus Single-Track Sell-Outs: An Empirical Analysis of Competing Harvest Strategies, in: *Journal of Business Venturing*, Vol. 25, No. 4, pp. 389-402.

Burgstahler, David/Dichev, Ilia (1997): Earnings management to avoid earnings decreases and losses, in: *Journal of Accounting and Economics*, Vol. 24, No. 1, pp. 99-126.

Bushee, Brian (1998): The influence of institutional investors on myopic R&D investment behavior, in: *The Accounting Review*, Vol. 73, No. 3, pp. 305-333.

Butler, Marty/Leone, Andrew/Willenborg, Michael (2004): An empirical analysis of auditor reporting and its association with abnormal accruals, in: *Journal of Accounting & Economics*, Vol. 37, No. 2, pp. 139-165.

Callen, Jeffrey/Robb, Sean/Segal, Dan (2008): Revenue manipulation and restatements by loss firms, in: *Auditing: A Journal of Practice & Theory*, Vol. 27, No. 2, pp. 1-29.

Caylor, Marcus L. (2010): Strategic revenue recognition to achieve earnings benchmarks, in: *Journal of Accounting and Public Policy*, Vol. 29, pp. 82-95.

Cecchini, Mark/Jackson, Scott B./Liu, Xiaotao (2012): Do initial public offering firms manage accruals? Evidence from individual accounts, in: *Review of Accounting Studies,* Vol. 12, pp. 22-40.

Chan, Albert/Chan, Ada (2004): Key performance indicators for measuring construction success, in: *Benchmarking: An International Journal*, Vol. 11, No. 2, pp. 203-221.

Chen, Jeff Zeyun/Rees, Lynn/Sivaramakrishnan K. (2010): On the Use of Accounting vs. Real Earnings Management to Meet Earnings Expectations – A Market Analysis. Working paper, University of Colorado at Boulder.

Cheng, Tom Y./Firth, Michael (2000): An empirical analysis of the bias and rationality of profit forecasts published in new issue prospectuses, in: *Journal of Business Finance and Accounting*, Vol. 27, No. 3-4, pp. 423-446.

Claussen, Carsten (2006): Stock Options - Quo Vadis?, in: Berger, Klaus Peter/Borges, Georg/Herrmann, Harald/Schlüter, Andreas/Wackerbarth, Ulrich (Eds.): Zivil- und Wirtschaftsrecht im Europäischen und Globalen Kontext. Festschrift for Norbert Horn, pp. 313-327. De Gruyter, Berlin, Germany.

Cohen, Daniel A./Dey, Aiyesha/Lys, Thomas Z. (2008): Real and Accrual-Based Earnings Management in the Pre- and Post-Sarbanes-Oxley Periods, in: *The Accounting Review*, Vol. 83, No. 3, pp. 757-787.

Cohen, Daniel/Mashruwala, Raj/Zach, Tzachi (2009): The use of advertising activities to meet earnings benchmarks: Evidence from monthly data. Working paper, Stern School of Business.

Cohen, Daniel/Zarowin, Paul (2010): Accrual-based and real earnings management activities around seasoned equity offerings, in: *Journal of Accounting and Economics*, Vol. 50, pp. 2-19.

Cohen, Daniel/Pandit, Shailendra/Wasley, Charles/Zach, Tzachi (2013): Measuring Real Activity Management. Working paper, University of Texas at Dallas, TX.

Collins, Daniel/Hribar, Paul (2002): Errors in estimating accruals: implications for empirical research, in: *Journal of Accounting Research*, Vol. 40, No. 1, pp. 105-134.

Comiskey, Eugene E. (1972): On the Value of R^2 in Regression Analysis: A Reply, in: *The Accounting Review*, Vol. 47, No. 2, pp. 358-359.

Damodaran, Aswath (2012): Investment Valuation: Tools and techniques for determining the value of any asset, 3rd edition. New Jersey: John Wiley & Sons.

Darrough, Masako/Rangan, Srinivasan (2004): Do insiders manipulate earnings when they sell their shares in an initial public offering?, in: *Journal of Accounting Research*, Vol. 43, No. 1, pp. 1-33.

Daske Holger/Hail, Luzi/Leuz, Christian/Verdi, Rodrigo S. (2008): Mandatory IFRS reporting around the world: early evidence on the economic consequences, in: *Journal of Accounting Research*, Vol. 46, No. 5, pp. 1085-1142.

Davis, Angela K. (2002): The Value Relevance of Revenue for Internet Firms: Does Reporting Grossed-Up or Barter Revenue Make a Difference?, in: *Journal of Accounting Research*, Vol. 40, No. 2, pp. 445-477.

DeAngelo, Linda (1988): Managerial competition, information costs, and corporate governance: The use of accounting performance measures in proxy contests, in: *Journal of Accounting and Economics*, Vol. 10, No. 1, pp. 3-36.

Dechow, Patricia M./Dichev, Ilia (2002): The Quality of Accruals and Earnings: The Role of Accrual Estimation Errors, in: *The Accounting Review*, Vol. 77, pp. 35-59.

Dechow, Patricia M./Hutton, Amy P./Kim, Jung Hoon/Sloan, Richard G. (2012): Detecting Earnings Management: A New Approach, in: *Journal of Accounting Research*, Vol. 50, No. 2, pp. 275-334.

Dechow, Patricia M./Kothari, Sagar P./Watts, Ross L. (1998): The relation between earnings and cash flows, in: *Journal of Accounting and Economics*, Vol. 25, No. 2, pp. 133-168.

Dechow, Patricia/Schrand, Catherine (2004): Earnings quality, in: *The Research Foundation of CFA Institute*. Charlottesville, Virginia.

Dechow, Patricia/Skinner, Douglas (2000): Earnings Management: Reconciling the Views of Accounting Academics, Practitioners, and Regulators, in: *Accounting Horizons*, Vol. 14, No. 2, pp. 235-250.

Dechow, Patricia/Sloan, Richard (1991): Executive incentives and the horizon problem: An empirical investigation, in: *Journal of Accounting and Economics*, Vol. 14, No. 1, pp. 51-89.

Dechow, Patricia/Sloan, Richard/Sweeney, Amy (1995): Detecting Earnings Management, in: *The Accounting Review*, Vol. 70, No. 2, pp. 193-225.

Dechow, Patricia/Sloan, Richard/Sweeney, Amy (1996): Causes and consequences of earnings manipulation: an analysis of firms subject to enforcement actions by the SEC, in: *Contemporary Accounting Research*, Vol. 13, pp. 1-36.

DeFond, Mark L./Jiambalvo, James (1994): Debt covenant violation and manipulation of accruals, in: *Journal of Accounting and Economics*, Vol. 17, pp. 145-176.

Demers, Elizabeth/Joos, Philip (2007): IPO failure risk, in: *Journal of Accounting Research*, Vol. 45, No. 2, pp. 333-371.

Demers, Elizabeth/Lev, Baruch (2001): A rude awakening: Internet shakeout in 2002, in: *Review of Accounting Studies*, Vol. 6, pp. 331-359.

Diamond, Douglas W./Verrecchia, Robert E. (1991): Disclosure, Liquidity, and the Cost of Capital, in: *The Journal of Finance*, Vol. 46, No. 4, pp. 1325-1359.

Dichev, Ilia/Graham, John/Campbell, Harvey R./Rajgopal, Shiva (2012): Earnings Quality: Evidence from the Field. Working paper, Goizueta Business School, Emory University.

Dong, Ming/Michel, Jean-Sébastien: Do Industry Growth Prospects Drive IPO Stock Performance? Working paper, Schulich School of Business, York University, Toronto, Ontario and HEC Montréal, Québec.

DuCharme, Larry L./Malatesta, Paul H./Sefcik, Stephan E. (2004): Earnings management, stock issues, and shareholder lawsuits, in: *Journal of Financial Economics*, Vol. 71, No. 1, pp. 27-49.

DuCharme, Larry L./Malatesta, Paul. H./Sefcik, Stephan E. (2001): Earnings management: IPO valuation and subsequent performance, in: *Journal of Accounting, Auditing and Finance*, Vol. 16, pp. 369-396.

Easton, Peter D./Harris, Trevor S. (1991): Earnings as an explanatory variable for returns, in: *Journal of Accounting Research*, Vol. 29, No. 1, pp. 19-36.

Enomoto, Masahiro/Kimura, Fumihiko/Yamaguchi, Tomoyasu (2012): Accrual-Based and Real Earnings Management: An International Comparison for Investor Protection. Working paper, Kobe University, Kobe, Japan.

Ertimur, Yonya/Livnat, Joshua/Martikainen, Minna (2003): Differential market reactions to revenue and expense surprises, in: *Review of Accounting Studies*, Vol. 8, pp. 185-211.

Ewert, Ralf/Wagenhofer, Alfred (2005): Economic Effects of Tightening Accounting Standards to Restrict Earnings Management, in: *The Accounting Review*, Vol. 80, No. 4, pp. 1101-1124.

Fama, Eugene F./French, Kenneth R. (2004): New lists: Fundamentals and survival rates, in: *Journal of Financial Economics*, Vol. 73, No. 2, pp. 229-269.

Fama Eugene F./MacBeth James D. (1973): Risk, Return and Equilibrium: Empirical Tests, in: *Journal of Political Economy*, Vol. 81, No. 3, pp. 607-636.

Fan, Quintao (2007): Earnings management and Ownership Retention for Initial Public Offering Firms: Theory and Evidence, in: *The Accounting Review*, Vol. 82, No. 1, pp. 27-64.

Fedyk, Tatiana/Singer, Zvi/Soliman, Mark (2012): The Sharpest Tool in the Tool Shed: Simultaneous Equations of Financial Statement Management Tools during IPOs. Working paper, Arizona State University, McGill University, and University of Southern California.

Feroz, Ehsan/Park, Kyungjoo/Pastena, Victor (1991): The Financial and Market Effects of the SEC's Accounting and Auditing Enforcement Releases, in: *Journal of Accounting Research*, Vol. 29, pp. 107-142.

Field, Laura Casares/Hanka, Gordon (2001): The Expiration of IPO Share Lockups, in: *The Journal of Finance*, Vol. 56, No. 2, pp. 1-106.

Fields, Thomas D./Lys, Thomas Z./Vincent, Linda (2001): Empirical research on accounting choice, in: *Journal of Accounting and Economics*, Vol. 31, No.1-3, pp. 255-307.

Financial Accounting Standards Board (FASB) (2013): Project – Revenue Recognition, available at: http://www.fasb.org/revenue_recognition.shtml#objectives, accessed May 2, 2013.

Financial Accounting Standards Board (FASB) (2010): Statement of Financial Accounting Concepts No. 8, Conceptual Framework for Financial Reporting. Norwalk, Connecticut.

Francis, Bill B./Hasan, Iftekhar/Zhou, Mingming (2012): Strategic Conservative Earnings Management of Technology Firms: Evidence from the IPO Market, in: *Financial Markets, Institutions & Instruments*, Vol. 21, No. 5, pp. 261-293.

Francis, Jennifer/LaFond, Ryan/Olsson, Per/Schipper, Katherine (2003): Costs of Capital and Earnings Attributes. Working paper, Duke University, University of Wisconsin and FASB.

Francis, Jennifer (2001): Discussion of empirical research on accounting choice, in: *Journal of Accounting and Economics*, Vol. 31, No. 1-3, pp. 309-319.

Friedlan, John (1994): Accounting choices of issuers of initial public offerings, in: *Contemporary Accounting Research*, Vol. 11, No. 1, pp. 1-31.

Ghosh, Aloke/Gu, Zhaoyang/Jain, Prem C. (2005): Sustained revenues and earnings growth, earnings quality, and earnings response coefficients, in: *Review of Accounting Studies*, Vol. 10, pp. 33-57.

Gompers, Paul/Lerner, Josh (2002): The Venture Capital Cycle. The MIT Press. Cambridge, MA.

Goncharov, Igor (2005): Earnings Management and Its Determinants: Closing Gaps in Empirical Accounting Research. Peter Lang, Frankfurt a.M. etc., Germany.

Gordon, Lawrence A. (1972): Comment on the Value of R^2 in Regression Analysis, in: *The Accounting Review*, Vol. 47, No. 2, pp. 356-357.

Joos, Peter/Plesko, George A. (2005): Valuing Loss Firms, in: *The Accounting Review*, Vol. 80, No. 3, pp. 847-870.

Joos, Philip/Zhdanov, Alexei (2008): Earnings and Equity Valuation in the Biotech Industry: Theory and Evidence, in: *Financial Management*, Vol. 37, No. 3, pp. 431-460.

Joos, Philip/Zhdanov, Alexei (2004): Examining the price-earnings relation in a real options framework with investor learning. Unpublished paper, University of Rochester.

Katz, Sharon P. (2006): Earnings Management and Conservatism in the Transition between Private and Public Ownership: The Role of Private Equity Sponsors. Ph.D. thesis. Columbia University.

Kothari, Sagar P./Leone, Andrew/Wasley, Charles (2005a): Performance matched discretionary accrual measures, in: *Journal of Accounting and Economics*, Vol. 39, pp. 163-197.

Kothari, Sagar P./Sabino, Jowell/Zach, Tzachi (2005b): Implications of survival and data trimming for tests of market efficiency, in: *Journal of Accounting & Economics*, Vol. 39, No. 1, pp. 129-161.

Kothari, Sagar P./Shanken, Jay/Sloan, Richard G. (1995): Another Look at the Cross-Section of Expected Returns, in: *The Journal of Finance*, Vol. 50, pp. 185-224.

Krolle, Sigrid/Sommerkamp, Jan-Dirk (2010): Bewertung von Unternehmen im Großanlagenbau, in: Drukarczyk, Jochen/Ernst, Dietmar (Eds.): Branchenorientierte Unternehmensbewertung, pp. 37-62, 3rd edition, Vahlen, München, Germany.

Lang, Mark/Lundholm, Russell (1996): The Relation between Security Earnings, Firm Earnings, and Industry Earnings, in: *Contemporary Accounting Research*, Vol. 13, No. 2, pp. 607-629.

La Porta, Rafael/Lakonishok, Josef/Shleifer, Andrei/Vishny, Robert (1997): Good news for value stocks: Further evidence on market efficiency, in: *The Journal of Finance*, Vol. 52, No. 2, pp. 859-874.

Leland, Hayne E./Pyle, David H. (1977): Informational Asymmetries, Financial Structure, and Financial Intermediation, in: *The Journal of Finance*, Vol. 32, No. 2, pp. 371-387.

Lerner, Josh/Hardymon, Felda/Leamon, Ann (2005): Venture capital and private equity: A casebook. 3rd edition, John Wiley & Sons, Hoboken, NJ.

Leuz, Christian/Nanda, Dhananjay/Wysocki, Peter D. (2003): Earnings management and investor protection: an international comparison, in: *Journal of Financial Economics*, Vol. 69, No. 3, pp. 505-527.

Lev, Baruch/Sougiannis, Theodore (1996): The capitalization, amortization and value-relevance of R&D, in: *Journal of Accounting and Economics*, Vol. 21, pp. 107-138.

Lévesque, Moren/Joglekar, Nitin/Davies, Jane (2012): A comparison of revenue growth at recent-IPO and established firms: The influence of SG&A, R&D and COGS, in: *Journal of Business Venturing*, Vol. 27, pp. 47-61.

Levitt, Arthur Jr. (1998): The Numbers Game, in: *The CPA Journal*, Vol. 68, No. 12, pp. 14-19.

Liu, Xiang (2009): Monitoring or Moral Hazard? Evidence from Real Activities Manipulation by Venture-backed Companies. Ph.D. thesis. University of North Texas.

Liu, Jing/Nissim, Doron/Thomas, Jacob (2002): Equity valuation using multiples, in: *Journal of Accounting Research*, Vol. 40, No. 1, pp. 135-172.

Lo, Kin (2008): Earnings management and earnings quality, in: *Journal of Accounting and Economics*, Vol. 45, pp. 350-357.

Lowry, Michelle/Schwert, G. William (2004): Is the IPO pricing process efficient?, in: *Journal of Financial Economics*, Vol. 71, No. 1, pp. 3-26.

Lowry, Michelle/Schwert, G. William (2002): IPO Market Cycles: Bubbles or Sequential Learning?, in: *The Journal of Finance*, Vol. 57, No. 3, pp. 1171-1200.

Marquardt, Carola A./Wiedman, Christine I. (2004): How Are Earnings Managed? An Examination of Specific Accruals, in: *Contemporary Accounting Research*, Vol. 21, No. 2, pp. 461-491.

Maksimovic, Vojislav/Pichler, Pegaret (2001): Technological Innovation and Initial Public Offerings, in: *The Review of Financial Studies*, Vol. 14, No. 2, pp. 459-494.

McNichols, Maureen F. (2002): Discussion of the Quality of Accruals and Earnings: The Role of Accrual Estimation Errors, in: *The Accounting Review*, Vol. 77, pp. 61-69.

McNichols, Maureen F. (2000): Research design issues in earnings management studies, in: *Journal of Accounting and Public Policy*, Vol. 19, No. 4, pp. 313-345.

McNichols, Maureen/Wilson, Peter (1988): Evidence of earnings management from the provision for bad debts, in: *Journal of Accounting Research*, Vol. 26, No. 1, pp. 1-31.

Mello, Antonio S./Parsons, John E. (1998): Going public and the ownership structure of the firm, in: *Journal of Financial Economics*, Vol. 49, No. 1, pp. 79-109.

Meyer, Conrad (2009): Umsatzerfassung als Instrument des Earnings Management, in: Meyer, Conrad/Pfaff, Dieter (Eds.), Jahrbuch Finanz- und Rechnungswesen 2009, pp. 57-73, WEKA-Verlag, Zürich, Switzerland.

Modigliani, Franco/Miller, Merton H. (1958): The Cost of Capital, Corporation Finance, and the Theory of Investment, in: *American Economic Review*, Vol. 48, No. 3, pp. 261-297.

Modigliani, Franco/Miller, Merton H. (1963): Corporate Income Taxes and the Cost of Capital, in: *American Economic Review*, Vol. 53, No. 3, pp. 433-443.

Morsfield, Suzanne G./Tan, Christine (2006): Do venture capitalists influence the decision to manage earnings in initial public offerings?, in: *The Accounting Review*, Vol. 81, No. 5, pp. 1119-1150.

Myers, Stewart C. (1984): Finance Theory and Financial Strategy, in: *Interfaces*, Vol. 14, No. 1, pp. 126-137.

Myers, Stewart C. (1984): The Capital Structure Puzzle, in: *The Journal of Finance*, Vol. 39, No. 3, pp. 575-593.

Nelson, Mark/Elliott, John/Tarpley, Robin (2002): Evidence from auditors about managers' and auditors' earnings-management decisions, in: *The Accounting Review*, Vol. 77, Supplement, pp. 175-202.

NYSE Euronext (2012): Listings Directory. Available at: http://www.nyse.com/about/listed/lc_all_overview.html, accessed May 2, 2013.

Ofek, Eli/Richardson, Matthew (2001): DotCom Mania: A Survey of Market Efficiency in the Internet Sector. Working paper, Stern School of Business, New York University.

Pae, Jinhan (2005): Expected Accrual Models: The impact of Operating Cash Flows and Reversals of Accruals, in: *Review of Quantitative Finance and Accounting*, Vol. 24, pp. 5-22.

Pagano, Marco/Panetta, Fabio/Zingales, Luigi (1998): Why Do Companies Go Public? An Empirical Analysis, in: *The Journal of Finance*, Vol. 53, No. 1, pp. 27-64.

Pagano, Marco/Röell, Ailsa (1998): The choice of stock ownership structure: Agency costs, monitoring, and the decision to go public, in: *The Quarterly Journal of Economics*, Vol. 113, pp. 187-225.

Parry, Helen (2012): Factbox: Facebook IPO and legal arguments ahead. Available at: http://www.reuters.com/article/2012/05/29/us-facebook-law-idUSBRE84S1DX20120529, accessed May 2, 2013.

Pastor, Lubos/Veronesi, Pietro (2005): Rational IPO Waves, in: *The Journal of Finance*, Vol. 60, No. 4, pp. 1713-1757.

Penman, Stephen H./Zhang, Xiao-Jun (2002): Accounting conservatism, the quality of earnings, and stock returns, in: *The Accounting Review*, Vol. 77, No. 2, pp. 237-264.

Penman, Stephen H. (2001): Financial statement analysis and security valuation. McGraw Hill/Irwin, New York, NY.

Pfaff, Dieter/Ising, Peter (2010): Earnings Management – Erscheinungsformen und Aufdeckungsmöglichkeiten, in: Seicht, Gerhard (Eds.): Jahrbuch für Controlling und Rechnungswesen 2010, pp. 291-312. LexisNexis, Wien, Austria.

Petersen, Mitchell A./Rajan, Raghuram (1997): Trade credit: Theories and evidence, in: *The Review of Financial Studies*, Vol. 10, No. 3, pp. 661-691.

Petersen, Mitchell A. (2009): Estimating Standard Errors in Finance Panel Data Sets: Comparing Approaches, in: *The Review of Financial Studies*, Vol. 22, No. 1, pp. 435-480.

Teoh, Siew Hong/Welch, Ivo/Wong, T.J. (1998a): Earnings management and the underperformance of seasoned equity offerings, in: *Journal of Financial Economics*, Vol. 50, pp. 63-99.

Teoh, Siew Hong/Welch, Ivo/Wong, T.J. (1998b): Earnings Management and the Long-Run Market Performance of Initial Public Offerings, in: *The Journal of Finance*, Vol. 53, No. 6, pp. 1935-1974.

Teoh, Siew Hong/Wong, T.J./Rao, Gita (1998c): Are Accruals during Initial Public Offerings Opportunistic?, in: *Review of Accounting Studies*, Vol. 3, No. 1-2, pp. 175-208.

Thomas, Jacob and Zhang, Xiao Jun (2000): Identifying unexpected accruals: a comparison of current approaches, in: *Journal of Accounting and Public Policy*, Vol. 19, No. 4, pp. 347-376.

Tobin, James (1969): A General Equilibrium Approach To Monetary Theory, in: *Journal of Money, Credit and Banking*, Vol. 1, No. 1, pp. 15-29.

Trueman, Brett (1986): The Relationship between the Level of Capital Expenditures and Firm Value, in: *Journal of Financial & Quantitative Analysis*, Vol. 21, No. 2, pp. 115-129.

Turner, Lynn/Dietrich, Richard/Anderson, Kirsten/Bailey, Andrew (2001): Accounting restatements. Working paper, Colorado State University.

UCLA (2013): Statistical Consulting Group, Stata Web Books: Regression with Stata, from: http://www.ats.ucla.edu/stat/stata/webbooks/reg/default.htm, accessed May 2, 2013, University of California Los Angeles.

U.S. Securities and Exchange Commission (SEC) (2013): Investor Bulletin: Investing in an IPO, available at: http://investor.gov/news-alerts/investor-bulletins/investor-bulletin-investing-ipo, accessed May 2, 2013.

Venkataraman, Ramgopal/Weber, Joseph/Willenborg, Michael (2008): Litigation risk, audit quality, and audit fees: Evidence from initial public offerings, in: *The Accounting Review*, Vol. 83, No. 5, pp. 1315-1345.

Venkataraman, Ramgopal/Weber, Joseph/Willenborg, Michael (2004): What if auditing was not 'a low margin business'? Auditors and the IPO clients as natural experiments. Working paper, MIT Sloan School of Management.

Wagenhofer, Alfred/Ewert, Ralf (2007): Externe Unternehmensrechnung, 2nd edition, Springer, Berlin etc., Germany.

Wagenhofer, Alfred/Dücker, Hannes (2007): Die Messung von „Earnings"-Qualität, in: Journal für Betriebswirtschaft, Vol. 57, No. 3-4, pp. 263-297.

Watts, Ross/Zimmerman, Jerold (1986): Positive Accounting Theory. Prentice Hall, Englewood Cliffs, New Jersey.

Wongsunwai, Wan (2013): The Effect of External Monitoring on Accrual-Based and Real Earnings Management: Evidence from Venture-Backed Initial Public Offering, in: *Contemporary Accounting Research*, Vol. 30, No. 1, pp. 296-324.

Wooldridge, Jeffrey M. (2002): Introductory Econometrics - A Modern Approach. 2nd edition, Thomson Learning, Mason, Ohio.

Zang, Amy Y. (2012): Evidence on the Trade-Off between Real Activities Manipulation and Accrual-Based Earnings Management, in: *The Accounting Review*, Vol. 87, No. 2, pp. 675-703.

Zhang, Feng (2012): Information precision and IPO pricing, in: *Journal of Corporate Finance*, Vol. 18, No. 2, pp. 331-348.

Zingales, Luigi (1995): Insider ownership and the decision to go public, in: *Review of Economic Studies*, Vol. 62, pp. 425-448.

Zucker, Lynne G./Darby, Michael R./Brewer, Marilynn B. (1998): Intellectual Human Capital and the Birth of U.S. Biotechnology Enterprises, in: *American Economic Review*, Vol. 88, No. 1, pp. 290-306.

Von der Promotion zum Buch

↗

WWW.GABLER.DE

Sie haben eine wirtschaftswissenschaftliche Dissertation bzw. Habilitation erfolgreich abgeschlossen und möchten sie als Buch veröffentlichen?

Zeigen Sie, was Sie geleistet haben.
Publizieren Sie Ihre Dissertation als Buch bei Gabler Research.
Ein Buch ist nachhaltig wirksam für Ihre Karriere.
Nutzen Sie die Möglichkeit mit Ihrer Publikation bestmöglich sichtbar und wertgeschätzt zu werden – im Umfeld anerkannter Wissenschaftler und Autoren.
Qualitative Titelauswahl sowie namhafte Herausgeber renommierter Schriftenreihen bürgen für die Güte des Programms.

Ihre Vorteile:

- Kurze Produktionszyklen: Drucklegung in 8-12 Wochen
- Dauerhafte Lieferbarkeit print und digital: Druck + E-Book in SpringerLink
- Umfassende Marketingaktivitäten: E-Mail-Newsletter, Flyer, Kataloge, Rezensionsexemplar-Versand an nationale und internationale Fachzeitschriften, Präsentation auf Messen und Fachtagungen etc.
- Zielgruppengerechter Vertrieb an Wissenschaftler, Bibliotheken, Fach- und Hochschulinstitute und (Online-)Buchhandel

▶ Möchten Sie Autor beim Gabler Verlag werden? Kontaktieren Sie uns!

Außerdem ganz neu:
DoktorArbeit | Das Promotionsforum.
Hier bieten wir News und Wissenswertes rund um das Thema Promotion. Seien Sie dabei:
www.facebook.com/promotionsforum

Marta Grabowski | Lektorat Wissenschaftliche Monografien
Tel. +49 (0)611.7878-237 | marta.grabowski@springer.com

KOMPETENZ IN SACHEN WIRTSCHAFT

GABLER

MIX
Papier aus verantwortungsvollen Quellen
Paper from responsible sources
FSC® C105338

If you have any concerns about our products,
you can contact us on
ProductSafety@springernature.com

In case Publisher is established outside the EU,
the EU authorized representative is:
Springer Nature Customer Service Center GmbH
Europaplatz 3, 69115 Heidelberg, Germany

Printed by Libri Plureos GmbH
in Hamburg, Germany